10⁰⁰

PRACTICAL UPHOLSTERING
AND THE
CUTTING OF SLIP COVERS

Practical Upholstering and The Cutting of Slip Covers

The Complete Guide to Authentic Renovation of Late 19th- and Early 20th-Century Furniture

With over 400 Illustrations

BY

FREDERICK PALMER

STEIN AND DAY/*Publishers*/New York

First published in the United States of America in 1980

Palmer, Frederick.
   Practical upholstering and the cutting of
slip covers.

   Originally published under title: Practical
upholstering and the cutting of loose covers.
   Reprint of the 1921 ed. published by Benn
Bros. Ltd., London, in series: The "Cabinet maker"
series.

   Includes index.
   I. Upholstery. 2. Slip covers. I. Title.
TT198.P3   1980   684.1'2   80-51766
ISBN 0-8128-2753-8

FOREWORD

by L. R. BEAGEN, F.A.M.U.

Past President, Association of Master Upholsterers

Although other books have been written about upholstery since *Palmer's Practical Upholstering* was published, none of them has come up to his. It is in a class of its own; a textbook for the tradesman; a must for both repairers and bespoke makers; invaluable for reference, and for training apprentices. In fact one could call it the upholsterer's "Bible".

It would be presumptuous to attempt to improve upon Palmer's work, but of course since the book was written in 1921 there have been some changes in methods and materials, and some explanation is necessary regarding these. Nevertheless it is worth pointing out that the methods and many of the materials Palmer described are still used in the trade today, and will be so used for some time to come.

Frames: The traditional frames depicted in the excellent sketches in the book are still used, even the iron backs, but in the modern suite, on the whole, the breakdown system is employed. This method enables the work to be carried out by less skilled workers, each person attending to different parts of the article and then the assembly being done by others. In fact, mass production. The frames of the past were mainly made of beech or birch; today the timber may be also chestnut, elm, oak, deal, or one of the many new imported woods. Plywood and chipboard are also used.

Castors: These have changed over the years, and the most popular today is the ball type castor.

Springs: The coil spring is still in use, while over the years we have had patent spring units, tension springs and, today, zig zag springing. The reliability of all springing is dependent upon the way the springs are fitted. They must be correctly placed, and lashed or clipped in position. The consideration of the gauge of the spring is essential; it is no use putting into a seat a spring which is intended for the back or arms.

Webbing: In Palmer's day 2 inch black and white webbing would have been the main type used. In recent years 2 inch jute webb has become the most common variety. Rubber webbing was at one time very popular, but is not so much used today. Polypropylene webbing is also used, but less successfully.

Fillings: In this field there has been great change. Polyether foam, pinhole latex foam, cotton felt, Dacron and terylene wadding have, in most cases, taken over from hair, fibre and wool.

Adhesives: Although animal glue is still used to some extent, most adhesives used today are the more recent products: in powder form, formaldehyde resin, which is damp resistant; epoxy resin, two part, is very strong; resorcinol resin does not deteriorate with age; contact adhesives are mainly for plastics; and polyvinyl acetate is a multi-purpose glue.

There are a number of adhesives for foam and fabrics. Dunlop make a range suitable for foam rubber and plastics, including the popular Multi-purpose S708. For

FOREWORD

fabric there is Copydex, but for trimmings a clear Bostik is more durable. The brush is still used, but many workshops now use the spray gun.

Tools: Most of the tools used in Palmer's day are still used, but the tack hammer has given way to the staple gun. The foam cutter is now part of the equipment, as are electric cloth cutters and steamers for taking the creases out of velvet. The sewing machine has changed also; the walking foot type has helped to solve the problems of dealing with the new materials. And the handy size electric glue gun is very useful for fixing trimmings.

Canvas: This seems to have disappeared from modern furniture, and strange looking, loosely woven bottom cloths are to be seen. It is most essential that between the zig zag springing and the foam there is some barrier – and canvas would be most suitable – to stop the springing cutting through the foam.

Cushions: At one time nearly all cushions were made of down or feathers. Then came pocketed spring units, then rubber cushions, and now it is mostly foam with a wrapping of Dacron or terylene.

Coverings: Here too change has taken place. Wool, cotton and silk have largely given way to manmade fibres, with all their problems. Nylon, viscose, polyester acetate, acrylic, polypropylene, and combinations of these have been a challenge to the upholsterer. It is important to follow the instructions of the manufacturer of a cloth when making up, and to use the right type of thread or cotton. Expanded vinyl has been a great improvement upon the old leather cloths, being much easier to deal with and having a pliable nature that makes it easy to work. Customers must be warned against using polish on it and told about the effects of greasy heads; both will hasten the cracking up of the cloth.

Loose Covers: There have always been various ways of cutting and making loose covers. In the past the most common was the method of going to the site and cutting in the half and then making up in the workshop, returning to the site for fitting. This is still done, but some upholsterers favour the idea of removing the furniture to the workshop and using the breakdown system of cutting and making up section by section. This way it is possible to use less skilled labour, training is easier, and the job can be checked for faults before the customer sees the work. Among the fabrics Palmer might have used were linen, damask, chintz and cretonne. Now all sorts of materials are employed.

This book has been the subject of much interest for many years. Some time ago I represented the Association of Master Upholsterers on a committee of the Furniture and Timber Trade Industry Training Board concerned with upholstery training, and it was discussed then. Many people have tried to get a copy through secondhand booksellers, but it has been a rare commodity, and it is gratifying to know that Messrs Benn have reprinted it. It will, I am sure, be of great interest to all upholsterers.

L. R. Beagen
F.A.M.U.

PREFACE.

It is customary for an author in his preface to explain how it came about that his work was begun and carried through. In my own case that can be very briefly stated. *Practical Upholstering* was written for the love of the thing. Having been associated with the craft all my working life as apprentice, journeyman, head foreman and instructor, it has been my good fortune to be of service to many of my fellow craftsmen. Many years ago I formed the habit of writing descriptions of the various processes of upholstery, and also of making sketches of chairs and settees at different stages of their construction. Having been appealed to so frequently on technical points, I thought it a pity that the experience I have gained as a really enthusiastic worker in the craft should not be set down in some permanent form for the benefit of others. Upholstery depends very largely on tradition. There is no trade which has been so little affected by modern machinery. It has always been and remains a handicraft, and moreover one in which a high degree of deftness and skill is needed. In *Practical Upholstering* it has been my task to lay bare all the inward parts, starting with the frame or skeleton and building up the structure process by process until the final covering. The reader who gets no farther than a perusal of the list of contents will, I venture to think, admit that I have dealt faithfully with the subject, and, if my book encourages my fellow craftsmen to carry on the fine traditions which have been bequeathed to us by the upholsterers of the past, I shall be morè than repaid for the time and trouble expended on the volume.

In the second part the Cutting and Making of Loose Covers has been dealt with exhaustively. Of this section I can say from considerable personal knowledge that there is a widespread demand for the detailed information which it contains.

Lastly, I should say that *Practical Upholstering* would never have seen the light of day but for the fact that Messrs. Benn Brothers, Ltd., the proprietors of *The Cabinet Maker*, placed at my disposal their experience and unrivalled resources as publishers of technical books.

F. PALMER.

LONDON, 1921.

CONTENTS.

PART I.

PRACTICAL UPHOLSTERING.

CONTENTS.

x

CONTENTS.

CONTENTS.

CONTENTS.

PART II.

SLIP COVERS (LOOSE COVERS).

CHAPTER 1.

THE WORKSHOP.

Essential Points that are Often Overlooked.

In no trade is a good supply of both natural and artificial light more essential than in that of the upholsterer.

It is impossible to accomplish good work in ill-lighted shops. Unfortunately, the upholsterer too often is the last to be studied in this respect. In small firms any out-of-the-way corner or even a basement is considered good enough for him. The writer recalls seeing upholstery work being done in a basement where the only daylight was that which struggled through an iron grating level with the pavement, and which was augmented by gas jets projecting from the wall. There are many reasons why this state of affairs does not exist to-day. First, the upholsterer is aware of the benefits, financial and physical, that accrue to him by performing his daily work amid healthy surroundings. Secondly, the attractions of the large upholstery firms with their ideal workshops provided with plenty of air, light, and space, appeal to him very strongly when seeking a berth.

Bad light is often the indirect cause of faulty construction in upholstery work, especially in the case of leather, velvet, and other shaded fabrics.

Shading and Blending Skins.

The upholsterer, although he may take great pains, will always work at a disadvantage in a bad light. In the case of leather work, it is impossible to shade and blend the skins. The reader may easily test this for himself. Let him examine, say, an easy chair in morocco, first in artificial light, and then in daylight. In the former the leather may appear to be of one colour; in the latter he will find, maybe, five or six different shades that cannot be toned together correctly in artificial light. The work in such conditions is liable to look patchy and to offend the eye.

THE MATCHING OF VELVETS.

Velvets are very difficult to match up by artificial light. Some of them possess four distinct shades by reversing back to front and right to left, and where many cuts are to be made mistakes soon occur.

All this shows how necessary it is that the upholsterer's shop should be one where a maximum of daylight prevails, and a minimum of articifial illumination.

The right to work in a good light is one upon which the upholsterer should always insist. It means all the difference between a good and a bad week financially, to say nothing of the inevitable effect on the quality of the work done.

BENCHES AND TRESTLES.

Next to light, a good benchway, with plenty of space, is important. It often happens that where coverings for the work in hand are not available, the upholsterer may have several jobs in progress at the same time unfinished. Hence, the need for plenty of room, especially where there are many men employed. A side-bench, about 4ft. 6in. wide and 3ft. 6in. high, fixed beneath the windows, with divided bins beneath for the various stuffings, serves the double purpose of a cutting-board and a place for unfinished work. The bins should be boarded up half-way, and divided into 5ft. or 6ft. lengths.

Trestles should be about 36in. wide and 30in. high with grooved tops, to insure a frame remaining rigid when placed on them. It is necessary to have a high pair and a low pair, the latter to be used for settees or chairs with extra high backs; they will also be found useful in many other ways.

Cutting-boards for marking out should be made about 6ft. 6in. by 4ft. for the large, and 3ft. 6in. by 5ft. for the smaller size. These should not be of too soft a wood, as with the constant hammering and pritchawl holes, the wood soon splinters, and the board becomes useless.

CHAPTER 2.

THE STOCK ROOM.

There is no trade that presents such a large field for economy as the upholstery trade ; hence the vital need for a stock-room, where the various hessians, springs, coverings, stuffings, and other materials may be kept, and regularly checked and tabulated.

Where possible this room should either be in or adjoining the actual workshop. In factories where many upholsterers are employed, a stock-keeper is kept, whose duties consist of sorting out the materials and stuffings required for various chairs, settees, and other work. Quantities are kept in a log book, in which is entered the number or name of each job applied for.

Neglect of Yard-stick and Scales.

Where only a few upholsterers are employed, economy is also necessary, and it is wise to have a place kept apart from the workshop itself—a kind of miniature stock-room. The writer, as a practical man, regrets to have to confess that upholsterers are frequently not very careful. To a piece-worker time is money in every sense, and if he is allowed to cut his own materials there is a temptation to neglect the yard-stick and weighing scales ; the result of this will be seen on visiting his particular bench. When the job is complete there will be found there remnants of material and stuffings, " to be used on the next," but which eventually find their way into the shop sweepings. When these small items are multiplied they amount to an appreciable quantity. We see, then, the need for economy in the shop. There are other avenues of waste which must be watched.

Where possible, materials should be made up beforehand for the standard jobs, marked, and given out as applied for. This is a good plan to follow in a large factory where an inexpensive class of work is manufactured.

Fittings for the Stock Room.

As mentioned above, the stock-room should adjoin the actual workshop. Baskets are best adapted for the conveyance of the materials and stuffings. The stock-room should have a long, wide board running the whole length of that side which is best lighted ; also tiers of fixtures for tapestries, cloths, etc., and centre tiers, accessible from all sides, if space permits.

Large open racks should be provided for the various qualities of hair, and closed ones for flocks, etc. ; downs, feathers, and kapok are most liable to waste and should be separated entirely from other stuffings. Springs should also be kept in racks, with the different gauges distinctly marked. Only just sufficient room should be allowed in width for each gauge ; if this is not done they very easily become entangled and useless.

Economy in Twines and Tacks.

Much waste will result from the indiscriminate serving out of twines and tacks. In old-fashioned workshops twines were sometimes kept in a long box with a glass front and a lid containing holes ; the ends of the twine hung down from the wall, within easy reach when required. A small bag will answer the same purpose. If the balls are allowed to lie about waste inevitably occurs.

Tacks are best obtained in large bags and served out in small ones. Packets are wasteful ; the many sizes used on one job render them liable soon to become mixed up and useless.

Buttons, studs, cords, and gimps are also liable to be wasted if not kept in proper compartments.

Relation of Stock Room to Shop and Office.

It is very important that everything kept in the stock-room should have a distinctive mark, and that a record should be kept. If this is not done, confusion will exist and the stock-room will be rendered useless as a time-saver. Given a well-regulated system, methodically carried out, the stock-room will act as a control for preventing waste, and be most useful both to the office and workshop. Numbers are best given to the different styles of chairs ; names sometimes cause confusion, especially in dealing with queries from customers. It has been found by experience that a number is more easily passed through correctly from the customer, office, stock-room and workman than a name. A log book of the quantities required for various work should also be kept in the workshop as well as in the stock-room.

CHAPTER 3.

THE POPULARITY OF STUFFOVER GOODS.

The growing popularity of stuffover work is one of the most notable features of the upholstery trade. If inquiry were made with regard to this preference on the part of the public, the reasons given might be summed up in one word "Comfort."

Take the gent's chair of a "suite," with its almost upright back, two small arm pads, and a seat which, if a reclining position be adopted, soons means a back-ache, and compare it with the modern "divan easy," consisting of a large, roomy seat, full stuffed arms, sloping back, with the full swell at the bottom which is so necessary for real comfort, spring edge, arms, and back ; no unbiassed observer can deny that the stuffover chair is the more inviting and comfortable piece of furniture.

Again, take the old-fashioned couch, placed so rigidly against the wall, with its open back and long pad, and contrast it with the modern chesterfield, which looks well in any position, and is frequently fitted with a drop end for extra comfort. The chesterfield allows of plenty of room for cushions—which impart a finishing touch to all stuffovers—and the occupant can recline at ease, as there are none of the awkward projections of the frame work so often found in the "suite" couch.

As far as "smalls" are concerned, the very adjective by which they are described calls attention to their inherent defect, viz., lack of seat room and consequent lack of comfort. Price-cutting has played a part here, and some "smalls" are so diminutive in size, and light in construction, that they cannot be regarded as real additions to the comfort of any home.

ERRORS IN CONSTRUCTION OF FRAMES.

The chesterfield and "divan easy" may be called the originals from which numerous other stuffover designs have been evolved, but these two original designs—doubtless because they conform to the requirements very closely—still remain popular. It is to be regretted, from the point of view of the practical upholsterer, that many stuffover frames are very poor in construction, and some upholstered furniture, reaching a high standard as far as outward appearance is

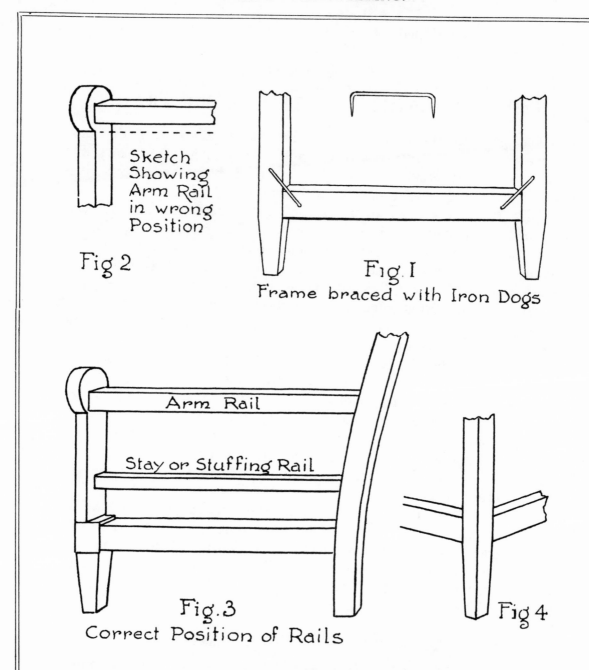

Sketch
Showing
Arm Rail
in wrong
Position

Fig 2

Fig. I

Frame braced with Iron Dogs

Arm Rail

Stay or Stuffing Rail

Fig. 3

Correct Position of Rails

Fig 4

DETAILS·OF·UPHOLSTERY·FRAMES

concerned, once stripped of its expensive covering, reveals a frame with badly-fitting joints and wood which has never seen a spokeshave or plane. This is not as it should be. Upholstering is a skilled trade, and in the making of frames as much care and attention to detail is required as in the subsequent building up and finishing. There are many technical errors in the construction of modern stuff-over frames that are irritating to the upholsterer, and which might be easily rectified even in the cheapest of frames.

Reason for Using a Tough Wood.

The many tackings necessary to secure the various materials used, some of which must be affixed to the extreme edges of the frame, make it necessary to use a tough wood, which will not split easily, for it is obvious that any weakening of the hold of the tacks, especially those which secure the webbing and spring covering, is inimical to proper workmanship.

Formerly upholstery frames were made of beech, with mortised joints, pinned and closely braced. At present, birch is the recognised wood for good-class work. This timber takes stain well, and no difficulty is experienced in the polishing shop in finishing the legs or cup-feet either oak, mahogany, walnut, or satinwood colour.

The dowel-joint is the one now most generally employed in frame-making. In larger frames, such as chesterfields, settees, and divans, four dowels should be used to each joint, but for slighter frames three will suffice, although the base should always have four if the wood is strong enough to take this number.

The Use of Braces.

Braces are most important for giving added strength, and should be used on all grades of upholstery frames. They are about $1\frac{1}{2}$in. thick, and shaped in such a way that screws may be driven in at right angles to the length of the rails, which the brace is used to support. Iron dogs are also used. They are easy to fix, obtainable in various sizes, and used as shown in FIG. 1. These iron dogs are also useful for strengthening frames needing repair which are weak from lack of bracing, as they can be fixed without too much stripping of the coverings.

The Proper Position of Arm and Stuffing Rails.

The best critic of a correctly-made stuffover frame is the upholsterer who has to build his work on it, and some errors of construction which affect his work adversely will now be described.

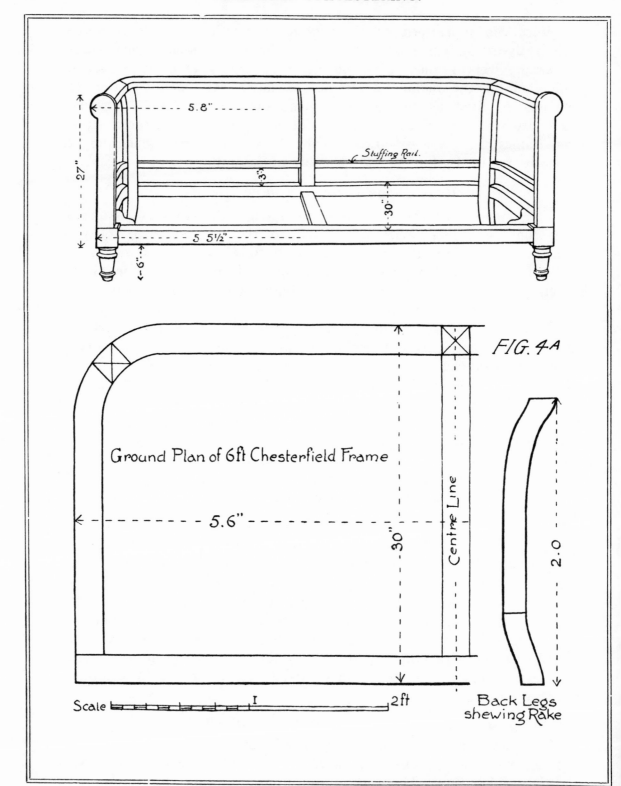

Stuffing Rail.

Ground Plan of 6ft Chesterfield Frame

Centre Line

FIG. 4A

Back Legs
shewing Rake

Scale

2ft

In stuffover settees or chairs the appearance of the outside of the arms is more noticeable than the inside, yet too often they are unsightly and irregular in finish, lacking the clean, direct line which one looks for in first-class work. This is frequently due to the placing of the arm rail too high in the front scroll, as shown in FIG. 2. The lower edge of this arm rail should be brought down to the level of the dotted line, otherwise it is well-nigh impossible for the upholsterer to maintain an even line directly underneath the arm. The same fault is sometimes found in the backs, and the unsightly and irregular surface of outside arms and backs is often due to badly-constructed frames.

The stay or stuffing rails should be sunk $\frac{1}{2}$in. to $\frac{3}{4}$in., to allow for the several layers of materials which will subsequently be tacked on them. In FIG. 3, both stuffing rail and arm rail are shown in their correct positions.

IMPORTANCE OF REGULAR LINE AT BASE.

Even a well-made chair may be ruined by inattention to minor details, for fine upholstery in the last resort consists of beauty in the finished lines. For instance, the braid or banding should present a regular line all round the base of the stuffover chesterfield or chair. In frames in which the legs are not dowelled on, such as those with taper legs as shown in FIG. 4, there is no guide by which the upholsterer can keep his line uniform when working on the leg itself. A man with a good eye will keep a regular, horizontal line, but careless workmen will fail to do so. This sometimes causes an unsightly corner. Frames with legs such as that indicated in FIG. 4 should have a deep chisel mark squared off from front to side rail, as a guide to the upholsterer.

CHAPTER 4.

SPRING–EDGE FRAMES.

A frame for an upholstered chair which is to be finished with a spring-edge seat requires a wider front rail than an ordinary frame, as this provides a stronger and better foundation for the front springs. This is important, for new chairs are sometimes returned as faulty, as a result of the front rails being made too narrow adequately to support the edge-springs, which soon become loose ; this weakens the front, and causes the seat to sag and look unsightly. In a badly-built frame in which the front rail is not wide enough for the edge-springs, it should be supplemented by another rail to make it up to the required width. Upholsterers will find this more satisfactory in practice than the webbing extension which is sometimes used for this purpose.

SHORTER FOOT FOR SPRING-EDGE CHAIRS.

In spring-edge upholstered work greater depth is needed than in an ordinary frame from the top of the seat to the bottom of the front rail in order to allow for the spring. To gain this required depth the foot of a spring-edge frame should be shorter than that of a firm-edge frame (FIGS. 5 and 6). If this rule is not followed, the height of the seat will be too great, and the correct proportion between the height of the seat and the arms will be lost (FIGS. 7 and 8).

DOUBLE-SPRUNG FRAMES.

Frames which are to be finished with double-sprung or imitation double-sprung seats require an extra stuffing-rail, as shown in FIG. 9. It is imperative that these rails should be strong, because in the upholstering they take the place of the base rails, the extra depth occasioned by the use of springs rendering this feasible, without detracting from the ultimate buoyancy of the seat. This is a detail which is sometimes disregarded by frame-makers and upholsterers, but the best opinion tends to the view that the extra stuffing-rail should be used in double-sprung work instead of the seat-rail.

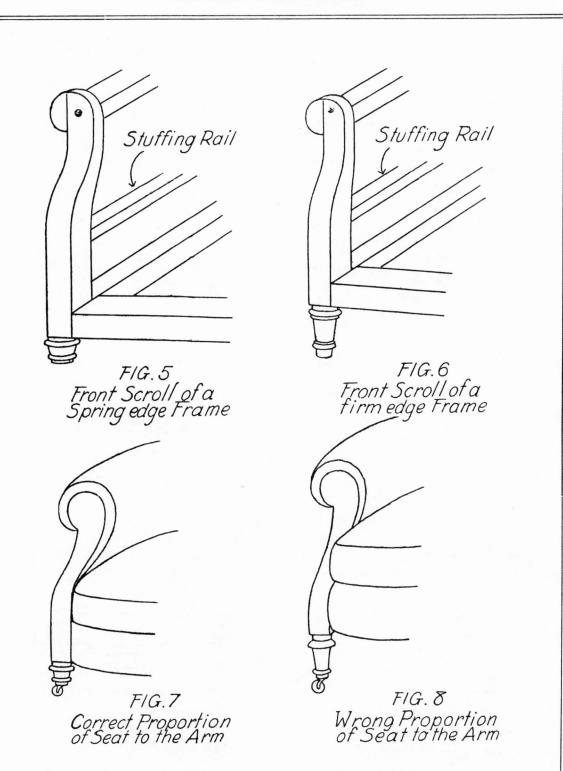

FIG. 5
Front Scroll of a
Spring edge Frame

FIG. 6
Front Scroll of a
firm edge Frame

FIG. 7
Correct Proportion
of Seat to the Arm

FIG. 8
Wrong Proportion
of Seat to the Arm

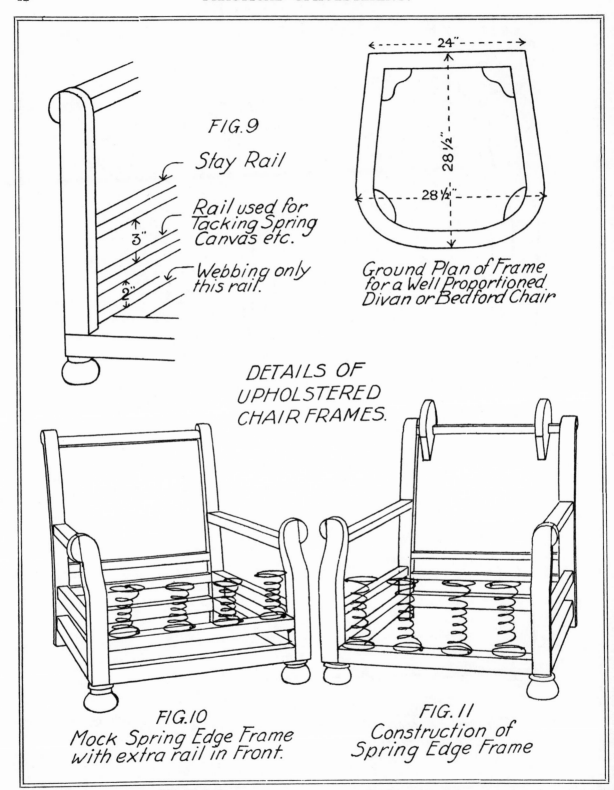

FIG. 9

Stay Rail

Rail used for Tacking Spring Canvas etc.

3"

Webbing only this rail.

2"

24"

28½"

28½"

Ground Plan of Frame for a Well Proportioned Divan or Bedford Chair

DETAILS OF UPHOLSTERED CHAIR FRAMES.

FIG. 10
Mock Spring Edge Frame with extra rail in Front.

FIG. 11
Construction of Spring Edge Frame

Though a double-sprung upholstered chair is luxurious and comfortable, unless made on a correctly-built frame, in which the rails are neither too high nor too low, it is apt to become faulty sooner than medium-class work. The reasons for this will be given in greater detail in those chapters in which the methods employed in double-springing are described.

The rule which has been laid down here with regard to chairs also applies to settees which are to be upholstered in real, double, or mock-sprung seats—namely, they should be fitted with a stout rail (as shown in Fig. 9) two or three inches above the base rails.

Imitation or Mock-Sprung Edge Frames.

Frames to be upholstered in the mock-sprung style are made with an extra rail in front, as shown in Fig. 10. This affords additional strength, and serves to support the arms; built of stout wood, such frames are very strong and reliable, though when upholstered they lack something of the buoyancy of the genuine double-sprung chair. This will be clear by comparing Fig. 10 with 11, and noting the extra depth of spring in.the latter.

Frames built in this way are sometimes upholstered with firm or stuffed seats instead of springs, and it is doubtless on account of the absence of springs that they are described in the trade as mock-sprung.

CHAPTER 5.

IRON AND WOOD STRETCHERS.

Frames for settees and chesterfields are generally made, in order to give added strength, with one or more wood stretchers in the seat according to length. While these add rigidity and durability to the frame, they frequently cause the upholsterer some difficulty for one or more of the following reasons :—

(1) The settee may require a low spring with insufficient resistance to avoid the rail causing discomfort to the person sitting on the settee or chesterfield when finished ; (2) a wood rail placed too high creates doubt in the upholsterer's mind as to whether the webs should be strained over or underneath it ; (3) the position of the wood rail renders it difficult to arrange the springs, and may cause an inconvenient gap liable to weaken the seat. The enthusiastic critic, anxious to test the workmanship of a settee seat, who bounces up and down on it is apt to be painfully aware of a wooden centre rail and in use, the owner of such a settee, knowing its defect, will be prompted to request a visitor to avoid sitting in the centre.

Sufficient reasons have already been given to show that wooden stretcher rails are not always to be recommended, and it is at least an open question whether the old-fashioned iron stretcher (FIG. 12) is not preferable to the wood stretcher mostly used in modern stuffover frames. (FIGS. 13 and 14).

Iron Stretchers and Loose Cushion Settees.

The use of an iron stretcher is recommended for strengthening the frame of a loose cushion settee because the upholstering of the seat of such a settee must be kept low, necessitating the use of a small spring without much resistance. By the placing of the stretcher below the web, free play for the springs is obtained without the risk of discomfort when the seat slackens—a risk that it would be difficult to avoid if a wooden rail were used.

It will be seen from the foregoing remarks that wood stretchers on settee frames may be used with safety where a deep seat is required, but iron stretchers may be recommended with confidence for small settees and loose cushion work. Not only is the possibility of the rail being uncomfortably felt avoided by the use of the iron

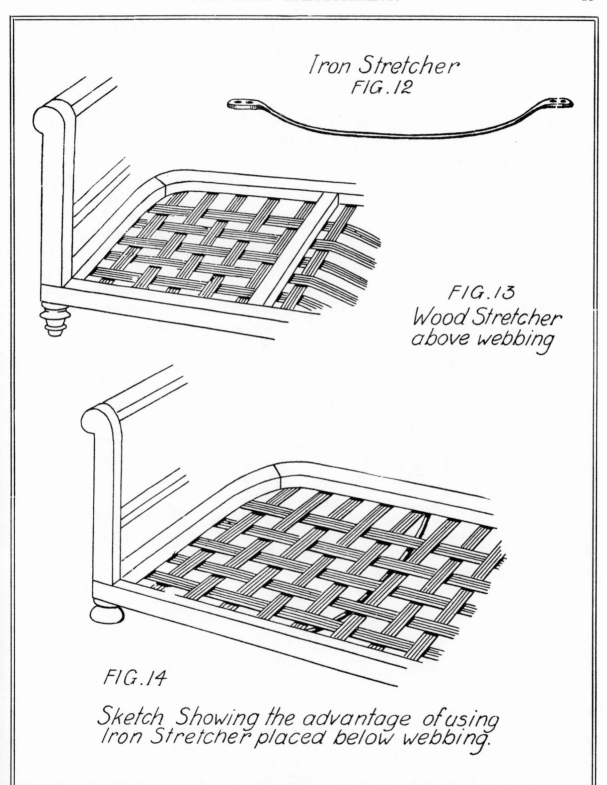

Iron Stretcher
FIG.12

FIG.13
Wood Stretcher
above webbing

FIG.14

Sketch Showing the advantage of using
Iron Stretcher placed below webbing.

stretcher, but more freedom is allowed the upholsterer in placing the springs. There is another disadvantage in connection with the use of a wood rail which should be mentioned. In inexpensive work the upholsterer, to save material, is tempted to fix both web and springs to it. This will produce a firm and level upholstered seat for a while, until the webs slacken on either side of the rail and the seat then sags at the ends, while the centre, on account of the rail to which the springs are fixed, remains firm and rigid. This is sometimes the cause of upholstered settees becoming irregular and unsightly. A stuffover chair frame may be adapted or turned into a spring chair frame by removing the legs. A second frame of exactly the same dimensions as the chair seat is prepared and used as a base (see sketch Fig. 12a). Chairs of this type are comfortable when upholstered, but there is always a tendency for chairs constructed in this way to appear " out of true," the reason being that the springs tend to weaken on the side mostly used, which creates a noticeable tilt difficult to remedy. Such frames are made like ordinary stuffovers, but it is important that the base frame should be of exactly the same size as the chair seat, otherwise it is difficult for the upholsterer to produce a good effect. A square frame, as sketched, is better adapted for a spring frame stuffover than a shaped one.

FIG.12a Spring Chair Frame

CHAPTER 6.

THE DOUBLE-SPRUNG CHESTERFIELD FRAME.

The real or genuine double-sprung seated chesterfield frame is a new departure in upholstery and is much in demand.

It is proposed to describe these frames in detail, and it should be pointed out that the upholstering of such pieces should only be undertaken by skilled workmen. The writer has often seen settees with luxuriously soft seats, for which long prices have been paid, returned as unsatisfactory, the faults having been caused by the incorrect position of the rails, which results in the materials being either over-strained or under-strained.

The double-sprung, or deep-seated, chesterfield frame should be constructed differently to the ordinary spring-edge frame to allow for the deeper seat. This is effected by lowering the base of the frame to within three or four inches of the floor. An additional stuffing-rail is required, to which the coverings are fixed, instead of to the base frame. This rail should be of stout wood, at least $1\frac{1}{2}$in. birch. As a rule such rails are not made strong enough for heavy tacking. The position of the rail is also very important. It should be neither too high nor too low, as otherwise the buoyancy of the seat is affected. If in the former position, there is too little resistance, and the seat binds; in the latter position there is too much resistance, and the springs are liable to shift their position at the surface, whilst the base remains rigid. This tendency will be fully described in the chapter dealing with the final processes of the upholstering of genuine double-sprung work.

Frames such as these are also adapted for mock spring-edge work, namely, half wood and half spring or stuffing. In such cases an additional rail is used in the front, about $2\frac{1}{2}$in. above the base rail (see sketch).

Cup feet are generally used for double-sprung frames, and flat, well-proportioned cups are superior to those which are round or half-round in shape. These cups may be dowelled on after the frame is made, but the best method, and that which gives the neatest finish, as far as the upholsterer is concerned, is to fix the cups with screws after the work is fully upholstered. Care should be taken by the upholsterer that the wood is kept clear of tackings at the angle of the frame

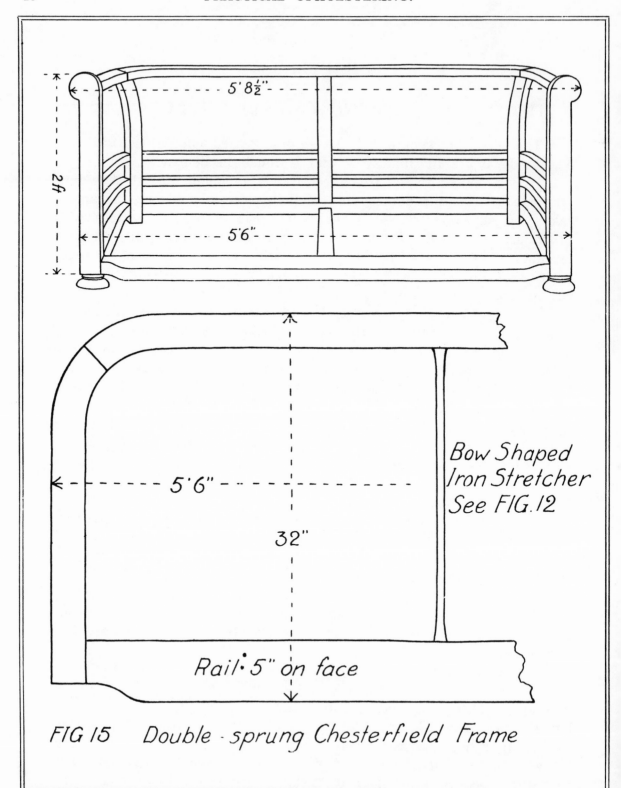

FIG 15   Double · sprung Chesterfield Frame

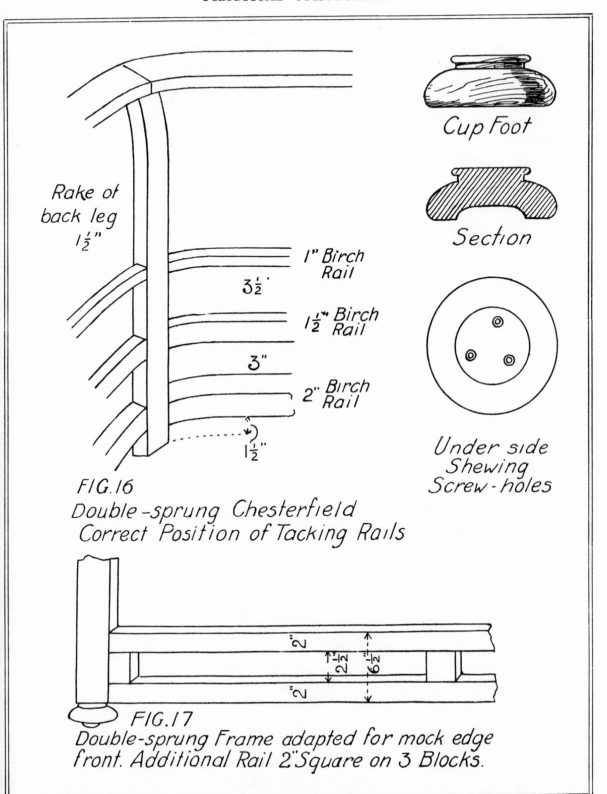

Cup Foot

Section

Rake of
back leg
$1\frac{1}{2}$"

1" Birch
Rail

$3\frac{1}{2}$'

$1\frac{1}{2}$" Birch
Rail

3"

2" Birch
Rail

$1\frac{1}{2}$"

Under side
Shewing
Screw-holes

FIG.16
Double-sprung Chesterfield
Correct Position of Tacking Rails

2"

$2\frac{1}{2}$"

$6\frac{1}{2}$"

2"

FIG.17
Double-sprung Frame adapted for mock edge
front. Additional Rail 2"Square on 3 Blocks.

on the underside, to allow for glueing as well as screwing on of the cup. As already pointed out in previous chapters, iron stretchers fixed underneath the base of the frame are preferable to wood when a low edge is required for loose cushions. A real double-sprung seat constitutes the last word in comfort, but unless the frame of a double-sprung chesterfield is correctly made, the work will soon become unsightly.

CHAPTER 7.

STANDARDISED CHAIR FRAMES.

The seven chair frames illustrated here are variations of the square chair frame sketched at A, formed by fixing pieces of wood of different shapes to the arms and back. The principle of standardisation is applied; the square chair frames may be made in quantities, and at the same time, by the addition of the shaped pieces, the outline of the chair may be altered as desired. A range of chairs may thus be offered by the retailer, so that the public may exercise its faculty of selection. The ability to offer a diversity of patterns is a real advantage, for, other things being equal, the public will patronise the shop at which the greatest number of designs may be seen.

From the point of view of the works manager, the advantage of standardisation need not be insisted on. It enables him to arrange long "runs" instead of short ones, and at the same time to produce several different patterns at about the same price. The traveller, who has two or more customers in the same town, is enabled to reserve some of the designs to one furnisher, and the remainder to another in the same neighbourhood, and the tendency to price-cutting by competitors in the retail trade is thus sensibly diminished.

Frames such as those illustrated are generally used for an inexpensive class of upholstery with a minimum of stuffing; the wood line of the arms and back is the finished cord line. Details and various styles of upholstering will be illustrated and described in subsequent articles of this series.

The principal dimensions are given at A, and, in the absence of a complete cutting order, the following sizes may also be useful :— The base frame should be made of 2in. by 1½in. birch; the back uprights 1½in. by 2in.; and the fronts and arms 1in. on the face by 2in. The thickness of the shaped loose pieces is governed by the parts to which they are applied.

The examples B, C, E, and F—the shaped pieces—should be fixed to backs and arms by glueing and nailing. The wing-pieces in D, G, and H should be dowelled or screwed from the back. As regards example F, two pieces only are needed for the back; the shape of the arms is obtained by the use of the spokeshave on the square interior edges until the required section is produced, the line

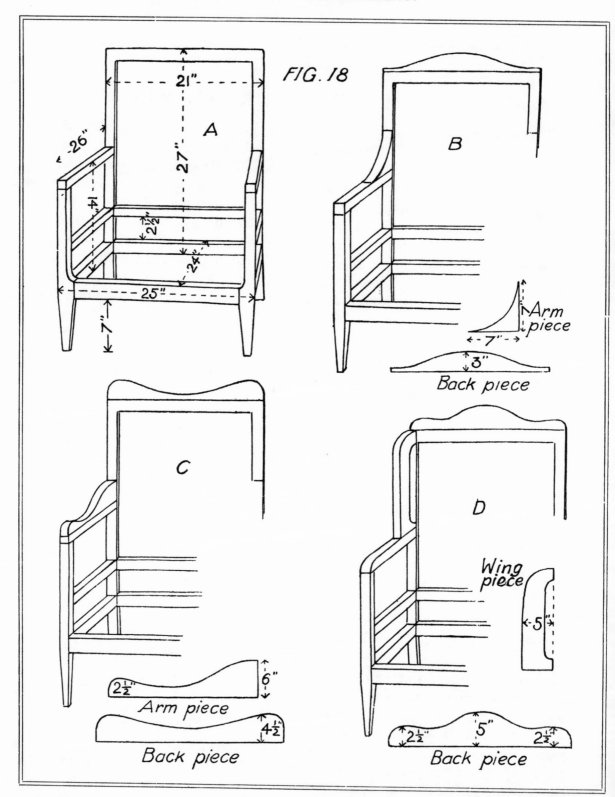

FIG. 18

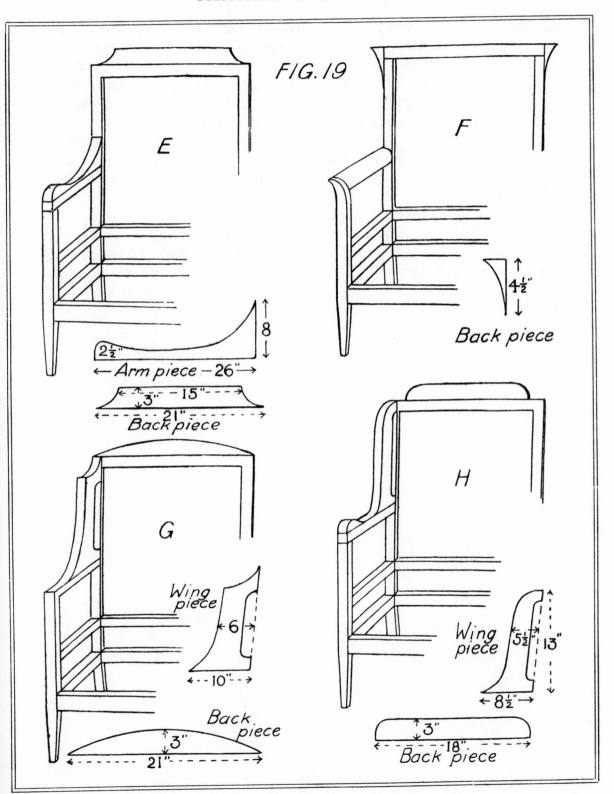

FIG. 19

E

F

8

2½"

← Arm piece — 26" →

3" — 15"

21"

Back piece

4½"

Back piece

G

Wing piece

6

10"

Back piece

3"

21"

H

Wing piece

5½" 13"

8½"

3"

18"

Back piece

of the upholstery being carried out in the same proportion. This example is interesting, as showing how radically the character of a frame may be altered by very simple means. A, F, and G are so dissimilar in outline in their finished state that the customer would scarcely believe, even if he were told, that he is choosing between frames which in all essential respects are exactly the same.

The principle of standardisation has been applied more generally to carcase goods than to chair-frame making, but we think readers will agree, with the examples we publish this week before them, that there is a great deal to be said for its adoption.

It certainly facilitates rapid and economical production, and the objection that it makes for dullness and uniformity, or tends to a limitation of the number of available patterns, may be successfully met by the exercise of a little ingenuity on the part of the frame-maker.

CHAPTER 8.

FRAMES FOR SPRING CUSHION WORK.

In spring cushion work the upholstery of the seats, and in some cases of the backs also, is detached from the frame and removable from it at will. Frames for this class of work should be well and stoutly built, as an upholstered chair or settee of this kind is essentially a high-class article. Seeing that both construction and material are to a large extent visible when the cushions are removed, badly constructed copies of good spring cushion work are rarely put on the market. Frames made in this way have much to commend them from a hygienic point of view, for, when the seats and backs are removed, complete access is obtained to those parts of a chair where dirt and dust usually accumulate.

In actual construction the frames differ very little from those used for the ordinary stuffover. The base of the frame is fitted with wood laths fixed at equal distances (see FIG. 21); this forms a foundation for the loose cushion, and webbing is entirely dispensed with. In frames of the best character the laths are polished, presenting a clean, neat appearance when the cushions are detached.

It will be obvious to the reader, that practically any style of stuffover may be converted into a spring cushion frame by substituting wood laths for webbing, but plenty of room should be allowed from the top of the arm to the base, as the maximum of comfort is obtained by using two spring cushions, one on the top of the other, as shown in FIG. 20. It will be noted that this chair has a loose cushion in the back, as well as the two loose cushions which form the seat. The actual construction of the cushions themselves is shown at FIG. 22. The cushion consists of two frames of strong wire, with spiral springs securely fixed top and bottom by zigzag wire, the whole bound together with metal fasteners. These wire spring frames can be made to any given measurement. It is claimed for spring cushion upholstery that the maximum of resilience and comfort is obtained owing to the number of springs that can be placed in the frame without fear of their becoming twisted, as might be the case if they were attached by means of twine to webbing; the number of springs in a large divan easy sometimes runs into three figures. It is questioned in some quarters whether spring cushion upholstery does represent the last word in comfort, but here the construction of frames only is dealt with, and this point will be discussed more freely in the chapters which bear directly on the finishing processes of upholstery.

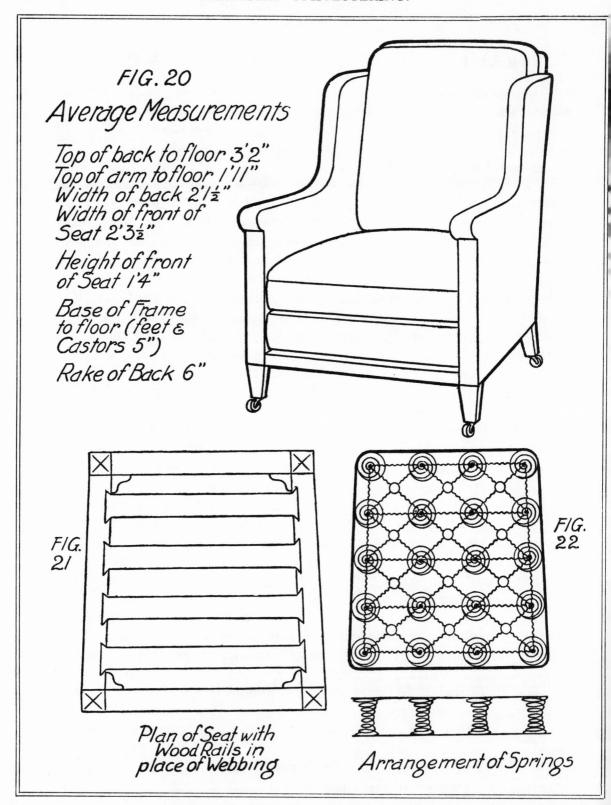

FIG. 20

Average Measurements

Top of back to floor 3' 2"
Top of arm to floor 1' 11"
Width of back 2' 1½"
Width of front of
Seat 2' 3½"

Height of front
of Seat 1' 4"

Base of Frame
to floor (feet &
Castors 5")

Rake of Back 6"

FIG.
21

*Plan of Seat with
Wood Rails in
place of Webbing*

FIG.
22

Arrangement of Springs

CHAPTER 9.

IRON BACK FRAMES.

Though there is no chair more comfortable when skilfully upholstered than the iron back easy, such frames have been little employed during recent years. As regards the appearance of the finished article iron back frames have much to commend them, for the metal rod which forms the outline of the chair may be fashioned into subtle concave or convex lines with greater ease than wood. Another feature of this type of chair is that the back, being constructed in one piece, and afterwards fixed securely to the seat frame, has no joints to work loose; after a little usage, also, the metal frame becomes less rigid, and assumes a slight "give" or spring which adds greatly to the comfort of the chair without detracting from its strength.

It is probable that such frames were first introduced as being cheaper than those of wood, for twenty or thirty years ago a good, strong iron back frame might be purchased at from 3s. to 4s. For such backs $\frac{5}{8}$in. iron rods are generally used; any gauge smaller than this is liable to get out of shape with use. The rod is beaten out on a wood mould to the required shape and 1in. iron laths are then fixed to it. (See FIG. 23). The lower ends of these are shaped step-like in order that they may be firmly attached to the top and inside of the wood seat frame with clout nails. This method of fixing the stretchers makes the frame rigid, and the bottom stretcher that runs parallel with the wood seat frame is placed high or low for spring or firm edges in the manner already described when dealing with the stuffing rails of wood frames. For spring edge work the average space between the seat frame and the stuffing stretcher is 6in.; for firm edge upholstery $2\frac{1}{2}$in. would suffice. FIG. 25 shows the method of fixing the stretchers to the inside of the wood frame; the method shown in FIG. 26 is also used in cheaper work; in this case the stretcher laths are fixed to the outside edge of the wood seat frame.

Settees and frames of shapes other than those we illustrate are made on the same principle. FIG. 27 shows an iron back used in conjunction with wood arm uprights dowelled to the seat frame. The iron rod (a) and the stretcher lath (b) are fixed with clout nails in the same manner as shown in FIGS. 25 and 26. From a study of diagram 23 it will be seen that the ends of the $\frac{5}{8}$in.

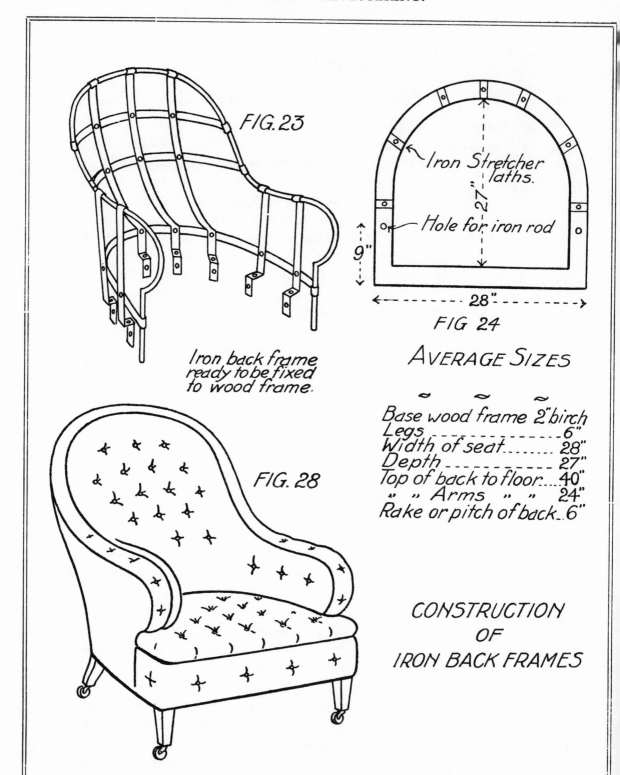

FIG. 23

Iron back frame
ready to be fixed
to wood frame.

Iron Stretcher
laths.

27"

Hole for iron rod

9"

28"

FIG 24

AVERAGE SIZES

FIG. 28

Base wood frame 2" birch
Legs _ _ _ _ _ _ _ _ _ _ 6"
Width of seat _ _ _ _ _ _ _ 28"
Depth _ _ _ _ _ _ _ _ _ 27"
Top of back to floor _ _ _ 40"
"   " Arms " "   24"
Rake or pitch of back _ 6"

CONSTRUCTION
OF
IRON BACK FRAMES

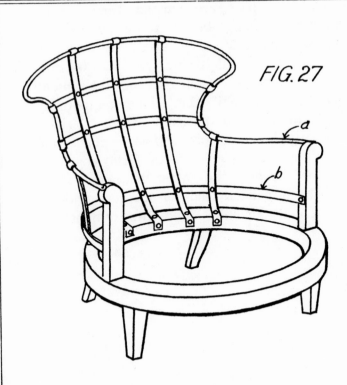

FIG. 27

AVERAGE SIZES

Legs..................6"
Seat depth..........26"
    " Width..........25"
Outside measurement
of arms, scroll to scroll..27"
Top of back to floor...34"
Top of Arms to floor 22"

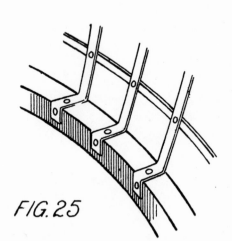

FIG. 25

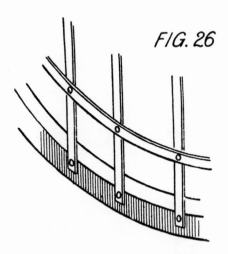

FIG. 26

Sketch shewing stretcher
  laths fixed to inside edge
  and top of seat frame.

Another Method of placing
  the iron back frame, shewing
  the stretcher laths fixed to
  the outside edge of seat frame

iron rod forming the outline of the chair are carried through the wood seat frame, holes in the frame being bored to receive them, so that they fit tightly, additional strength being given by wedging with clout nails. Iron backs require careful fixing, for if the outlines, etc., are not symmetrical, difficulties occur in the subsequent upholstery. The proper method is to nail the frame temporarily on the wood base with the stretchers in position, then overhaul the back with a rule to obtain the true proportions before final fixing. Iron back chairs may be upholstered with firm edges or spring edges; the sketch, FIG. 28, shows the latter method. From the upholsterer's point of view, the iron back chair is not very popular, as all materials have to be sewn, and this takes more time than nailing.

CHAPTER 10.

LOOSE SEATS.

In a stuffover chair or settee defects of material or faulty construction of the frame, when they exist, may be covered by the subsequent work of the upholsterer. In the show-wood frame this is not the case to the same extent, and the frame-maker who carefully follows the hints given in this chapter will materially aid the upholsterer in finishing the work satisfactorily.

Show-wood frames are not so heavily built as stuffovers, and for this reason the joints should receive special attention. Many are made with inadequate mortice joints or dowels to save wood, and braces, if any, are fixed with nails instead of screws. It cannot be insisted on too strongly that braces are necessary to show-wood frames of any description, and that they should be securely glued and screwed.

Show-wood frames, in modern practice, are usually made with loose seats, these being economical in the subsequent upholstery both in material and labour. It is important that the loose seat frame should fit accurately, and in this respect the upholsterer frequently has reason to complain of some carelessness on the part of the frame-maker. Some faults which occasion a good deal of extra trouble when they occur are described below. The frame-maker, in setting out the loose seat, has to decide what margin to allow for the upholstery materials that will ultimately cover it. If he leaves about ⅛in. all round, and the final covering happens to be a thin material, a badly fitting seat will result; whereas a thick, heavy material would ensure a perfect fit. It is, therefore, important where possible that the frame-maker should be informed as to the kind of covering to be employed in order that he may be able to adjust the measurement between the loose seat and the chair frame. In practice he rarely possesses this knowledge, and in cases of doubt as to the materials to be used the safe margin is to allow between the two frames $\frac{1}{16}$in. all round.

At FIG. 30, a well-fitting frame is sketched in contrast to FIG. 31, in which only one side of the loose seat is exactly parallel with the frame. The practical upholsterer, in dealing with a badly fitting frame of this kind, attaches pieces of material to its sides with the

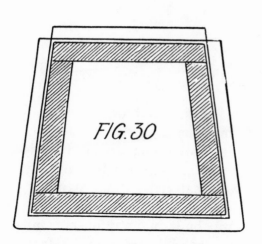

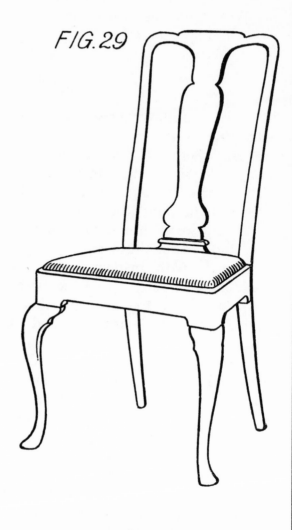

FIG.29

Plan of chair frame
with loose seat.

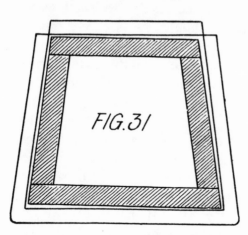

Plan of frame with
badly made loose seat

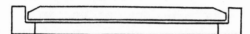

FIG.32

Shewing a badly made
seat with chamfered edge
below the edge of frame.

FIG.33   SECTION

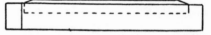

SIDE VIEW

Properly constructed
loose seat raised slightly
above the chair frame.

view to making it fit better, but the final effect is, in such cases, never so good as when the loose frame is made to the correct size with a proper margin all round.

The section given at Fig. 32 shows a fault sometimes met with in this style of chair. It will be seen that the chamfered edge of the loose seat falls below the line of the chair frame. This not only presents an unsightly appearance in the finished work, but renders the chair uncomfortable in use. The trouble may arise from one of two causes—(a) the loose seat frame may not be of sufficient thickness; (b) a too liberal use of the spokeshave, whereby a seat of sufficient thickness is so much reduced at the edge as to bring it below the level of the chair frame. This fault when it occurs must be rectified by the upholsterer, but it requires some skill, as the deficiency in thickness has to be made up with stuffing.

Before commencing work on chairs with loose seats the upholsterer should examine his frames, numbering each one, and noting the loose seats which need rectification before he proceeds with the work of upholstering them.

CHAPTER II.

DROP SCROLL SETTEE FRAMES.

The idea of constructing a settee so that one end may be adjusted at various angles between the vertical and the horizontal is not new. The best known early example is the Knole settee, but the principle on which the adjustment is made is quite different from that adopted by the modern frame maker. In the old pieces the end of a settee or the back of a chair was raised or lowered by means of a toothed quadrant. Applied to a chair back this was effective because support was obtained on either side, but in the case of a settee the drop end when horizontal was only supported by the toothed quadrant at the back, and had to rely for its rigidity to some extent on the iron hinges fixing it to the frame.

Modern drop-end scrolls differ largely in detail, but the underlying principle, whether they are made of wood or metal, is much the same. It is not possible to describe the numerous variations, but experts hold that there is still room for improvement, and that the perfect action has not yet been put on the market. The frame-maker must not be credited with all the faults to which drop scrolls are liable; these are sometimes due to defects in the subsequent upholstering. The mere fact that the drop scroll is detachable, and necessitates the use of hinges, springs and ratchets, renders it more liable to get out of order than a fixed end, though it is not thereby suggested that a drop scroll settee cannot be recommended as a satisfactory piece of furniture or that it will necessarily be a source of trouble to the user. On the contrary, when care is exercised, a well-made drop-end settee should last many years in perfect condition.

It may be helpful to describe some of the faults most commonly found in order that frame-makers may endeavour to eliminate them.

A drop-end scroll when in the upright position should be perfectly rigid and perpendicular. After some usage it frequently becomes loose and inclined to fall outwards an inch or two. When viewed from the front the settee then appears faulty. The iron action is more liable to this fault than the wood, because the former must be detached and upholstered independently and subsequently fixed with bolts when complete (see FIG. 35); if these bolts are not carefully and correctly fitted by the upholsterer the nuts become loose and the

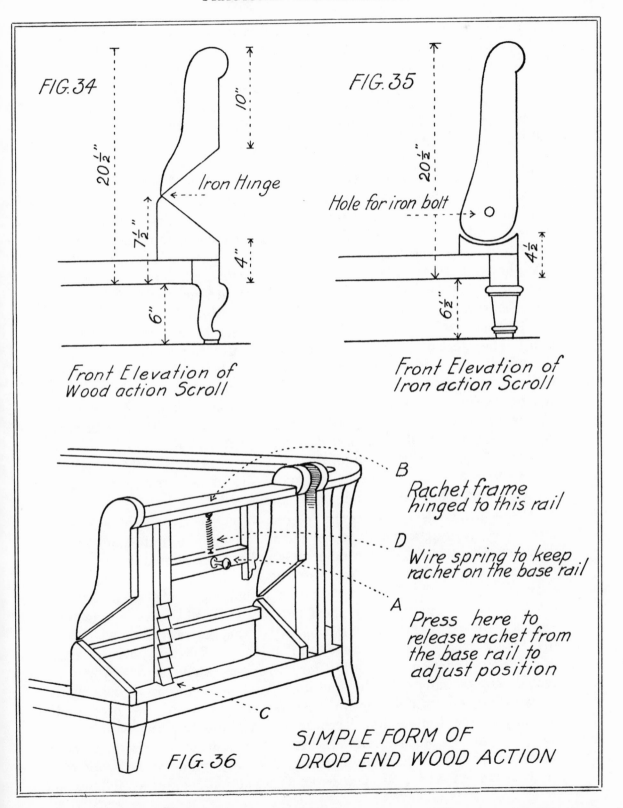

FIG. 34

20½"

10"

7½"

Iron Hinge

4"

6"

Front Elevation of
Wood action Scroll

FIG. 35

20½"

Hole for iron bolt

4½"

6½"

Front Elevation of
Iron action Scroll

B Rachet frame
hinged to this rail

D Wire spring to keep
rachet on the base rail

A Press here to
release rachet from
the base rail to
adjust position

C

FIG. 36

SIMPLE FORM OF
DROP END WOOD ACTION

scroll consequently loses its rigidity. In cases of difficulty the fault can sometimes be remedied by untacking the lower portion of the covering of the outside scroll and readjusting the bolts. In the wood action the scroll is essentially part of the frame, and need not be detached from it to be upholstered, and the fault is thus obviated to a great extent. Before commencing the work of upholstering, drop-end scrolls should always be carefully examined to see that the action works correctly.

It occasionally happens that a finished scroll is difficult to adjust to position, and that undue pressure is necessary to release the ratchet when the scroll is to be lowered; this is sometimes due to the outer covering (called the outside scroll) being stretched too tightly from top to bottom, and the ratchet consequently is pressed down so tightly on to the frame that it is difficult to move (FIG. 36, C.). A loosening of the covering of the outside scroll either at the top or base will allow the ratchet to leave the frame more easily.

The wood or brass knobs attached to scrolls are frequently unsightly, and do not convey by their form any indication as to how they are to be used, that is, whether they should be pushed, pulled, raised or depressed; as a result of this the outside scroll covering through constant mishandling of the knob becomes damaged, untacked or shows a tendency to sag. Whatever form of handle is necessary for adjusting the scroll, the best position for it is immediately beneath the head or as near the top of the outside scroll as possible, and it is very desirable that the style of handle should indicate clearly at sight how it should be used for adjusting the scroll.

Drop-end scrolls are generally placed at one end only of a settee, namely, at the right hand when facing or on the left hand when sitting on the settee. The aim of the upholsterer should be to make both ends appear exactly alike from the front. It will be seen by a study of FIG. 34 and FIG. 36 that this is only possible when a wood action is used, as in this case the front of the scroll (called the facing) may be covered without interfering with the adjustment, which is effected by means of the hinge and ratchet. This is not the case with the iron action (FIG. 38), for here the whole scroll, which is pivoted, moves independently, and to cover the front, as is done with the wood action, would prevent the free movement of the drop end. In FIG. 38 the iron action scroll is shown in a vertical position; a space of $\frac{3}{4}$in. should be allowed between the back and scroll where shaded on diagram; a wider opening than this renders the work unsightly when viewed from the end. The action works as follows :—

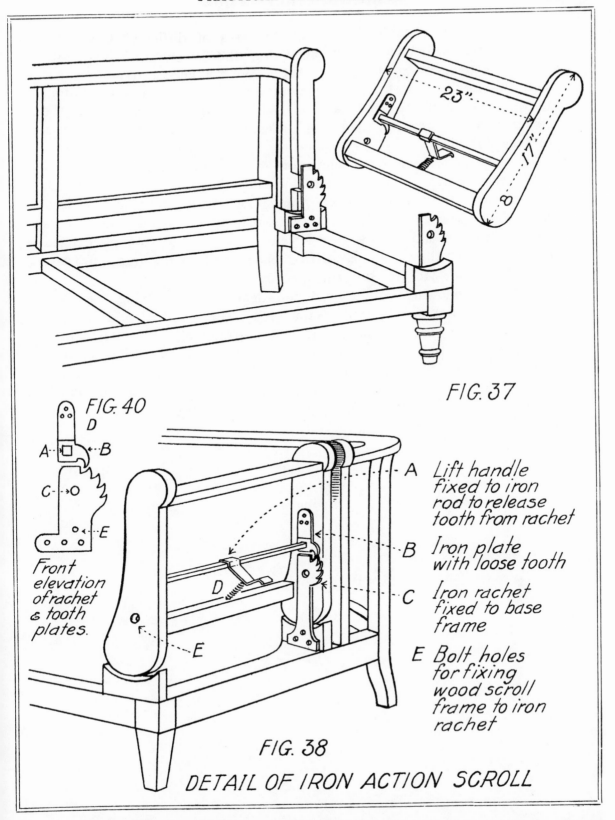

FIG. 37

FIG. 40

D

A —□— B

C ·· O

E

Front
elevation
of rachet
& tooth
plates.

D

E

A Lift handle
fixed to iron
rod to release
tooth from rachet

B Iron plate
with loose tooth

C Iron rachet
fixed to base
frame

E Bolt holes
for fixing
wood scroll
frame to iron
rachet

FIG. 38

DETAIL OF IRON ACTION SCROLL

The lifting of the handle A releases the tooth B from the ratchet C, and the scroll will then fall either to a horizontal position level with the top of the seat or to one of the various angles governed by the tooth and ratchet ; a spring, D, connects the iron rod and the bottom rail of scroll, and ensures that the tooth engages properly with the ratchet. When strongly made and accurately adjusted these actions are very durable.

FIG. 40 gives the front elevation of the iron tooth and ratchet to a larger scale. A is the hole for the square iron rod to which is connected the tooth B ; the round hole C is to take the iron bolts which hold the scroll in position, one on each side, and act as pivots when the end is raised or lowered ; D is a flat iron plate fixed to the inside of the scroll ; E an iron plate fixed to the frame. These plates are from $\frac{1}{16}$in. to $\frac{1}{4}$in. thick.

All the following points need consideration in evolving the ideal action for a drop-scroll settee frame :—(1) The scroll should be perfectly rigid at each adjustment. (2) Capable of easy adjustment by a person sitting on the settee. (3) Method of adjustment clearly indicated. (4) The elimination of spiral springs. (5) Outside scroll free of handle or knob. (6) Construction which allows of the upholstering of scroll without detaching from the frame ; and (7) the elimination of hinges.

CHAPTER 12.

SHOW WOOD FRAMES.

In small chair frames the seat rails should be wide enough to allow sufficient space for the fixing of the webbing and the final coverings. In drawing-room or fancy chairs, the rails frequently lack the width necessary to enable the upholsterer to fix the webs in the proper position to ensure the maximum strength. FIG. 41 shows the correct method and FIG. 42 the difficulties which the upholsterer has to surmount when the seat rails are too narrow. Another unsightly effect resulting from narrow seat rails is indicated at FIG. 42a; here the folded ends of the canvas are seen projecting beneath the polished moulding, and an uneven line is the result, a fault that is sometimes found even in good-class upholstery.

The rails of a small chair which is to be webbed on the top (top stuffed) or the bottom (spring stuffed) should not be less than $1\frac{1}{4}$in. in width. It is in the lighter types of chair known in the trade as occasional or fancy chairs that the faults due to narrow seat rails are most pronounced. The upholstery of a seat which is pin-cushion stuffed often becomes detached after very little use, because an insufficient margin has been left for the tacking of the webs; top stuffed upholstery of this kind entirely depends for strength on the amount of space allowed for tacking, which should never be less than 1in. in width. In some show-wood frames the whole surface is polished, and it is left to the upholsterer to trace a line of finish; this is not a satisfactory method, as will be explained in the subsequent chapters on upholstery. The surface of the space for tacking should never be more than $\frac{1}{8}$in. below the polished edge.

The remarks which have been made above with reference to adequate margins on the seat rails apply with equal force to the backs of chairs which are to be stuffed. These also should have at least 1in. clear space allowed for upholstering (FIG. 43), to prevent the cramping of materials—hessian, covering and gimp (see FIGS. 44 and 45); this is especially necessary where leather is used as a covering material. FIG. 45 shows the upholstering of a back finished with a banding and studs.

Show-wood frames with panel backs have the reverse side or outside back entirely polished (see FIG. 47). In frames such as these the outside back covering is attached first before the inside, and the need for plenty of margin for the upholsterer to work on is obvious. These polished

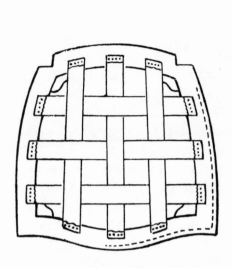

FIG 41

Frame with rails wide
enough to take webs
and allow sufficient
space for final covering

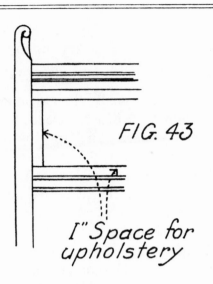

FIG. 43

I" Space for
upholstery

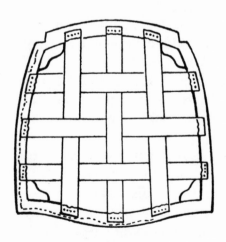

FIG. 42

Result when rails
are too narrow

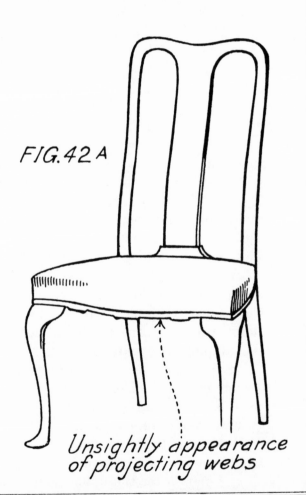

FIG. 42 A

Unsightly appearance
of projecting webs

panel backs give a very smart appearance to the small chair in comparison with the ordinary upholstered back, FIG. 46, which is rather clumsy in appearance, and may be unsightly when the outside back covering begins to sag with use and the material projects at the back. With a polished panel back any sagging of the material is hardly noticeable, and this finish

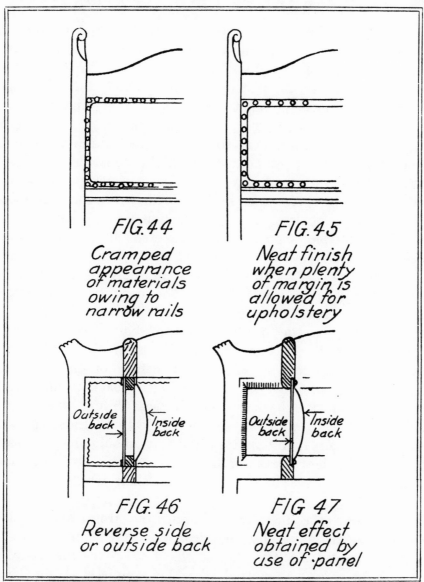

FIG. 44
Cramped
appearance
of materials
owing to
narrow rails

FIG. 45
Neat finish
when plenty
of margin is
allowed for
upholstery

FIG. 46
Reverse side
or outside back

FIG 47
Neat effect
obtained by
use of ·panel

may be regarded as indispensable in the highest class of chair. It will be seen from the above that the frame maker, who, in an endeavour to save wood, cuts down the space which should be left available for tacking, is responsible for faults which the upholsterer, however skilled he may be, finds it difficult and even impossible to rectify.

CHAPTER 13.

K.D. FRAMES FOR EXPORT.

K.D. or loose frames for export are constructed in such a way that they may be taken apart to save space in packing, and assembled with the minimum of trouble and expense on arriving at their destination. A number of systems are employed, but the one illustrated here is the most popular. Frames of this kind held together by iron bolts must be strongly made and carefully fitted, otherwise complaints are likely to arise as to their lack of rigidity when in use. Show-wood frames are more adapted to K.D. construction than stuffovers, as they are not so bulky, and the various parts being more accessible, the bolts, etc., can be adjusted with the minimum displacement of the upholstery. Each section of a chair constructed on the K.D. principle should be upholstered as an individual unit and carefully fitted to ensure a neat finish when the various parts are finally fixed for use. FIGS. 48 and 49 show the method of construction employed for a small chair. The back frame is fitted with projecting dowels, and the centre of the rail is morticed as shown in plan at A to take the head of an iron bolt. FIG. 49 gives the construction of the seat frame with the ends of the side rails bored to receive the dowels and a hole in the centre of the back rail for the bolt. In order to hide the mortice in the back frame into which the bolt is dropped, the back rail of the seat frame projects in such a way that it fits over it as shown in section, FIGS. 49 and 50. This overlapping rail is often too frail; it should be at least $\frac{5}{8}$in. thick, to allow sufficient space for fixing the various covering materials, gimps, etc. FIG. 51 is a back view of the chair when the seat frame is fixed.

FIG. 52 shows the method of fixing the front and back scroll of a couch such as is usually supplied with K.D. suites. Bolts and dowels are employed to fix the scrolls firmly to the base frame, and the head of a bolt is slotted into the armpiece at the back and bolted to the back scroll, the construction being similar to that already explained in connection with a small chair. In the arm-chair dowels and bolts are also employed, but there is one part of the construction of such an arm-chair that needs a note of explanation, namely, the arm at B, which is fixed to the back by means of dowels and a strong

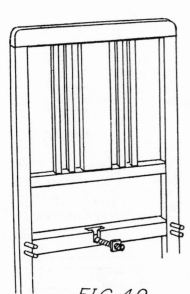

FIG. 48
Back frame with
dowels and bolt

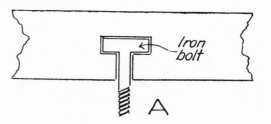

Iron bolt

A

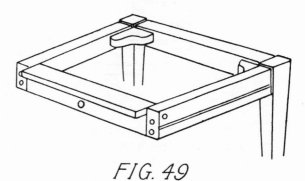

FIG. 49
Seat frame shewing
hole for bolt and
projecting rail at
back to cover mortice

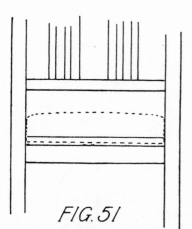

FIG. 51
Back view of
seat when fixed.
dotted line shews
outline of covering

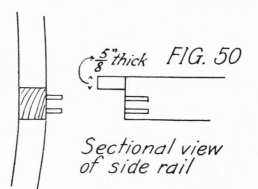

$\frac{5}{8}$" thick   FIG. 50

Sectional view
of side rail

CONSTRUCTION OF
K.D. FRAMES
FOR EXPORT.

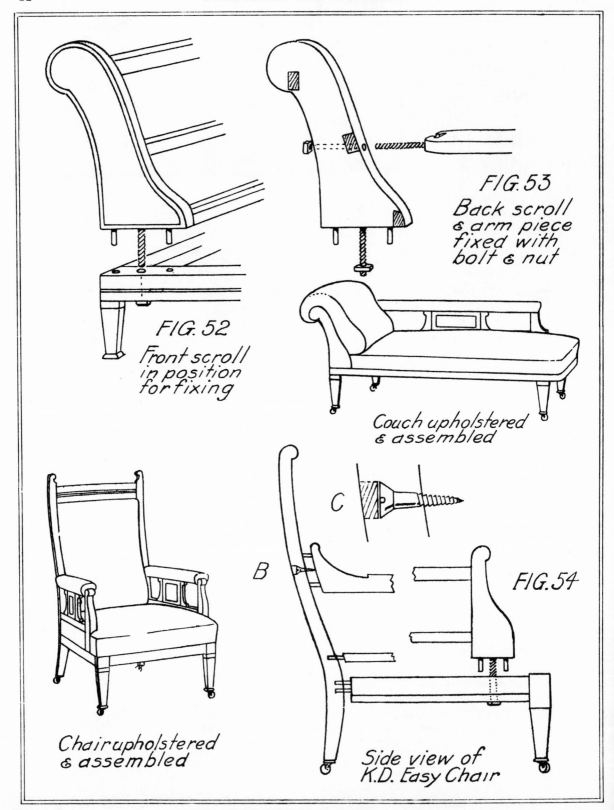

FIG. 52
Front scroll
in position
for fixing

FIG. 53
Back scroll
& arm piece
fixed with
bolt & nut

Couch upholstered
& assembled

C

B

FIG. 54

Chair upholstered
& assembled

Side view of
K.D. Easy Chair

screw; the screw is countersunk as shown in section at C, and the head is hidden by a turned wood button, or "pip," as it is termed in the trade.

The bolts underneath the seat frames which hold K.D. furniture together are often visible from the front, and show at a glance that the construction differs from that of ordinary frames; this fault might be remedied by sinking the bolts, but this is seldom, if ever, done. In K.D. furniture of all varieties care should be taken that the devices used for holding the different parts securely together are not unsightly when the work is finished. There is room for further experiment in this class of frame, and the following points deserve consideration :—

1. The construction should be so arranged that the least possible displacement of upholstery is occasioned if the work has to be taken apart after it is assembled.

2. The method of construction and fixing the various parts together should be clearly indicated.

3. In the case of stuffed seats the material that covers the webs must be left undone at the back, so that access may be obtained in order to screw on the nut shown in FIG. 48. In an upholstered suite there are a dozen or more bolts and nuts, and the upholstered parts round these must be all left unfinished and completed when the work is finally glued and cramped. This is one of the disadvantages which must be put against the many advantages of K.D. frames. The ideal construction would be some system so simple that the work might be assembled by unskilled labour, no completion of the upholstery round bolts, etc., such as we have described being necessary.

CHAPTER 14.

SCROLLS AND FACINGS.

A well-proportioned scroll is of great assistance to the upholsterer in building up his lines of stuffing, though this is sometimes overlooked by frame-makers when setting out their moulds. A skilful upholsterer is really better qualified to set out a mould for a scroll than the frame-maker because he knows the exact difficulties with which he will have to contend in the various tackings. Being conversant from long experience with the correct lines of the finished work, he can see at a glance when the shape is such as to allow him to enlarge in correct proportion. For these reasons the shapes and sizes given in the diagrams accompanying this chapter should be closely studied by the frame-maker. The term scroll is in general use for describing the ends of a couch or settee, but it also applies to the arms of a chair-frame. The front of a scroll when finished, *i.e.*, when covered with stuffing and material, is termed the facing. In stuffover work the line of the finished scroll either offends or pleases the eye acccording to the skill with which the work is carried out, though unfortunately for the upholsterer he may take the greatest care to build up careful lines which are soon spoilt by rough handling. Generally speaking, stuffover frames lack finish, and it is no uncommon thing to find frames when stripped of their rich outer covering made in the roughest style and without any evidences of the use of a spokeshave. This should not be; a stuffover frame (or overstuffed frame as American upholsterers call them) should be carefully finished by the frame-maker, and should be just as good a piece of craftsmanship as a frame as it will be eventually when finished by the upholsterer. Careful shaping and finish is essential, particularly in those chairs in which the outline of the wood is the finished line for the upholsterer. The above remark applies more particularly to modern reproductions of the antique, which consist of a skilful combination of show-wood and stuffover work.

It is possible for the expert upholsterer so to build up his materials that the most fanciful shapes are obtained without any assistance from the frame-maker. (See chapter on Standardised Frames). But this is not satisfactory in large and important pieces of work. A stuffover frame should be (1) of well cleaned wood; (2) the joints should be true and fit perfectly; (3) the shaped parts,

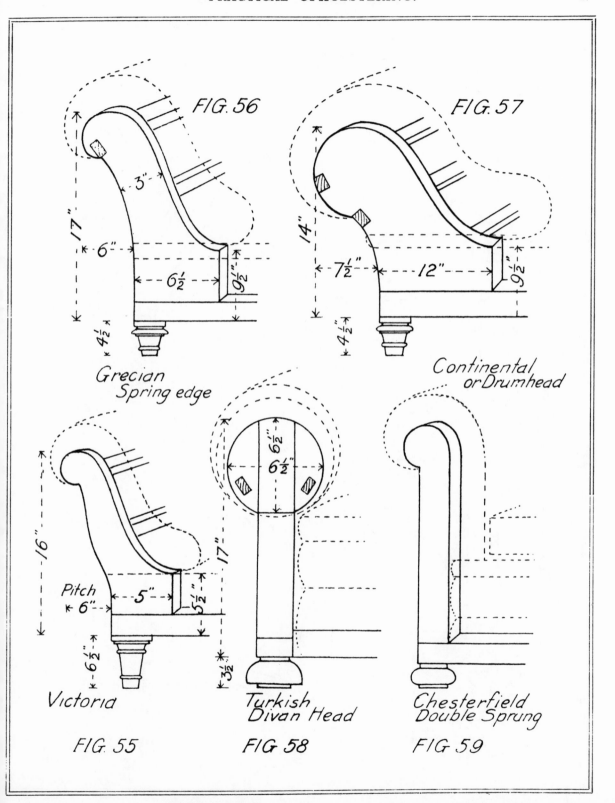

FIG. 56

17"

3"

6"

6½

9½"

4½

Grecian
Spring edge

FIG. 57

14"

7½"

12"

9½"

4½

Continental
or Drumhead

16"

Pitch
6"

5"

5½"

6½"

Victoria

FIG. 55

6½

6½"

17"

3½

Turkish
Divan Head

FIG 58

Chesterfield
Double Sprung

FIG 59

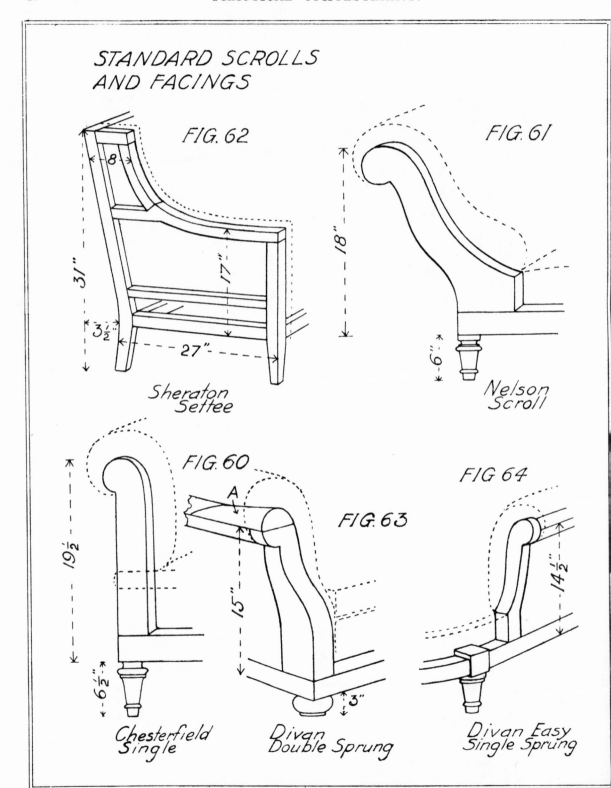

STANDARD SCROLLS
AND FACINGS

FIG. 62

Sheraton
Settee

FIG. 61

Nelson
Scroll

FIG. 60

Chesterfield
Single

FIG. 63

Divan
Double Sprung

FIG 64

Divan Easy
Single Sprung

such as the back and front scrolls, should be shaped to the finished line of the upholstery as nearly as possible (see diagrams). The need for insistence on good joints is demonstrated by frequent complaints, more especially in regard to the arms, which soon get rickety in inferior frames as they are subjected to a deal of hard wear compared with the other parts. Stuffover frames get faulty sooner than show-wood frames, probably because the joints of the former are hidden while the latter are exposed to view, and must therefore be properly made.

To produce a pair of well-balanced facings or scrolls they must be shaped approximately to the lines the upholsterer will create when finishing the work. It is a mistake to place the scroll or head of a couch in too upright a position. Such scrolls should be well pitched and not too high in proportion to the length of the piece.

A frame-maker sometimes finds himself in a dilemma as to what measurement to allow for upholstery when given a finished size to work to. In the case of Chesterfields and the heavier kind of frames the following approximate sizes will be of service. Say a Chesterfield settee, as FIG. 60, is to be made 6ft. 9in. over all, viz.: outside stuffing measurements, the frame should be 6ft. 3in. from scroll to scroll outside measurement, this will allow the upholsterer 3in. for stuffing at each end; the size of the bed of the frame at seat would be governed by the size and pitch of the scrolls.

The Victoria scroll, shown in FIG. 55 is a well-known type, such couches are usually made about 5ft. over all, with a seat frame of 25in. back to front. FIG. 56 (the Grecian) is a bolder scroll, and usually more heavily built than the Victoria for upholstery with spring edges; it should be well pitched, but not quite so pronounced as FIG. 57; the width on the face must not be less than 3in. in the upper part for the convenience of the upholsterer, who usually finishes with what is termed double-facing as compared with the single facing on the Victoria. The usual length of the Grecian couch is 5ft. 3in. seat frame, 26½in. back to front.

The Continental scroll shown in FIG. 57 is very comfortable when finished; it should be kept low, and much beauty of outline may be obtained by a frame-maker with well-proportioned moulds. The dotted line shows the finished upholstery. A couch of this type finished with high back (which will be described later) and wide seat presents a very bold appearance; the length should be about 5ft. 6in. end to end, and seat frame 27in. back to front. As such couches are usually upholstered with spring edges the seat rails should be widened by adding 1in. rails to the inside of the seats as described in Chapter 4.

The divan head shown at FIG. 58 is used in connection with settees, which are called Turkish divans or bolster settees, so named on account of their shape. They are usually of heavy construction and made to special sizes, the feature of such a frame being the well-proportioned head. A frame of this kind, which is less than 6ft. end to end when upholstered, does not give the bold effect which such a piece of work should possess ; the depth of the frame back to front should not be less than 30in. This type of scroll is fixed upright, and the head shaped as a complete circle.

FIGS. 59 and 60 are Chesterfield frames of the type so universally used as to call for little comment. The scrolls are of the same shape as those used for easy-chair frames, and the width of the wood about 3in.

FIG. 61 is the well-known Nelson scroll. The length of the couch over all is approximately 4ft. 9in., and the seat frame back to front 25in. FIG. 63 shows a spring edge frame and 64 a common divan or Bedford chair. This type of scroll, when properly upholstered, is bold and imposing. That shown in FIG. 63 should be constructed of very stout wood. An additional piece A, which is shaped and tapered, is placed on the arm to aid the upholsterer, as the facings are built higher than in inexpensive frames ; this tends to alter the shape of the scroll from a circle to an oval. The scroll of the small divan easy, FIG. 64, is a type which is usually associated with inexpensive chairs, such scrolls look much better when they are set back as sketched than when upright.

Early in this chapter the approximate out-to-out sizes to which frames should be made when a finished upholstery size was stated on an order were given. In making a calculation of this kind when applied to easy chairs more care must be taken than in the case of a couch or settee, for if the measurements allowed for the outward curve of the scroll, plus the thickness of the upholstery are too great it may be found that the seat space is so contracted as to be quite out of proportion to the arms and back. In subsequent chapters the various sizes of complete frames for designs such as accompany this article will be given.

In FIG. 65 the wood at the top is increased in width to aid the upholsterer in getting the outline he requires. The frame should be of stout wood without feet (the castors being fitted direct to the

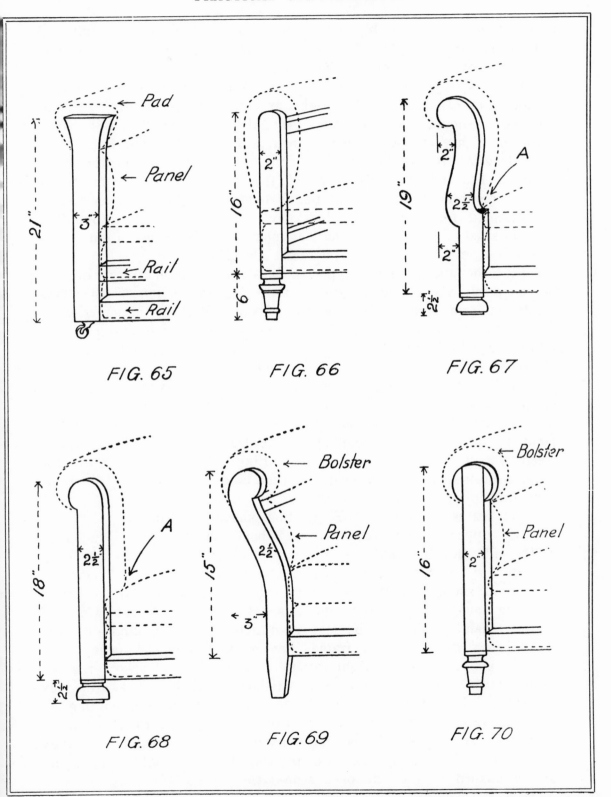

FIG. 65

FIG. 66

FIG. 67

FIG. 68

FIG. 69

FIG. 70

frame), and it should be strengthened by means of an additional rail placed at a height of about 6in. from the base of the frame. The width of a frame of this kind is about 26in. over all.

What is known as a skittle arm is sketched in FIG. 66. A scroll of this sort can be placed upright or set back as in FIG. 73, and the frame should measure 25in. over all. A type of scroll which allows of plenty of seat room is shown at FIG. 67. If the line of the upholstery at A in this type is compared with that at the same point in FIG. 68, the advantage of the curved scroll, where plenty of seat room is desirable, will be obvious. A scroll such as this is not adapted for small easy chairs, but shows to greater advantage on full-sized frames. The measurement of the front from scroll to scroll over all should not be less than 28in.

FIGS. 69 and 70 show types of bolster head upholstery; in FIG. 69 the scroll has a rake of 3in., a form of construction which allows plenty of arm space. Of the two designs FIG. 69 is superior in appearance in cases where the upholstery is carried down nearly to the floor level, as in a double sprung frame. A frame of this kind should measure 24in. in the bed and 30in. at the scrolls.

In FIG. 71 the line of the frame at the top is the finished line of the upholstery. The edges at A and B need careful shaping, chamfering, and rounding off, and the shaping, etc., should graduate from the point C upwards. This shaping of the frame will assist the upholsterer who usually places but little stuffing on this style of arm. The usual measurements for a chair of this kind are 26in. on the base, 31in. out to out at top of scroll.

FIG. 72 is a similar scroll to that shown at FIG. 63.

The upper portion should be set back about $3\frac{1}{2}$in. as indicated in the side elevation.

FIG. 73 is finished with slightly rounded edges at A and B. The wood should be $2\frac{1}{2}$in. in width and well set back, and the top of the arm must be quite flat for this style of frame; the width of such a chair should not be less than 26in. and this kind of scroll looks better on a full-size frame than a small one. A facing such as this placed in an upright position, with the upholstery finished in a similar way, makes a very satisfactory chair. The arm may be widened by fixing a rail on the outside at C for the stuffing.

FIG. 74 is a type of frame that can be adapted to many styles of upholstery. It should be constructed of stout wood and heavily built; the rail forming the arm projects to the front about $2\frac{1}{2}$in., and is shaped to the line of a semi-circle.

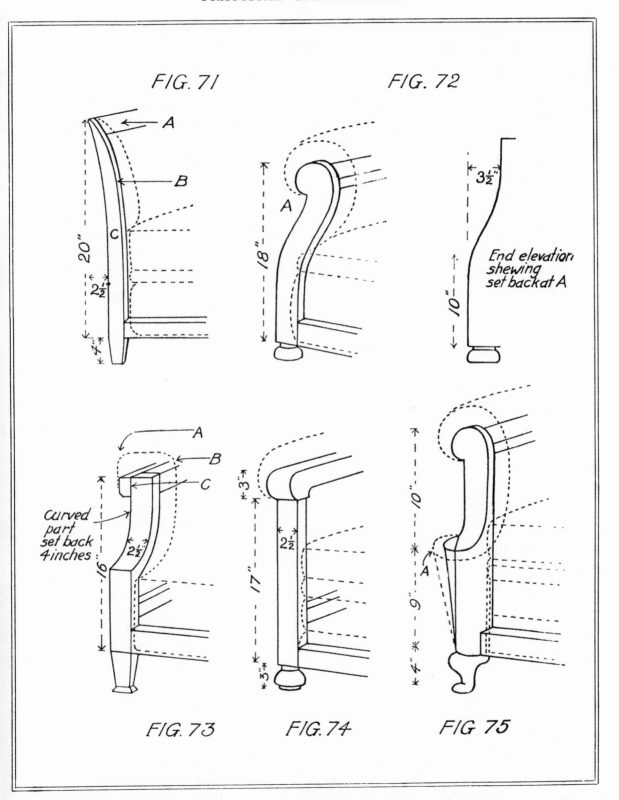

FIG. 71

FIG. 72

End elevation
shewing
set back at A

Curved
part
set back
4 inches

FIG. 73

FIG. 74

FIG 75

FIG. 75 shows a curved scroll which breaks from the horizontal plane at the seat level to a vertical plane above. Such a scroll is very pleasing when upholstered on a well proportioned mould, but it may easily be overdone and made to appear clumsy on an unsatisfactory mould. Frame-makers, when adding additional pieces at A, are very liable to overdo it, consequently, the upholsterer finds it difficult to build his outlines in proportion. The applied piece at A should project at a very slight angle (about $1\frac{1}{4}$in. at top), and should taper off to a feather edge about 1in. above the base of seat frame. Whenever possible scrolls should be shaped out of one piece and not built up, as they gain both in outline and proportion when this method is followed. The upper portion should be set back as in FIG. 72. The width of the frame at the scrolls should be about 28in., and a cabriole leg gives a better finish than a tapered or turned leg.

CHAPTER 15.

FEET FOR STUFFOVER FRAMES.

A selection of the many different designs for cups and feet used on stuffover frames is given at FIG. 76. The height of the foot for an ordinary single sprung frame should not exceed 6in. exclusive of the castor, which varies from 1in. to 2in. Deep-seated or double-sprung frames, such as divans, lounges, or settees, in which the finished line of the upholstery is only a few inches from the floor, are usually fitted with turned, polished cups, which may be either screwed or dowelled to the frame.

From the upholsterer's point of view the former is the more satisfactory method, as they can then be fixed after the work is fully upholstered. As pointed out in a previous chapter, care should be taken by the upholsterer that the wood to which the cup is ultimately fixed is kept clear of tackings on the under side to allow for glueing as well as screwing on the cup. Another point in favour of screwing, as opposed to dowelling, is that bruising or scratching of the polished cup when dowelled on cannot always be avoided by the upholsterer in finishing the work, however careful he may be.

A cup of any design when raised too high from the floor is not so pleasing to the eye as when in a low position. A well-shaped cup adds much to the appearance of a deep-seated frame, and a first-class piece of work is often spoilt by an ugly semi-ball cup with the castor fixed on the flat surface beneath. FIG. 77 shows a cup with the castor fixed on the flat surface, and FIG. 78 an example turned or gouged out to allow for the sinking of the under side of a cup to leave sufficient space for the bowl of the castor to revolve freely without touching the wood. The dotted line A, FIG. 77, shows the contour of the underside after being turned or gouged out to allow for the sinking of the castor. Sometimes the castor is sunk in the brace, as indicated at FIGS. 81 and 82, when the designer does not wish to use a cup or foot.

The cups shown at FIGS. 77 and 78 are about 2in. in depth and 4in. in diameter; they are suitable for settees or heavy frames. The cup marked X in FIG. 76 is a high-class design, which adds greatly to the appearance of a good piece of work. The diameter should not be less than 4in. and the depth 2½in. A cup of this type is a good finish to upholstery covered in morocco.

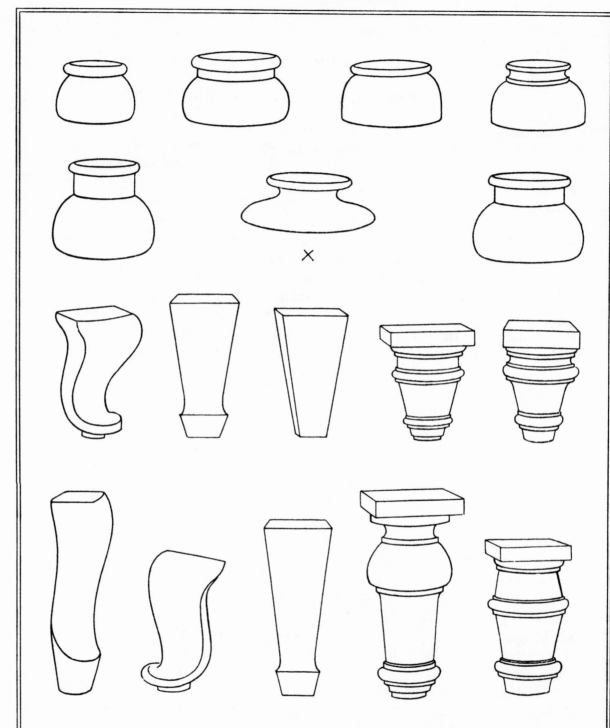

FIG 76   FEET FOR STUFFOVER FRAMES

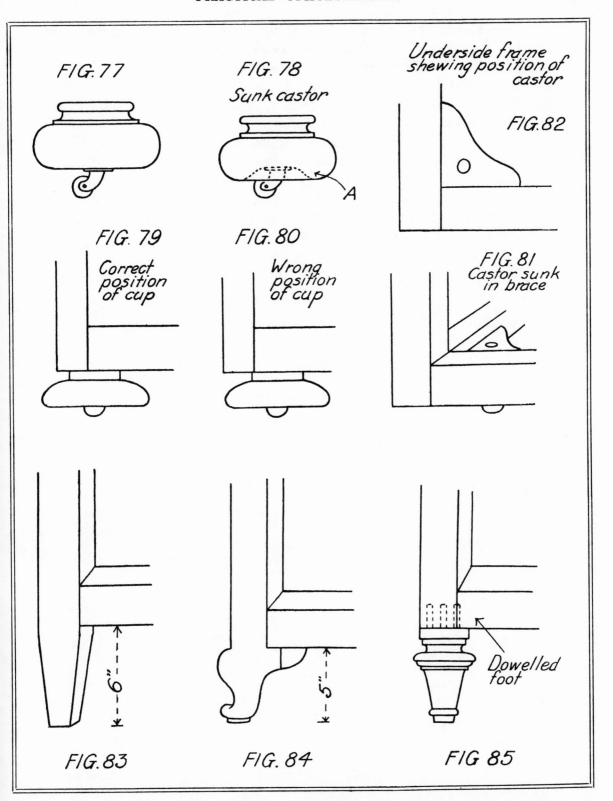

FIG. 77

FIG. 78
Sunk castor

A

Underside frame
shewing position of
castor

FIG. 82

FIG. 79
Correct
position
of cup

FIG. 80
Wrong
position
of cup

FIG. 81
Castor sunk
in brace

FIG. 83

FIG. 84

FIG 85
Dowelled
foot

Care should be taken when fixing cups to avoid placing them too far underneath the frame, otherwise much of the effect of the shape is lost. The correct and incorrect positions to fix cups are shown at FIG. 79 and FIG. 80. Cups which are too spherical or ball shaped, fitted to stuffover frames, produce a clumsy effect, and give the work a common appearance.

Castors form a very important finish to any piece of upholstered furniture, and here, as has been mentioned in connection with drop-end settees, there is a field for something new. This is proved by the many patents that have been placed on the market recently. In the opinion of the writer nothing has yet surpassed the old-fashioned cabriole castor for strength and durability.

CHAPTER 16.

THE FIXING OF CASTORS.

In many workshops, as soon as a settee or easy chair leaves the upholsterer's hands, it is regarded as finished, and insufficient care is taken in minor details such as the fixing of castors. In heavy upholstery a good deal depends on a suitable, well-fitted castor, and, apart from this, all manufacturing firms suffer to a greater or lesser degree from complaints of damaged castors. The damage may consist of a broken bowl, the wood of a leg split through careless boring, or a broken rivet caused by inefficient fixing. These defects are very troublesome, as in some cases it is necessary to provide a new leg. For instance, when the castor becomes detached, leaving the upper portion in the leg, it is very difficult to remedy the trouble without causing further damage.

The method of fixing castors varies according to the style of work. The socket, the plate, and the cabriole castor each requires different handling. The socket and the cabriole are generally used for lighter work, and the plate castor for heavier pieces, such as divans, settees, and ottomans that are raised only a few inches from the floor. The ball-bearing castor is an easy-running variety, serviceable when applied to heavy work.

When circumstances permit, castors should be fixed with the chair or settee turned bottom upwards on a low bench, well padded to prevent any damage to the covering or polished wood. In practice a chair or settee is frequently placed on the outside back with the legs in a horizontal position; this facilitates boring for the castors, but is not a satisfactory method for obtaining the true positions for the castors. FIG. 86 is a diagram of a chair placed correctly for castoring, with the legs in a vertical position. Before boring, the workman should first true or square the legs. This is necessary, because sometimes the frame may have warped or the joints given slightly. The method adopted to true or square the legs is to place a straight edge across the front legs from A to B, having first ascertained that they are of equal height. (See FIG. 86). If the upholsterer takes up a position midway between the front legs, with his eye a few inches from the straight edge, he will be able to prove the back legs and make any necessary adjustment. After selecting the castors, which should not be less than 1⅛in. for an easy-chair

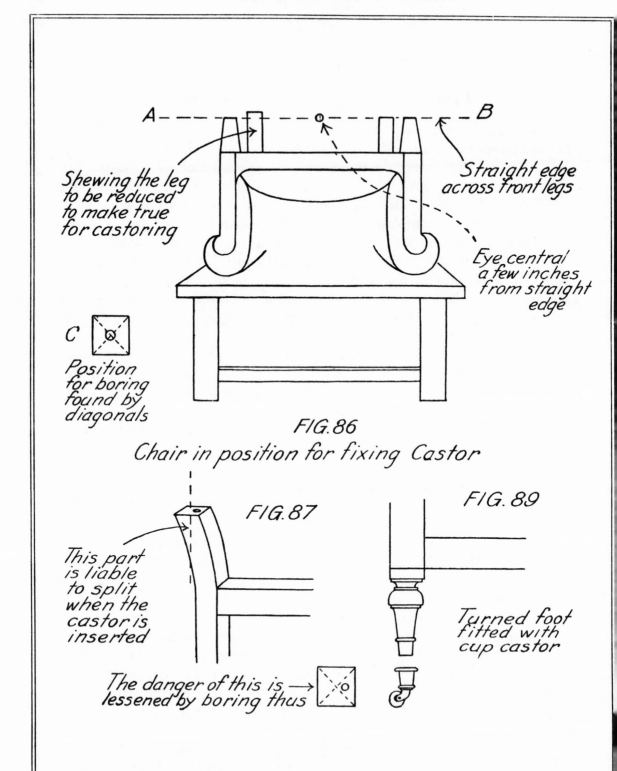

A - - - - - - - - - - O - - - - - - - - - - B

Shewing the leg to be reduced to make true for castoring

Straight edge across front legs

Eye central a few inches from straight edge

C

Position for boring found by diagonals

FIG. 86

Chair in position for fixing Castor

FIG. 87

This part is liable to split when the castor is inserted

FIG. 89

Turned foot fitted with cup castor

The danger of this is → lessened by boring thus

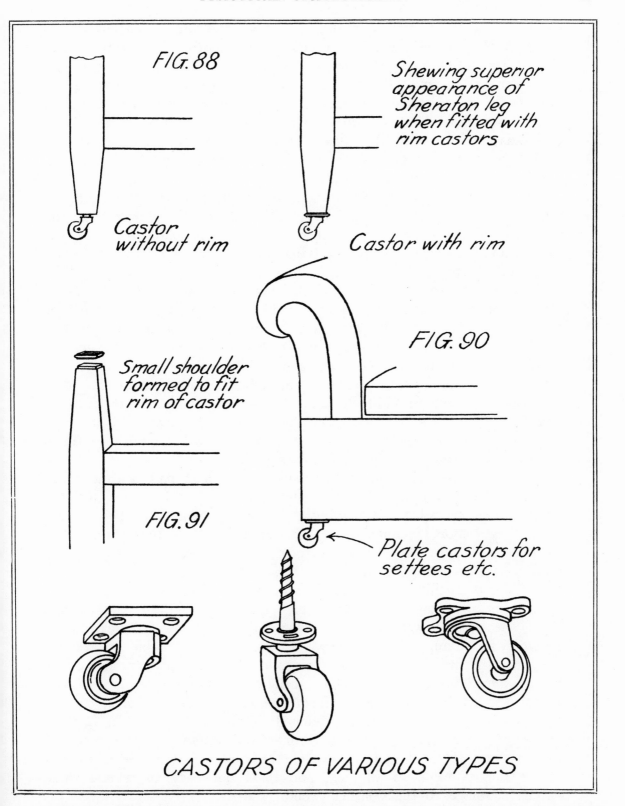

FIG. 88

Shewing superior
appearance of
Sheraton leg
when fitted with
rim castors

Castor
without rim

Castor with rim

FIG. 90

Small shoulder
formed to fit
rim of castor

Plate castors for
settees etc.

FIG. 91

CASTORS OF VARIOUS TYPES

frame, a hole slightly less in diameter than the widest portion of the screw of the castor should be bored in the centre of each front leg. The centre is obtained by drawing a pencil line diagonally from corner to corner, as shown at C, FIG. 86. The back legs of chairs and settees are frequently shaped as shown in FIG. 87, and in preparing these for castors care must be taken to bore the hole in that part of the wood best adapted to bear the strain which the castor imposes on it. Back legs may be weakened and rendered liable to split by boring too deeply or exactly in the centre.

It is an open question theoretically whether a castor should be screwed on or hammered in. In practice it is safe to say that the general method is to hammer them in until the plate rests on the surface of the wood, makers relying for the necessary strength on the smaller screws in the plate.

For socket castors, FIG. 89, the leg need not be bored. Such castors are made either round or square to fit exactly the turned or square wrought leg; they give a good finish, but must not be too large, or they appear clumsy and heavy. The cup of the castor should be of such a size as to allow of its being gently hammered into position and finally screwed through the holes made for that purpose. This is an old-fashioned style of castor, but very durable, and its advantages are :—(1) The leg is not weakened by boring; (2) the cup fitting tightly round the wood of the leg binds the fibres together, and thus adds greatly to its strength.

Plate castors are made either with or without ball bearings, and as with the cup castor the leg need not be bored except for the small screws necessary for holding the plate in position. The appearance of a castor is enhanced by the addition of a brass rim fitted to the leg before the castor is fixed. (See FIG. 88). These rims require careful fitting, as shown in FIG. 91.

While the utility of castors is unquestioned, they have disadvantages as well as advantages. For example (1) the strength of the wooden leg is necessarily weakened by the number of holes, at least four, required for fixing; (2) the bowl of the castor is liable to become clogged with dust, especially if it is oiled; (3) the appearance of the leg in some styles, such as the cabriole and square leg, is to some extent spoiled by being raised from the floor by means of a castor; (4) castors are, unless carefully packed, liable to breakage in transit; (5) when a rivet is defective or broken the whole castor is rendered useless; and (6) a detached bowl of the castor leaves the plate and screws in the wood of the leg, and it is not easy to release these without damage to the polished wood.

CHAPTER 17.

WEBBING.

Having dealt with the construction of frames for upholstering, the reader's attention will now be called to the first of the actual processes of upholstering, namely, webbing. The tools required for upholstering are few in number compared with those necessary for other trades, and they are inexpensive. In a subsequent chapter, they and their uses will be described in detail, together with the characteristics of materials and stuffings.

It is not absolutely necessary to use webbing. The reader is referred to Chapter 8, where at FIG. 21 he will find a plan of a seat with wood rails in place of webbing. This construction is used, as was then described, in connection with spring cushion work. Chair frames are also sometimes fitted with small woven wire spring mattresses, such as are usually associated with beds. Others are made with three-ply seats fitted to the chair-frame, and with springs attached. These forms of construction aim at dispensing with webbing, though it is safe to assert that webbing will always be associated with upholstery of all grades.

The upholsterer who wishes to become a competent craftsman should make a study of the properties and characteristics of all the materials he uses—this applies especially to webbing, which is subjected to much wear and tear.

English or Scotch webbing is generally used for the seats, while the cheaper Belgian or Continental variety is considered suitable for the webbing of backs, arms, and other parts not subjected to so great a strain as the seat. Webbing is a stout braid made in various widths, and has a herring-bone pattern running right through it, a well-made web being a very strong and durable material.

It would be difficult to insist too much on the need for care as far as the process of webbing is concerned. It is the actual foundation of the upholstery, and if not properly done may be the initial factor in a bad piece of work. For example, the stuffing of a seat may sag and become unsightly for the following reasons connected with the webbing :—(1) Insufficient webbing, even though the material is of a good quality. (2) Poor quality webbing that will not bear the pressure of a strong spring. (3) The over-straining of good quality webbing.

It is the placing of the webs in correct position and stretching them properly that give strength to the work, rendering it capable of resisting the wear and tear of daily use. It should be noted that seats may sag from causes which have nothing to do with the webbing, but these will be described in future chapters.

For the process of webbing the upholsterer needs a strainer—either a spiked stretcher or bat and roller stretcher may be used (see FIGS. 92 and 93). The spiked strainer is condemned by many upholsterers because the holes caused by the spikes (see FIG. 97a) weaken the webbing and render it liable to tear. The bat and roller stretcher is the ideal tool, because the leverage on the webbing can be adjusted to a nicety, and the danger of scratching polished work by means of the spikes is eliminated. FIG. 94 is an iron webbing pincer used for stretching short lengths of webbing in the backs and arms of frames. Nothing like the same leverage is obtained by the use of this tool, but, as will be shown in subsequent chapters, it can be employed for work in connection with which it would be impracticable to use the others. The above will be understood more clearly after studying various methods of webbing. The tools required for webbing are a hammer, scissors, a webbing stretcher, and ⅝in. tacks. The spiked webbing stretcher is simpler to use than the bat, but the danger of spoiling and tearing the webbing is greater. A common fault with beginners is to overstrain the webbing in their efforts to make it as taut as possible, but this is overcome by practice. A small chair is the best kind to commence upon, and these may be webbed on top (top-stuffed) or underneath the frame (spring-stuffed). The number of webs should not be less than five.

A chair which is to be spring-stuffed should be placed upside down on the board or trestle, as shown in FIG. 86, Chapter 16. For top-stuffing (the process which will now be described), the frame may be webbed as it stands on the floor or a low board. (See FIG. 95). First of all mark off the centre line of the back rail D, FIG. 95. (*Sketch 95 shows the webbing parallel with the front rail, merely to demonstrate the process more clearly, but webbing should always start on the back rail in top-stuffed work*). Having obtained the centre point of the back rail D, take one end of the webbing, fold over about ¾in. and fix it with a temporary tack, and proceed similarly with the ends of the other webs on the back rail. Having decided the exact position of the webs, four ⅝in. tacks should be driven home as shown at A, care being taken to tack nearer the outer than the inner edge of the frame. Then take the stretcher in the right

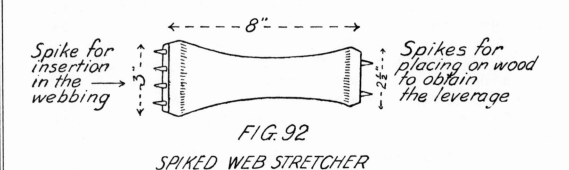

Spike for insertion in the webbing →

8"

3"

2½"

Spikes for placing on wood to obtain the leverage

FIG. 92

SPIKED WEB STRETCHER

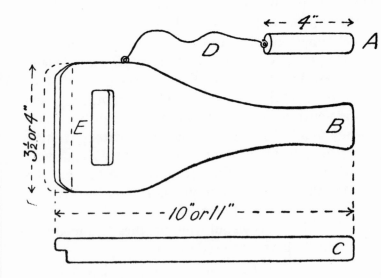

4"

A

D

E

B

3¼ or 4"

10" or 11"

C

Wood roller

FIG. 93

BAT & ROLLER STRETCHER

D. Cord or chain to which roller is attached

E Dotted line shews end padded to avoid scratching the polished wood

FIG. 97ᴬ

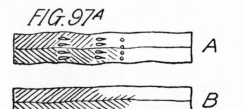

A

B

Webbing. A. after use of spiked stretcher. B. after bat stretcher

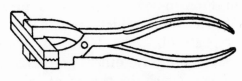

FIG. 94

Iron web pincer for straining short pieces of webbing

hand, place the smaller end with the two spikes against the frame at F, avoiding any polished moulding; hold the stretcher at an angle of about 45 deg., push the web on to the spikes with the left hand, still holding the stretcher with the right, and the position should be exactly as shown in FIG. 95, except as before mentioned, that the stretcher should be in the centre of the front rail E. To stretch the web, grasp both it and the stretcher firmly with the left hand, press it firmly down to a horizontal position as shown by the dotted line C, and, with the stretcher still horizontal, fix the webbing with three or four tacks, cut off the webbing, leaving one inch for folding, and turn back the fold and secure with one or two tacks.

Though this operation sounds simple, the beginner will experience minor obstacles which can only be overcome by practice. The first is the difficulty of fixing the tacks while the web is in a horizontal position. To take up each tack singly and individually is a slow and clumsy method, but the ease with which the more experienced craftsman produces tacks from his mouth just as a bootmaker does will prompt the beginner to do the same. Then, again, an inexperienced worker in endeavouring to strain the webs tightly places the stretcher nearly perpendicular. If the web is very strong it may stand this strain, but there is always a danger of its breaking away from the tacks on the further side or tearing from the spikes on the stretcher (see FIG. 98). Another very common fault, by no means confined to learners, is failure to drive home the head of the tack. This is important, as it is the flat surface of the tackhead embedding itself in the material that really gives the strength.

After straining the two other webs, one on either side of the centre, the side ones should be fixed in the same manner. It is easier to tack on the right side and strain on the left, as shown in FIGS. 95-97. There is a point here in connection with the position of the webs which run parallel to the front rail which should be emphasised. The front of a seat is subjected to greater wear and tear than any other portion. It is the practice, therefore, to keep all webs well to the front—that is to say, the middle web connecting rails A and F would be nearer the front rail E than the back rail D.

Subsequent chapters will explain the position of the webs connecting the side rails more clearly.

In the interests of economy unnecessary cutting must be avoided when using webbing. FIG. 101 shows a diagram of a chair seat with six webs, for which a length of three yards is sufficient; if this length is cut in half it will give four ends to work from, but this should not

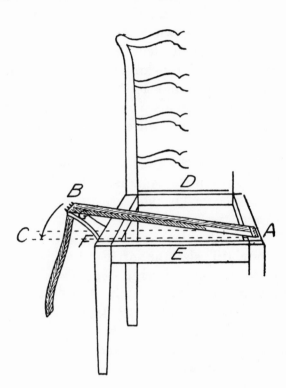

FIG. 95

A. Web folded and tacked with 3 or 4 $\frac{5}{8}$" Tacks

B. The strainer in position with spikes inserted in the web

C. Dotted line shewing position of web, with pressure from B to C

N.B. Webbing should commence from back rail. The sketch shews treatment of side rail merely to indicate process clearly

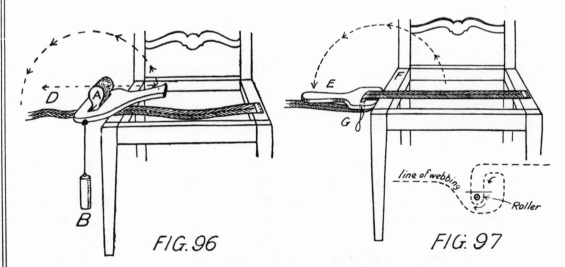

FIG. 96

FIG. 97

SHEWING USE OF BAT STRETCHER

be done, as it results in waste, for the simple reason that if there
is any balance of web left over when the work is completed it will
be in two short lengths of very little service, whereas if the three-yard
length is worked from in one piece, a useful length of web may be
left over.   A single length of web is sufficient for small work of any
description, and the beginner should realise that too many cuts always
result in waste.   This is important, for economy is absolutely essential
in the upholstery trade, in which so many different materials are
used in the making of a single article.

In larger pieces of work, such as settees or easy chairs, more
ends may be used with a lesser possibility of waste, as the short
lengths of web left over are useful for backs, arms, etc.   Many
firms adopt the principle of allowing the upholsterer a certain number
of yards of web and material for each piece of work, and this is
practical where replicas of a standard size or style of frame are
constantly made : it works well for the upholsterer, who soon accus-
toms himself to " cutting his garment according to his cloth," and for
the employer who is enabled to get accurate costings, knowing exactly
the amount of web used on any particular work.   The insistence laid
on this matter here is to impress upon the upholsterer that economy
results from working with one length of web, and that to divide it
into one or more pieces before commencing work often spells waste.

The Bat Web Strainer.

The bat web strainer is a little more complicated in construction
and use than the spike strainer, FIG. 93.   Powerful leverage may be
obtained with it, and the beginner is often tempted to overstrain,
and as a result the web breaks away entirely.   This is by no means
an uncommon fault whilst the trade is being learnt.   First tack
the web in the same manner as already explained, and place the
stretcher in position as shown at FIG. 96, the handle always pointed
towards the inside of frame and the slot clearing the outer edge of
rail (see A), so as to allow of the web being passed through freely
from underneath.   Place the roller B in the loop formed by the web
at A (FIG. 96).   The beginner will now realise the ease with which
the stretcher can be adjusted.   By grasping the handle firmly with
the right hand and tightening the web D (FIG. 96) with the left, the
stretcher moves along the web to any position or at any angle as the
roller revolves.   To strain the web, grasp the handle and the web
after the roller has been inserted and pull as indicated by the arrows

B. Shews web stretched & tacked
ready for cutting & folding: when cut
fold over & secure with 2 tacks.

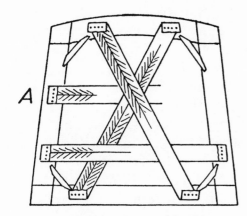

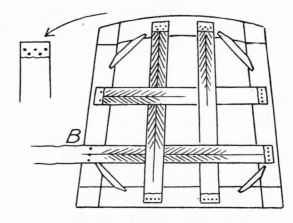

FIG. 98 Method of
webbing common chairs.
For placing 3 springs.
The web A is sometimes
dispensed with

FIG. 99 Method of
webbing for 4 springs.
It is important that
the webs should be kept
well to the front

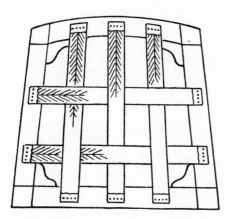

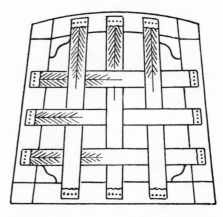

FIG. 100. Another method
of webbing with 5 webs

FIG. 101. A seat correctly
webbed for placing any
number of springs up to 9

into a horizontal position as FIG. 97. As will be seen, here the bat is now completely turned over, and the web is stretched in a horizontal position for tacking.

The web pincers (FIG. 94) are very serviceable for straining short lengths. They are used much in the same way as ordinary pincers, being placed in exactly the same position prior to stretching. Care must, of course, be taken to avoid damaging any polished surface with the sharp edges of the pincers when straining the web by levering with this tool. If a pad or loose fold of web is first placed on the polished surface or rail before straining commences the danger is considerably reduced. It is important to grip the handle of the pincers firmly while tacking, otherwise the web may gradually slacken and the efficacy of the straining process be reduced. With pincers the web cannot be strained so effectively as with the spike stretcher or bat stretcher. If the piece of web to be strained is of sufficient length to allow of its being folded over and placed in the teeth of the pincers doubled, a much better grip is obtainable. The use of the pincers in practice will be described from time to time in dealing with other materials used in upholstering.

DISPOSITION OF THE WEBBING.

As will be seen from the diagrams (FIGS. 98 and 101), the cross webbings, that is, those that are tacked to the side rails, are interlaced with those that are tacked to the back and front rails. There are three reasons for this :—(1) It keeps the web in a more rigid position for the sewing on of the springs; (2) it adds additional strength to the whole seat, and (3) it prevents the sagging of any web, or webs, not strained as well as the others. In placing the side webs on a small chair frame they should be tacked on the right and strained to the left, and should be so disposed as to divide the chair frame into regular spaces, as shown in FIGS. 99, 100 and 101 ; but the importance of webbing close to the front rail must not be forgotten. FIG. 98 is a diagram showing a method of webbing with three webs often employed in connection with inexpensive furniture ; though not so strong as the other methods shown, the amount of wear that a frame webbed in this way will stand is astonishing if reasonable care is exercised by skilled men. It is webbed to carry three springs placed triangle-wise where the webs cross each other. The fourth web, A, is frequently dispensed with, though when employed it, of course, gives additional support. FIG. 99 is the method of webbing employed to carry four springs ; FIG. 100, another method for four

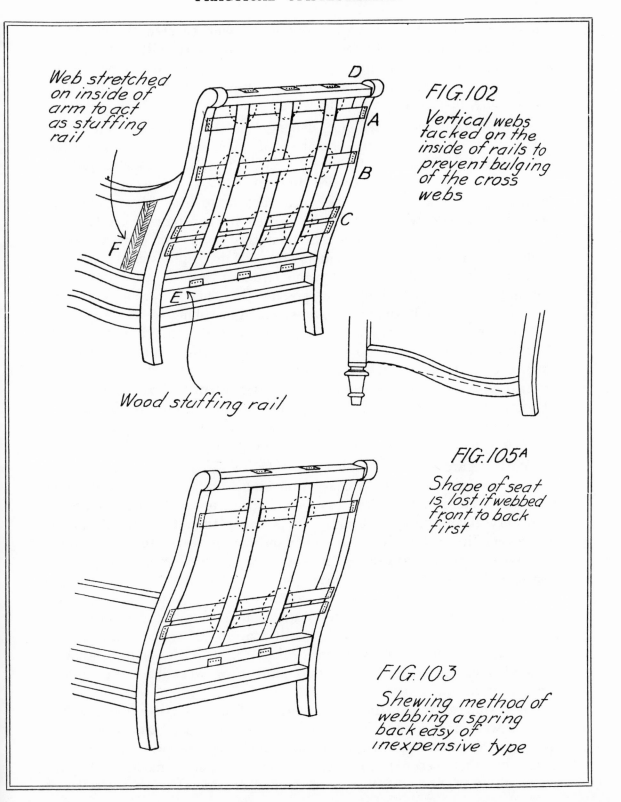

Web stretched on inside of arm to act as stuffing rail

F

Wood stuffing rail

E

D

A

B

C

FIG. 102

Vertical webs tacked on the inside of rails to prevent bulging of the cross webs

FIG. 105A

Shape of seat is lost if webbed front to back first

FIG. 103

Shewing method of webbing a spring back easy of inexpensive type

springs; FIG. 101 shows a seat correctly webbed to give the maximum of resiliency and wear. A seat treated in this way with good quality web, either for top stuffing or spring stuffing, should allow of the other parts of the upholstery being renovated two or three times without any displacement of the webs.

The efficiency of webbing depends more upon the care taken in stretching than upon the quantity of webs used. It is important that the webs should not be over-strained; if they are, extra pressure on the seat when in use causes the strands of the web to become slack at the points where they are tacked to the frame, and this tendency increases with the friction caused by constant use. It would be difficult to lay too much stress upon this point, yet it is frequently overlooked or not properly understood. Many upholsterers, if asked as to how to obtain the best value from a web seat, would reply, " Stretch the webs as tightly as possible." This is wrong, and good work is often spoilt because over-strained webbing gives way after a little use. The web should first be strained taut, but the secret of durability lies in slackening slightly before finally tacking. Experience will prove the truth of this statement. When a web is strained almost to the breaking point and then tacked it retains no buoyancy or give, and its life is thereby shortened, but by first obtaining a good leverage with the stretcher, and then slightly relaxing, the web responds to pressure and a good seat is obtained.

With regard to the number of webs required on any given seat, there is no hard and fast rule. A medium or high-class chair should not require more or have less than six. (See FIG. 101). In Continental upholstery the webbing is usually much wider than the English variety and covers the seat entirely. These Continental seats are very durable, and have a further advantage in requiring no further covering underneath, but this method is better adapted to show-wood upholstery than to stuffover work. Given good webbing, which is the main consideration, it matters little what actual number be used, and if the material is of excellent quality a chair webbed as FIG. 98 might last as long as one webbed as FIG. 101. With common webbing it is obvious that the greater the number of webs used the greater the strength.

A divan easy-chair frame is shown in FIG. 102, with the positions of the webs indicated. The side rails of the back are curved, and in order to retain the shape in the upholstery the webs A, B and C must be first secured in position, and strained moderately taut, whilst the upright ones must be slackened considerably after stretching,

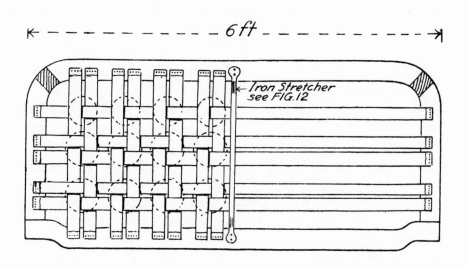

FIG.104. SETTEE WEBBED FOR 8 ROWS OF SPRINGS
When number of springs is known and their
approximate positions much advantage will
accrue by webbing in pairs

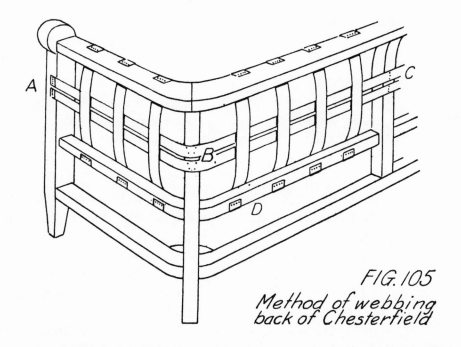

FIG.105
Method of webbing
back of Chesterfield

otherwise the requisite shape will be lost. This must also be remembered when webbing any seat frame that is shaped. (See FIG. 105a). The webs must be first placed from side to side, and the general rule, which is to fix from the front of the frame, must not be followed.

In tacking the back webs the upholsterer is sometimes in doubt as to whether they should be folded or tacked on the raw edge without folding. There an advantage to be gained by following the latter method, which is of considerable importance when the subsequent outer cover is placed over the webs, but the former method, namely, folding before tacking, is certainly the correct way for strength and durability. In high-class upholstery the outside backs being well padded with a thin layer of hair and wadding, there is no danger of the thickness of the folded web causing an uneven surface of the covering material spoiling the effect of what should be a perfectly flat surface. This defect does occur when the webs are folded on inexpensive furniture, the folds causing irregularities or bulges which look unsightly. This will be explained more clearly in a subsequent chapter.

In dealing with the upright webs they are first tacked on the stuffing rail E, and strained and tacked on the top rail D. Two webs are usually placed at C, because in this position they are required to support larger springs than are used at A and B. The web at F must be tightly strained, as it acts as a substitute for the wood rail which was used in old-fashioned stuffovers, but is dispensed with entirely in modern frames.

An inexpensive method of webbing a spring back easy is shown at FIG. 103. Once more the reader is reminded of the importance of placing the cross webs first. It is unnecessary to lace the webs of backs that are curved, the aim being so to arrange them that in addition to being taut they conform to the shape of the frame as far as possible.

Double webbing, that is, the placing of webs side by side in pairs, is the method followed in cases in which the exact number of springs required is known. (See FIG. 104). This is the ideal method of webbing for work of this kind. A study of the diagram will show how well the springs (shown by the dotted lines) are supported. The two methods may be compared by referring to FIGS. 12 and 14 of this series. The number of webs in FIG. 104 suffice for a settee 6ft. 6in. over all. Given a good quality web, upholstery treated in this way is very durable and lasting.

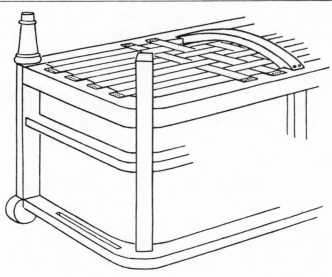

FIG. 106 A curved wood stretcher rail
sometimes used with good effect

FIG. 107
Double sprung chairs
are sometimes webbed
on top edge of seat frame
instead of underneath

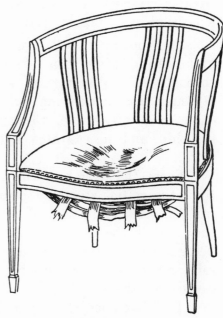

FIG. 110
A possible result
of tacking webbing
without folding end
of the web

Billiard seats, settees, or frames that are of great length should always have the short webs placed first. When a frame such as this is turned upside down for the process of webbing, the lengthwise webs are placed beneath the curved iron stretcher, as shown at Fig. 104. In cases where wood stretchers are used the lengthwise webs would come into contact with them, but must not be fixed to them, otherwise much of the buoyancy of the seat will be lost. This tacking to the stretcher is very common in practice, but absolutely wrong in principle.

Chesterfields and settees usually have spring backs. The method of webbing varies, but Fig. 105 shows a correctly webbed back. The short vertical webs are not laced, but are placed on the outside of the long double webs and tacked top and bottom. This gives adequate support to the springs and material subsequently used. Other webs are required to complete a webbed back, which will be described in the chapters on springing. To fix the double web first tack on the left-hand scroll facing, and strain at A, being careful to keep the webs horizontal. Then secure with tacks at B and C. Greater strength is sometimes given at the points B and C by a short length of web placed vertically and tacked over the horizontal webs.

The beginner will probably have been engaged in the craft of upholstering some time before he feels himself competent to carry through the webbing of a large, complicated piece of work, for although the underlying principles are the same in webbing a small chair or a big settee, the latter calls for judgment and skilful workmanship and necessitates knowledge of the subsequent stages of the work.

From the sketches which accompany this chapter it will be noted that the initial stages of webbing on spring-stuffed frames are different from those of top-stuffed work—that is, frames that are webbed on the top of the seat rail instead of beneath. A spring-stuffed frame being turned upside down, the webs are first tacked on the front rail and strained to the back rail, whilst in a top-stuffed frame the reverse is the case.

The stretcher rails of settees and couches were not such a cause of trouble and inconvenience to the upholsterer of 50 years ago as they are to-day, because, instead of being straight as in modern frames, they were generally curved, as shown in Fig. 106. This form of construction kept the lengthwise webs when strained well clear of the rail, the intervening space being ample to allow for the eventful sagging of the webbing. When a frame is constructed thus with a curved wood stretcher or curved iron rod, a clear run of web is presented for the setting of the springs, and as the stretcher rail is well below them no inconvenience is caused by it, as is sometimes the case with modern seats with straight stretcher rails. Sometimes a person who sits down heavily is painfully reminded of the fact that certain parts of the seat are more comfortable than others, and experience will teach him that the ends of a settee constructed with a straight stretcher rail are more comfortable than the centre.

Double sprung stuffover frames—that is, those that are upholstered with deep seats with the stuffing extended to the base of the frame—are sometimes webbed on the top of the seat rail (as FIG. 107). The reason for this is that more rigidity is thereby given to the seat, and greater value is obtained from the 12in. springs used owing to the fact that they are raised the depth of the seat rail, generally about 2½in. This is, however, a method of construction that cannot be recommended, and whenever possible it should be avoided. Where webbing is applied to the top edge of seat rails it is important to cover the top of rails with folded pieces of material prior to webbing. This lessens the friction between the wood and the web, and unless this precaution is taken the sharp edge of the frame soon cuts through the web. A great strain is placed on seats that are top-webbed; therefore nothing but webbing of the best class should be used.

To return once more to the question of webbing in connection with a straight wood stretcher, the webbing is sometimes tacked on to this stretcher (see FIG. 108). This is a practice which should be avoided, as there is always a danger of the webs breaking away from it entirely, as shown in FIG. 111, causing the springs to drop and the seat to sag. The possibility of this damage is, of course, greater when webbing of inferior quality is used. A support for the lengthwise webs is obtained by placing a further piece of webbing at right angles to them and tacking in the spaces between the webs at 1, 2, 3, 4 and 5 instead of on the web as at A.

By adopting this method of supporting the webs in the centre additional buoyancy is given to a seat of great length, and it also lessens the tendency of the covering material to slacken in cases where a heavy stuffing such as white flock is used. On either side of the stretcher rail and close to it should be placed one of the short webs running from back to front.

Few upholsterers, whether manufacturers or shopkeepers, are free from complaints with regard to the giving way of the seats of light pin-cushion-stuffed furniture. Such chairs are generally con-

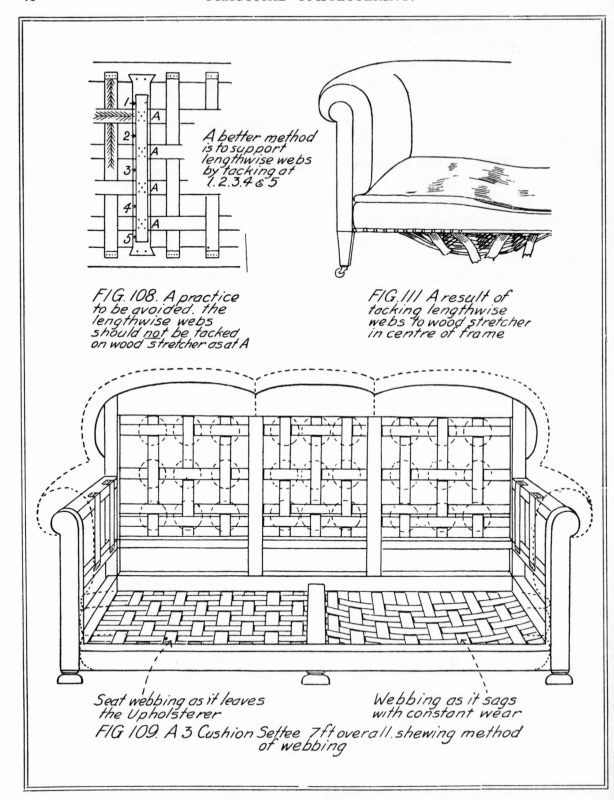

A better method
is to support
lengthwise webs
by tacking at
1. 2. 3. 4 & 5

FIG. 108. A practice
to be avoided. the
lengthwise webs
should *not* be tacked
on wood stretcher as at A

FIG. III A result of
tacking lengthwise
webs to wood stretcher
in centre of frame

Seat webbing as it leaves
the Upholsterer

Webbing as it sags
with constant wear

FIG 109. A 3 Cushion Settee 7ft overall. shewing method
of webbing

structed with slight rails not strong enough to stand heavy tacking, and it is quite possible for the upholsterer while working to split the wood without knowledge of having done so. The webs will sometimes break away for reasons mentioned in chapter 12. There is also another cause of failure of such chairs. The upholsterer, in his endeavour to obtain a regular, even surface, frequently tacks the web on the raw edge and neglects to fold it. This is done to the detriment of the strength of the seat, although probably a better finished appearance is thereby obtained. The results of tacking on the raw edge are not long in making themselves apparent. They are indicated in Fig. 110. The damage is put right by stripping the seat and then folding the web, but a better method still, which involves very slight additional expense, is to apply the web to the under side of the seat frame. This will be described more fully in the chapter on pin-cushion work.

Fig. 109 depicts a modern three-cushion settee webbed ready for springing. In subsequent chapters frequent reference will be made to this style of upholstery. The aim of the craftsman in such work should be resiliency and softness with well-finished lines, a combination of two qualities that requires considerable skill, it being quite easy to sacrifice the former to obtain the latter. Webs other than those shown are also required; these will be mentioned in the chapters on springing.

In large work the length and depth of the seat are such that the use of first-class webbing is imperative. The ultimate sagging of the web with wear will not interfere with the appearance of the seat as a whole if care is taken—first, to avoid tacking the webs on the stretcher rail; second, not to overstrain the webbing. The back webs are all tacked on the outside back of frame, the top row of springs either being tacked on the wood rail or alternatively sewn to the webbing. There is no hard and fast rule with regard to placing the webs, and the same outward appearance could be obtained with webbing for five springs in each division of the back, instead of nine as shown in the sketch, although this would entail a sacrifice of softness and durability.

Skill in webbing a large settee consists in knowing how to economise material and how to place the webs in the most advantageous position to take the springs. An experienced workman seems to know these things intuitively, while the younger man sometimes has to do a good deal of hard thinking before commencing a large piece of upholstery, the construction of which is new to him.

CHAPTER 18.

SPRINGS.

Webbing having been accomplished, the next process in the manufacture of upholstery is the placing and sewing of the springs in position. In modern pieces of large size considerable skill is necessary for this process, together with mature judgment in selecting the correct gauge and height of the springs and setting them correctly in position. The beginner finds it comparatively easy to sew the springs to the web after having been shown the correct method, but the "setting" of them in correct position on seats and backs of varied shape can only be learnt by experience.

The springs used in upholstery vary in size, ranging from 4in. to 12in. or 14in., the large sizes being used for deep-seated upholstery. Spring makers are now fully alive to the requirements of the upholsterer, and springs of various sizes are obtainable in wire of different gauges. Special springs are made for arms, others for backs, an extra strong variety for particular types of settees, and so on. The springs measuring from 4in. to 8in. are obtainable in three grades, namely, light, medium, and strong; these, in addition to those measuring from 10in. to 14in., will give a range of about two dozen varieties for selection. The weakest part of a spring is the waist or centre; if made too narrow at this point they are liable to become weakened, and the value of the whole spring is thereby lost. A well-proportioned spring is sketched at FIG. 112.

Twines for sewing the springs must be strong; three grades are generally used—fine, medium, and stout. The fine or buttoning twine is used chiefly for the quilting of cushions and button work, the medium for the stitching of edges, and the stout or spring twine for sewing springs, heavy materials, hessians, etc.

The knotting and tying of the twine plays a very important part in upholstery. A careless worker may be the cause of all kinds of faults that will accrue through his not having paid sufficient attention to tying his knots in the proper way, and firmly securing the end of the twine when tying the final knot. This is especially the case in button work, as will be described in the chapter dealing with that subject.

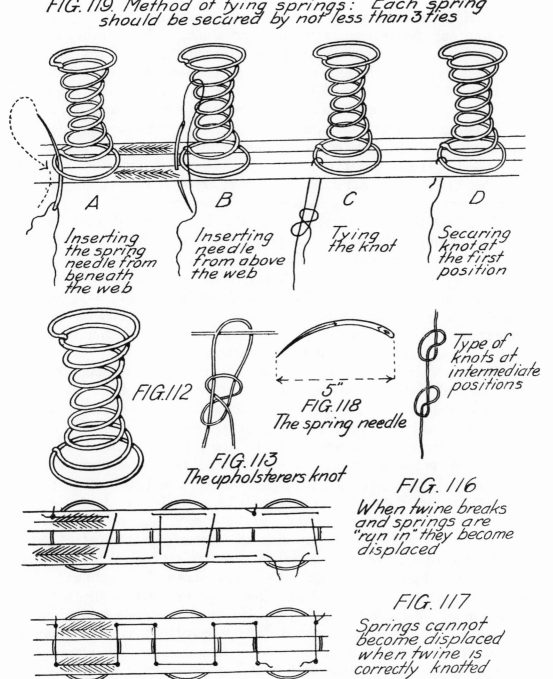

FIG. 119. Method of tying springs: Each spring should be secured by not less than 3 ties

A — Inserting the spring needle from beneath the web

B — Inserting needle from above the web

C — Tying the knot

D — Securing knot at the first position

FIG. 112

FIG. 113
The upholsterers knot

5"
FIG. 118
The spring needle

Type of knots at intermediate positions

FIG. 116
When twine breaks and springs are "run in" they become displaced

FIG. 117
Springs cannot become displaced when twine is correctly knotted

Retail furnishers frequently receive compliants from irate customers about buttons becoming detached or loose, such complaints generally being accompanied by a request to rectify the fault as soon as possible.   In large pieces of work, such as chesterfields and settees, loose buttons present an unsightly appearance.   The outline of the upholstery is spoilt and the shape of the surrounding parts affected. Buttons occasionally break and become detached from other reasons, but it may be safely asserted that in five out of six cases the cause of failure is due to the knot.   The tying of a correct knot is a small but important matter, and the writer has sometimes been astonished on examining work executed by excellent craftsmen to find a treacherous knot used.   The beginner should practise the knot shown in FIG. 113 until he ties it quite naturally without effort.   It is very useful, and suitable for all purposes, especially for button work.

After webbing is complete and the frame turned over on its feet the springs are placed in position.   Small chairs should have not less than five nor more than eight in number.   Strong 6in. springs should be used for ordinary seats with the exception of drawing-room chairs, when a lighter and smaller spring may be used with advantage.   The springs must be placed correctly or an ill-proportioned seat will result ; if they are crammed too closely in the centre a hard seat will result.   They should be equally distributed so that each spring will give freely under pressure without coming into contact with the others.   In the chapter on webbing we noted that the webs should be kept well towards the front rail, and in FIG. 114 it will be seen that the springs follow the same rule, there being considerably more space at the back than at the front.   An unavoidable projection occurs at the top and bottom of springs where the ends of the wire are doubled over.   These projections should always rest on the webs, and should be placed towards the centre of seat as indicated by the dots in FIG. 120 ; the smoothest parts of the springs will then lie towards the outer edge of seat.

Unless this precaution is taken the projections will soon wear through the hessian covering.   FIG. 115 shows five springs placed in position and sewn to the web, four ties or knots being used for each spring.   A definite knot should be made at each of the points at which the spring is attached to the web.   It is not sufficient to run the twine as a seamstress does when tacking and secure with a knot at the end.   FIGS. 116 and 117 will show the wisdom of this.   If the twine is simply run through, a cut or damaged twine may result in all the springs becoming loose or detached, whereas

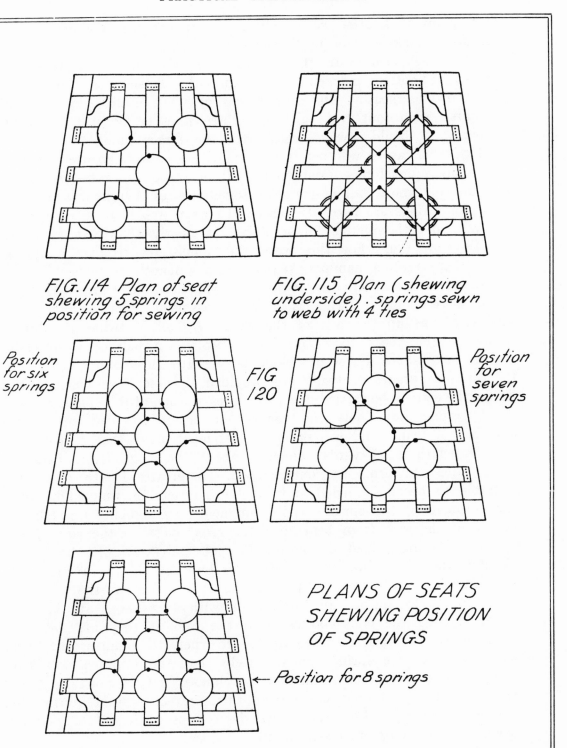

FIG. 114 Plan of seat shewing 5 springs in position for sewing

FIG. 115 Plan (shewing underside). springs sewn to web with 4 ties

Position for six springs

FIG 120

Position for seven springs

PLANS OF SEATS SHEWING POSITION OF SPRINGS

← Position for 8 springs

if each point is knotted separately no great damage is done if the twine does break at any particular point.

In old-fashioned work the twines were sometimes run first and each point knotted independently before the hessian or "bottom" was fixed underneath. In large pieces of work each spring should be secured with four ties; although three may be deemed sufficient the beginner should always learn with the larger number. It is a vexed question as to whether it is absolutely necessary to use the four ties; many upholsterers insist on it. It is quicker to run the twines and omit the knots, but faulty seats sometimes result from this practice. After the springs are correctly placed the next step is to sew them to the web, and the method of so doing is clearly shown at A, B, C and D, FIG. 119. For this work the upholsterer requires a spring needle (FIG. 118), a hammer, scissors, and a length of twine.

In connection with the twine he will need to learn a further lesson in economy. Twine is a very expensive item, and if used carelessly runs up the cost of the work. A ball of twine, if allowed to lie on the bench loose, inevitably becomes a ball of waste ends, and in some shops a row of oblong boxes with glass fronts containing the different grades of twine are provided. These have holes in the lid for the ends to be carried down within easy reach of the upholsterers.

Beginners have only the vaguest notion as to what constitutes a length of twine, and will often cut off much more than is required. A safe length is $1\frac{3}{4}$ yards, which is about the length from hand to hand when the arms are outstretched. A greater length than this is liable to become tangled and involve a waste of time and twine. After threading the spring needle commence by stabbing through the centre of the web from beneath (FIG. 119A) close to the coil of the spring. Having passed the needle through stab vertically downwards through the web (FIG. 119B). Tie the knot as shown in FIG. 113, and draw it tightly until in position as at D. Repeat the operation from spring to spring, and finish off with two knots at the end. Avoid cutting the ends too close to the web as they are liable to work loose. There is no fixed rule as to where to commence or finish the sewing of the springs on the webs, but the beginner will soon find out the most economical way for himself. Care must be taken that the springs do not move from their correct position during the process of sewing. FIG. 120 shows the correct setting of 6, 7 and 8 springs respectively on a seat frame.

Modern practice compares unfavourably with the methods and principles followed by upholsterers of an older school. For instance, the question of the running of twine would never have occurred to the craftsmen of half a century ago, as it is so obviously important, even to a non-technical mind, that the springs should be secured firmly to the webs. This rigidity is the more necessary because the web, which is the foundation on which the springs rest, must eventually sag and become somewhat flexible. The upholsterer, therefore, who is anxious to do good work should always tie at every point rather than run the twine. Running the twine, in the way shown at FIG. 116, may be done with more facility but at the risk of an unsatisfactory seat.

CHAPTER 19.

THE LACING OF SPRINGS.

After the springs are securely sewn to the webs the next procedure is to reduce their resiliency by tying or lacing them down to a given height. There are two ways of doing this : (1) by covering with hessian, as shown in FIGS. 127 and 129, or by lacing with cords, as in FIG. 123. For upholstered work that is made for wear and not merely to sell the latter method is always adopted. For lacing the springs a stout cord is used, called laid-cord, and the top coil of each spring is knotted, a process which takes considerable time, especially in large pieces of work.

Springs in upholstery are laced for three reasons :—(1) The top coils of the springs are held firmly in such a position that the axis remains perpendicular ; (2) any given row of springs may be compressed independently of the others ; for instance the back row may be kept lower than the two front ones, as shown in the side elevation at FIG. 125 ; (3) the friction and wear on the hessian covering subsequently used is reduced to a minimum by the process of lacing.

FIG. 121 shows the front row of springs on a seat with temporary tacks fixed ready for lacing. The tacks are placed exactly opposite each spring in the centre of the rails. The length of cord required for lacing is difficult to gauge with accuracy, and it is a good plan to lay the cord loosely over the springs, as from A to H, FIG. 122 ; allowing sufficient for knotting and the return cords, indicated at A and G, FIG. 123. The return should be long enough to tie from the tack to the top coil A, FIG. 123. Such return cords are not always necessary in small work where 5in. or 6in. springs are used, but in large work they are imperative. Before lacing is commenced all the cord should be cut and laid ready to hand. Cords are then looped over each temporary tack on the back rail, and on one of the side rails A and C, FIG. 126, and the tacks are driven in securely leaving sufficient cord for the return. Some upholsterers do good work by following methods contrary to those generally accepted. For instance, in lacing, the right to left worker often gets better results than the left to right, and so on, although one method may be generally adopted. The lacing of the springs of small chairs and easy chairs should be commenced from the side

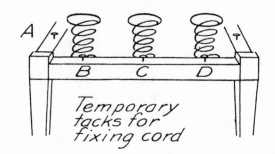

FIG. 121
Springs as they appear before lacing

Temporary tacks for fixing cord

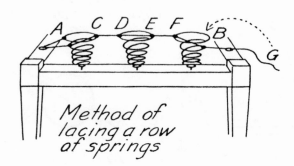

FIG. 122
Springs laced for straining down to position

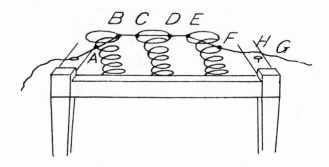

FIG. 123
Springs pressed down to a given height

Method of lacing a row of springs

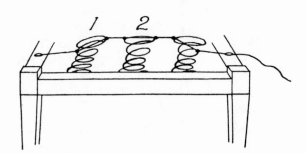

FIG. 124
Springs laced incorrectly

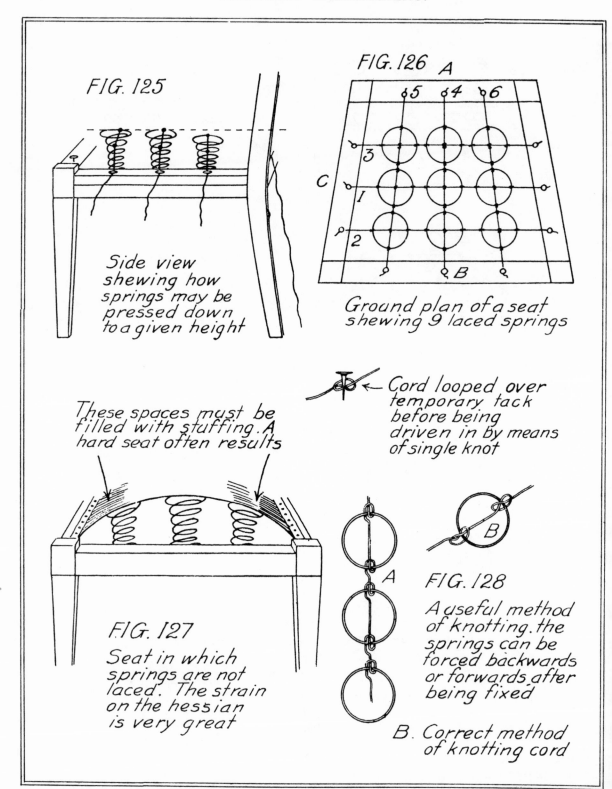

FIG. 125

Side view
shewing how
springs may be
pressed down
to a given height

FIG. 126 A

Ground plan of a seat
shewing 9 laced springs

Cord looped over
temporary tack
before being
driven in by means
of single knot

These spaces must be
filled with stuffing. A
hard seat often results

FIG. 127

Seat in which
springs are not
laced. The strain
on the hessian
is very great

FIG. 128

A useful method
of knotting. the
springs can be
forced backwards
or forwards after
being fixed

B. Correct method
of knotting cord

rail, tacking the centre cord first and working from left to right; the others are then laced in rotation, as indicated by the Nos. 1 to 6, FIG. 126. In settees and couches the short cords running from back to front are laced first and the lengthwise ones afterwards. In knotting the procedure is as follows :—Hold the cord in the left hand and make the first knot on the second coil of spring with the right hand, see A, FIG. 122, drawing the spring a little out of the perpendicular. Repeat the operation on the top coil of first spring at B, and so on as indicated. The distance between B—C and D—E should be a little more than the corresponding distance between the springs on the web. The springs should now appear as shown at FIG. 122 before being strained down to a given height. Hold the end of the cord G with the right hand pressing the springs with the left. To measure the height required, place a rule between C and D on to the web, and when the right height is obtained the cord should be strained taut and looped round the temporary tack H, which is then driven in. A 6in. spring should be compressed to 4½in. in the centre and the back row always slightly lower, this latter rule applying to seats of all kinds.

FIG. 128 shows two methods of knotting for the lacing of springs. B is the old-fashioned method, although many upholsterers still insist on its use. In cases where a long row of a dozen or more springs are laced the craftsman often finds it necessary to adjust a spring that is not true. This is not possible when the knot B is employed without the whole being unlaced, whilst in the knot A it is possible to make an adjustment of a few inches either way without unlacing.

A correctly sprung seat should be characterised by the following points :—(1) The height of the springs should be in correct proportion to the subsequent height of seat when upholstered ; (2) the springs should be set true and evenly balanced, and in forming the finished line of upholstery they should require no additional adjustment by means of the hessian covering. It is most important that the spring should stand true and perpendicular. FIG. 124 shows the result of incorrect lacing. From this it is clear that after spring No. 1 loses some of its resiliency owing to wear, the top coil will touch the coils of the spring No. 2 when in use. This is a bad fault of which beginners in upholstery are often guilty, and their work should always be examined before the hessian covering is tacked into position. FIG. 123 shows a row of springs correctly placed, the spring in the centre perfectly upright, those on either side strained slightly out of the perpendicular.

The next process is to cover the springs with hessian, FIGS. 129 and 130. A tape measure laid over the springs from back to front and side to side (widest part), allowing 1in. all round, will give amount required. Apprentices should avoid the habit of guessing at measurements if they are allowed to cut their own materials. In small work waste is occasioned by thoughtless cutting, and the beginner will benefit considerably in the matter of gauging sizes if he is fortunate enough to be under the eye of a vigilant stock-keeper to check his measurements and quantities. Here also it is important to note that the woven threads of all materials used in

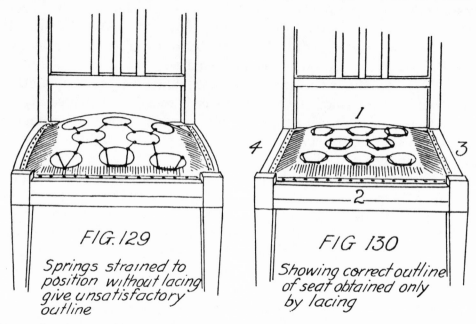

FIG. 129
Springs strained to
position without lacing
give unsatisfactory
outline

FIG 130
Showing correct outline
of seat obtained only
by lacing

upholstering should be kept perfectly straight and true. If this rule is carried out the work may be done more easily and quickly, for material which is set on the bias or diagonally is very difficult to manipulate. The spring hessian having been cut to size, as previously explained, it must be laid on the springs and placed in position, so that an equal margin is left on all sides. Place a temporary tack at 1, FIG. 130, strain slightly, and repeat at 2, 4 and 3. An extra strain on each of the four corners will set the canvas, and additional temporary tacks are required should any portion appear slack. To complete this process commence at the back, placing and driving in the tacks about 1½in. apart. Repeat at the front and finally at the sides, trim off the hessian evenly leaving about 1in. to be folded over and tacked for extra strength. These tackings must be in the centre of the rails.

To cover with hessian springs that have not been previously laced is a more difficult operation. The method of placing the hessian is the same and the springs are strained down to the height required. A good quality of material should be used in seats treated in this way. FIG. 127 shows a sectional view of this method of straining down the springs without lacing. By placing a rule between the space in the web from underneath the correct heights may be obtained. The springs must be kept true and fixed temporarily on the hessian before being finally sewn. The sewing is done by means of the spring needle, and three or four knots are used for each spring. The needle being curved enters the hessian from above and from beneath at one stab, and the two holes thus formed by the curved needle should be kept as close to the top coil of the spring as possible, as this ensures that the knot grips firmly.

CHAPTER 20.

SPRING EDGES.

Upholstered furniture, though constructed and finished in the best manner and with the greatest care to ensure that curves are well balanced and facings exact in every detail, may be spoilt in a moment by subsequent careless handling or bad packing. Front stitched edges are especially liable to become damaged and unsightly unless carefully handled, and the outline of an expensive morocco chair or settee may easily be spoilt through lack of knowledge or carelessness in packing. In large establishments, where quantities of upholstery are handled, the packers by long experience become conversant with the best methods of handling and packing, and exercise care in order that no undue pressure may be brought to bear on such parts as are liable to damage—for example, front edges, outside backs, arms, etc.

As regards front edges, the method of construction known as the spring edge renders the front less liable to damage by undue pressure, as well as making the seat more comfortable by substituting springs in part of the work which would otherwise be crammed with stuffing. Spring edges require careful workmanship, otherwise they soon become faulty. In spring edge work, in which the springs are insufficiently or incorrectly laced, the whole front sometimes projects or bulges forward in an unsightly manner. On the other hand, a well-set-up seat, with springs well selected and properly laced, is very durable, and will stand much hard wear. Figs. 131 to 136 illustrate the method of fixing springs on the front rail of a seat. The importance of securing them firmly by the various cords and twines should be insisted on, as this part of the seat is necessarily subjected to much wear. After springs of the correct size and strength are selected, the best plan is to place the seat springs first before commencing the edge springs. Fig. 137 represents the side view of an ordinary divan easy chair seat. (1) is a 6in. (2) and (3) 9in., and (4) 8in. spring. The apprentice will experience many difficulties in mastering spring edge work, and in his first attempt rarely avoids making mistakes which will assert themselves before he advances far with the work. An endeavour is made here to point out some of the things which he should endeavour to avoid. A common fault is the setting of the front row of springs at (2) (Fig. 137) too near the edge springs (1). When they are too near there is a tendency for them to clash together, or "talk," when pressure is applied to the seat. The seat springs should be put in position temporarily, so that the space between them may be judged accurately by tilting the springs to the positions they will occupy after they have been laced. Before commencing to fix the edge springs fix a piece of web or folded piece of canvas on the front rail with a few temporary tacks, and then secure the bottom coil of the springs firmly with staples—four to each spring, as shown in FIG. 131. Another method is to slide the bottom coil of the spring underneath the piece of web or canvas, then secure it with ⅝in. tacks, driving these through the material and on either side of the wire, so that the bottom coil is secured as firmly as if the staples were employed.

Another method of fixing the edge springs to the front rail is illustrated at FIG. 132. In this case the bottom coil is left projecting towards the front about 1½in. and when the coil is secured the projecting part is hammered down at right angles. This is a good method of fixing, as it precludes the danger of the springs becoming displaced.

Spring edges are of two kinds—independent and fixed. (See FIGS. 134 and 135). In the former method care must be taken that the springs are close to the upright arm pieces, have a clear space of ½in. (see A and B, FIG. 134) to ensure the free play of the springs. The next procedure is to drive in temporary tacks on either side of each spring at positions shown at A and B, FIG. 132. The end of a length of cord is fixed at C, looped over one of the coils of the spring at about one-third of its height. The spring is then drawn slightly forward by tension on the cord, which is secured by tacking at D, and the operation repeated with the other springs. During the work, each spring is measured with a rule to ensure uniformity of height. The resiliency of the springs must now be somewhat reduced, as shown by the dotted line (FIG. 133). Proceed as follows:—Cut four lengths of spring twine, take one of them and tie it to the centre of the bottom coil of spring A (FIG. 133). Loop over the top cord and knot at B, at the same time drawing the spring tightly downwards so that the top coil is in a horizontal position; knot again at D, see spring marked (2), FIG. 133, then strain down the twine from E to F, see spring (3), FIG. 133. The fourth spring shows the operation completed. The beginner should practice this operation constantly, as it will be some time before he will be able to manipulate the springs to bring them to a given height correctly.

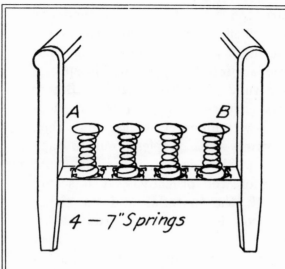

FIG. 131
Springs fixed on front
rail with staples

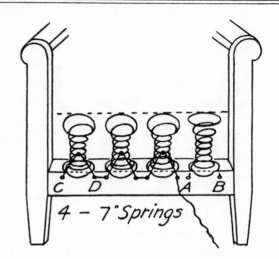

FIG. 132
One third of height
of springs drawn
forward with cord

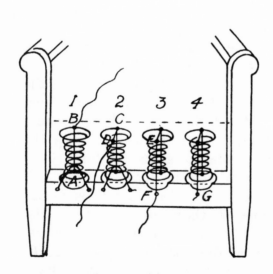

FIG. 133
Gauging height of
springs by return cord

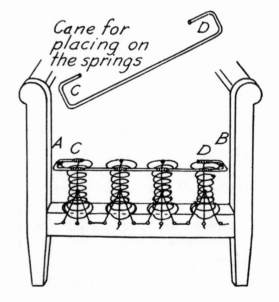

FIG. 134
Independant
spring edge

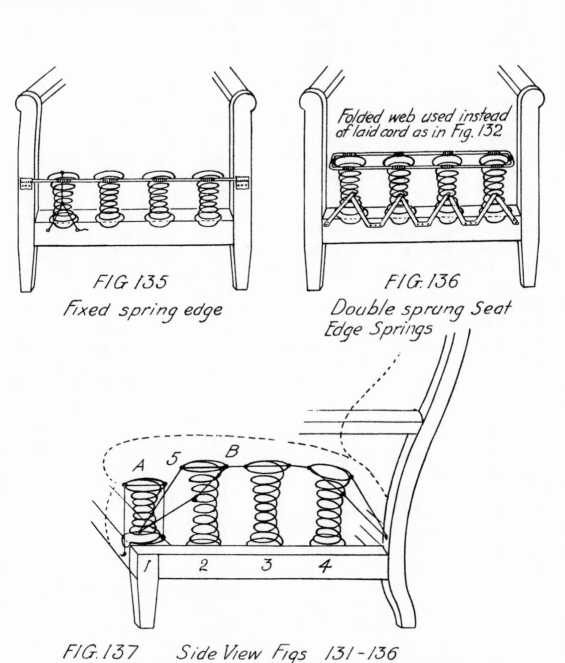

FIG 135
Fixed spring edge

Folded web used instead
of laid cord as in Fig. 132

FIG. 136
Double sprung Seat
Edge Springs

FIG. 137   Side View Figs 131-136
Dotted line shews finished upholstery

The next process is to strengthen and support the springs by a foundation acting as a substitute for the wood rail. (See following chapters on Stitching). This is done by the fixing of cane to the springs. Wire is sometimes used, as it is more easily bent to shape, but cane is preferable, as it presents a larger surface for the subsequent sewings than wire. In the case of a straight front, such as is shown at FIG. 134, the cane should be prepared first before fixing in position. First cut the length required by measuring the distance between A and B and allowing sufficient to grip each of the end springs at C and D. Some varieties of cane are more brittle than others, and to avoid wasting material it is a good plan to test a small portion before shaping. Bending with the web pincers (see FIG. 94) is preferable to cutting notches, as the latter method sometimes results in breakage. Soaking the cane in water before bending also facilitates the work. The importance of allowing ½in. space between the end springs and the upright arm pieces, in order to ensure freedom of action, must be remembered. Otherwise a bad set will result. After the cane is correctly shaped it must be secured to the front of the top coil of the springs. This is effected by binding with twine. When finished the cane rests on the top edge of the springs, and its ends must be properly secured by additional binding at C and D.

FIG. 135 shows a fixed spring edge, a method of construction used in inexpensive easy chairs and chesterfields. In this method the ends of the cane are covered with web and secured to the upright arm pieces by several tackings. Edges such as these will stand much hard wear, but it is obvious that the buoyancy of a seat constructed as shown at FIG. 135 is limited, as the ends are fixed and the springs have no independent action.

Double-sprung seats represent the last word in comfort. In work of this kind it is important that springs of the right size should be used. Double-sprung work requires much experience for the correct placing and lacing of the springs. The most expensive furniture with double-sprung seats sometimes develops faults after a little wear owing to bad judgment in the selection of springs, which causes the seat to sag, or faulty placing and lacing of the edge springs, causing the front to project or bulge forward.

Double-sprung seats can be made in one of two ways. First, by two layers of springs in the seat with a tall spring on the edge. Second, two layers of springs in the seat and one spring above another on the edge. The former method, if carried through correctly, produces a luxuriously soft and buoyant seat, equalling a loose cushion seat in comfort. The methods of constructing such upholstery will be described in subsequent chapters. FIG. 137 is a sectional view of a spring-edge seat. The space above the springs at A is larger than at B. This is necessary because of the stitchings that will be required to mould the front edge to the shape indicated by the dotted lines.

CHAPTER 21.

DOUBLE-SPRUNG WORK.

The young upholsterer while engaged in elementary work should endeavour to gain a knowledge of the principles underlying it, and learn as much as he can by observation. Elaborate work such as the springing and lacing of a large chesterfield will not then present so many difficulties. The underlying principles having been grasped he can deal with confidence with fresh problems and the variations from ordinary routine work which constantly occur. It is a good plan to keep and constantly use a notebook for jotting down sizes and other details, which will be useful for future reference. These notes may be made hurriedly, but should afterwards be put in order and classified from time to time. Such memoranda, arranged under headings for different grades of work, are invaluable. The note-book should contain measurements for standard size chairs, sizes of springs, quantities of materials, and particulars relating to special work. In the event of a repeat the note-book will settle all doubts as to the materials formerly used, height of springs, treatment of edges, and so on. The apprentice who keeps such a book will find that his fellow-workmen constantly appeal to him for information and particulars which have been forgotten.

The first operation in commencing the springing of a large chesterfield is to fix and "box up" the corner spring, as shown at FIG. 141. This spring is fixed and laced independently of all the others, then covered with hessian, which is folded round it, sewn with the spring needle, and fixed at the bottom with tacks. This is called a "boxed up" spring, and to it the hessian of the arm and back is subsequently sewn.

FIG. 138 shows the method of setting the springs in position: for medium and best-class work three rows of springs are used, two rows on the wood rail as indicated, and one row on the web. For inexpensive chesterfields the row of springs on the web is dispensed with, and stuffing is substituted. Where this method is employed the work tends to sag, and the buoyancy of the first and second row of springs is lessened. The number of springs indicated in the sketch are sufficient for a settee 6ft. 6in. over all. The first row may be fixed on to the top of the arm with staples or tacked with web, as explained in the previous chapter, and then laced exactly as described. To fix the second row of springs the bottom coil is bent over at right angles and tacked exactly as already described in connection with front edge springs. The springs in the second row are then raised into an oblique position by means of cords. The lengthwise lacing is clearly shown at FIG. 138. A piece of cane bent to shape and fixed on the outer edge of the springs is useful in preserving the outline of the upholstery and rendering it more durable. The cane need not be carried right round the back, but stop at B (FIG. 138). FIG. 140 is an end view showing the position of the springs when the hessian has been fixed in position. The distance between C and D is greater than that between A and B. In covering the back springs with hessian care must be taken not to reduce their height by straining the material too tightly. It should be tacked temporarily and set ; where much fulness of the hessian occurs it should be folded into a series of neat pleats.

The seats of chesterfields are sprung in various ways and require careful manipulation. FIGS. 142 to 145 show the essential differences between mock and real double springing. Genuine double-sprung seats have two distinct layers of springs. FIG. 142 shows the treatment of a 6ft. 6in. chesterfield. The numbers of springs required are as follows :—10 9in. strong springs for the edge, 40 7in. strong springs for the bottom layer, 40 6in. medium strong for the top layer. These are placed in ten rows of four, giving a total of eighty springs in all, exclusive of the front edge. After placing the edge springs at equal distances, the rows of 7in. must be placed in such a position that the laid-cords may be fixed in the spaces between the edge springs (See 1 and 2, FIG. 142). The method of gauging the height and reducing the resiliency of the springs is just as described in a previous chapter.

Strips of web, as shown at 136, should be used instead of cord, and the face should be placed at the back as well as the front of the edge springs as at FIG. 136. The springs of the bottom layer are laced each way and strained slightly, keeping them perfectly level.

If a double width hessian is to be used, measure the length required and tack the material where the fold occurs close to the back edge of the front rail from end to end of the settee, as shown by the dotted line 3 (FIG. 142). When the hessian is tacked thus, there will be two hessians to manipulate. One of them is laid temporarily over the edge springs, as indicated by the dotted line at 4 (FIG. 142), and the other fold is spread over the 7in. springs, set, tacked into position, and the springs sewn with four ties. The

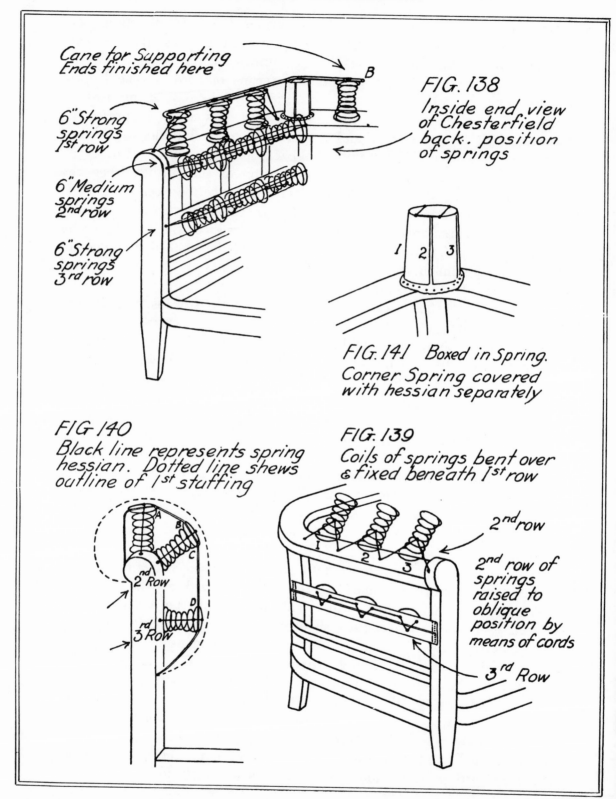

Cane for Supporting
Ends finished here

B

6" Strong
springs
1st row

6" Medium
springs
2nd row

6" Strong
springs
3rd row

FIG. 138
Inside end view
of Chesterfield
back. position
of springs

FIG. 141 Boxed in Spring.
Corner Spring covered
with hessian separately

FIG. 140
Black line represents spring
hessian. Dotted line shews
outline of 1st stuffing

2nd Row

3rd Row

FIG. 139
Coils of springs bent over
& fixed beneath 1st row

2nd row

2nd row of
springs
raised to
oblique
position by
means of cords

3rd Row

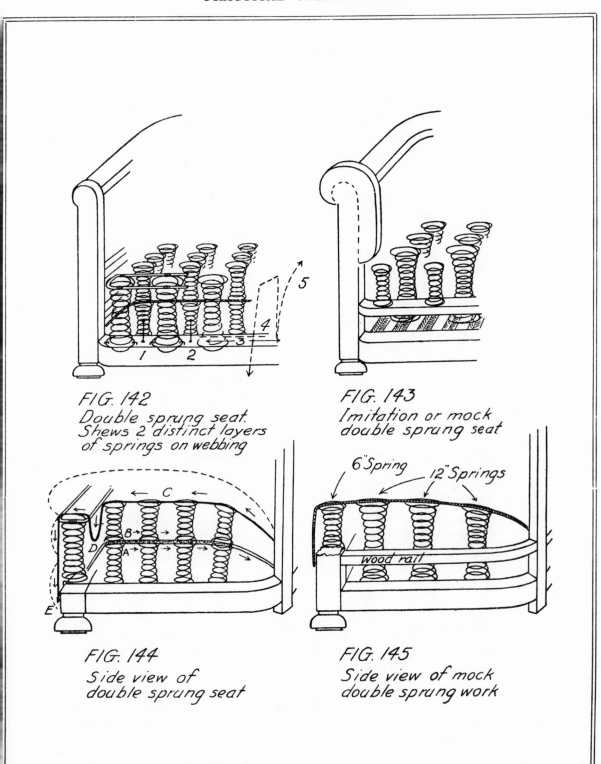

FIG. 142
Double sprung seat.
Shews 2 distinct layers
of springs on webbing

FIG. 143
Imitation or mock
double sprung seat

FIG. 144
Side view of
double sprung seat

FIG. 145
Side view of mock
double sprung work

bottom layer of springs will now be covered with a single layer of hessian as indicated by the arrows A (FIG. 144), while the second layer of hessian has been placed temporarily over the edge springs. A thin layer of stuffing is now spread lightly over the seat and the second hessian is folded back over this stuffing, strained fairly taut, and tacked. The side view at FIG. 144 indicates the two layers of hessian, A and B, with the stuffing between them. Hair is the ideal stuffing for double-sprung upholstery, other materials do not produce such satisfactory results.

The next operation is to fix the forty 6in. springs immediately above the 7in. springs already placed in position. In practice it

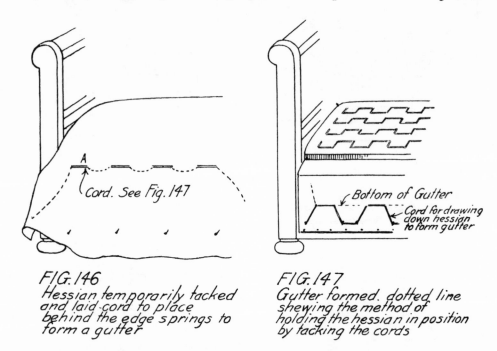

FIG. 146
Hessian temporarily tacked
and laid-cord to place
behind the edge springs to
form a gutter

FIG. 147
Gutter formed. dotted line
shewing the method of
holding the hessian in position
by tacking the cords

will be found best to commence with the third row from the front, working from left to right, and proceed as follows:—Place the hand firmly on the hessian when the top coil of the 7in. spring may be easily traced, the bottom coil of the 6in. spring is placed directly over it. The 6in. spring has now to be sewn to both hessians at one operation. This may be done with the spring needle or a long straight needle; the latter is used in exactly the same way as already described in sewing springs to the webs, but each of the four ties is knotted and cut independently. When the bottom coils of the 6in. springs are all fixed and the lacing has been accomplished, a thin cane is fixed to the top coils of those springs which are nearest the ends and back of the settee, and the work is then ready for the final hessian covering shown at C (FIG. 144). In estimating the amount of hessian needed for this, care must be taken to allow for the "gutter" at D. The reason for guttering is to lessen the strain on the front edge springs, and to relieve the wear and tear on the hessian, which is very great when the seat is subjected to compression in use. Start by temporarily tacking the hessian on the back rail. Spread it lightly over the spring, and tack temporarily on the front rail, as shown at FIG. 144. Then with the needle run a length of cord through the hessian from end to end (FIG. 146), leaving a long length of cord projecting at one end. In running in this cord care must be taken to avoid sewing the hessian to the springs, which must be kept quite clear. Having released the hessian by removing the tacks in the front rail, form the gutter by placing the cord A, which has been previously run through into the position shown at D in FIG. 144. The cord forming the gutter is now fixed down by means of tacks to the front rail, as shown at FIG. 147, and the remainder of the hessian is carried over the edge springs and tacked on to the front rail at E (FIG. 144). The springs are then sewn to the hessian, so also is the cane with stitches 1in. apart. It must be remembered that when drawing the hessian round the cane by means of the stitches, a foundation is formed on the outer edge to which is sewn the scrim, calico, covering, etc.; the hessian must not grip the cane too tightly, otherwise the threads are liable to break and the work becomes faulty. The hessian covered cane of a spring edge serves the same purpose as the wood for a firm stitched edge. In the former the various materials are fixed with skewers and sewn on the latter tacked to the wood.

Mock double-sprung work is less complicated. It is so very like the genuine article in appearance when upholstered that only an expert can discern the difference. In inexpensive work the guttering is dispensed with. This is a great mistake, as edge springs should always be arranged to work independently of those fixed on the webs. The only way of effecting this is to form a gutter as described. One way of ascertaining whether a spring-edge seat has been properly constructed is to sit well back in the seat. If the hessian has been strained without guttering the front edge will at once assume a pronounced concave shape, but if properly guttered very little difference in the line will be observed.

In mock-sprung the strain on the springs, edges and material used is very much greater, consequently they do not last as long as they do in genuine double-sprung work.

CHAPTER 22.

SPRINGING.

The springs in stuffover backs are arranged in three rows, as shown at A, B and C (FIG. 148). For the swell or bulge at the lower part of the back, C, 8in. or 7in. springs are used; for the row B, 6in. scroll springs, and the top row, A, 5in. light scroll springs, raised to an oblique position by means of cords as described. This portion of the back is subjected to much strain when the subsequent coverings are sewn into position.

The choice of springs, as far as size is concerned, is governed by the materials used: morocco, pegamoid, and other heavy coverings require a different gauge to such materials as cretonne, silk, or tapestry.

The hessian covering shown by the dotted line in FIG. 148 may be treated in one of two ways—first, by laying the hessian over the tops of the springs, as in ordinary chair seating (see dotted line and larger arrows), and second by guttering, as indicated by the shaded portions and smaller arrows. The latter method gives independent action to the springs and a more buoyant back results. The hessian is stabbed through to the web with a few ties, and the hollow spaces, or gutters, between the rows of springs are eventually filled lightly with stuffing.

FIG. 149 illustrates centre lacing. By this method the springs are knotted by means of cords at the waist of the spring instead of at the top. When upholstery is specified extra soft, centre lacing may be used with advantage, but in selecting springs for centre-laced work it must be remembered that by this method the spring cannot be reduced in height to the same extent as when top laced. In centre lacing the weakest portion of the spring, viz., the waist, is bound by cords, and thereby considerably strengthened, while the upper portion has freedom of action; it is therefore necessary, when placing the hessian covering, to make sure that the springs are in their true position before sewing to the hessian. Centre lacing, when correctly carried out, almost equals double-sprung work for softness and resiliency. It is not necessary to have return cords as in top lacing, and better results are obtained from large springs than small ones.

It is not an unusual occurrence, even in regard to the best-class upholstery, to hear complaints of seats being too firm or hard, although the finest materials have been used throughout, in addition to hair stuffing. In course of time the general slackening of various materials through constant use of the chair or settee will give the whole seat more buoyancy, but it is not easy to satisfy customers with this explanation, as having got a new piece of furniture they look for the maximum of comfort immediately. A seat that is too hard or firm may be the result of (1) over cramming of the hair; (2) bad selection as regards size of springs; (3) straining too tightly in top lacing. The last named fault is more general in small seats, where 8in. or 9in. springs have been used and reduced to such an extent that a hard seat results. By giving freedom to the upper portion of the spring by means of centre lacing the fault is at once rectified.

Backs that are concave in shape require careful springing. Fig. 150 is a diagram showing the method of springing a kidney-shaped seat. It is similar to the method employed in springing a chesterfield back, with the exception that a series of ties are stabbed through the hessian and web on each side of the springs, as it is only by this process that the desired shape may be obtained. Guttering by means of ties is applied to all concave surfaces, and the gutters may be formed either horizontally or vertically, as illustrated. The diagrams 151 to 154 show the importance of lacing the springs correctly. If they incline inwards when laced, as in Fig. 151, they have a tendency to bulge at the waist or centre when compressed (see Fig. 152), but springs that incline outwards, being placed slightly fanwise, as Fig. 153, assume a vertical position in compression, or, to use an upholsterer's phrase, they "ride true." Fig. 155 shows the method of lacing springs on a hollow-shaped arm. It will be seen that each spring is laced independently. This may be accomplished in various ways, two of which are shown on the diagram: (1) Triangular lacing to each side of the spring, and (2) guttering by means of laid cords.

Points which the beginner or apprentice should remember with regard to springing are summarised below: (1) Avoid placing springs too close to the woodwork of the frame. (2) Springs that are compressed without lacing (see Fig. 127) must be adjusted to position before final sewing. This is accomplished by viewing them from beneath. (3) The back row of springs in the seats of upholstered frames must always be kept lower than the front rows. This difference in height is obtained not by extra lacing or straining of the hessian, but by using smaller springs as follows:—If the front rows consist

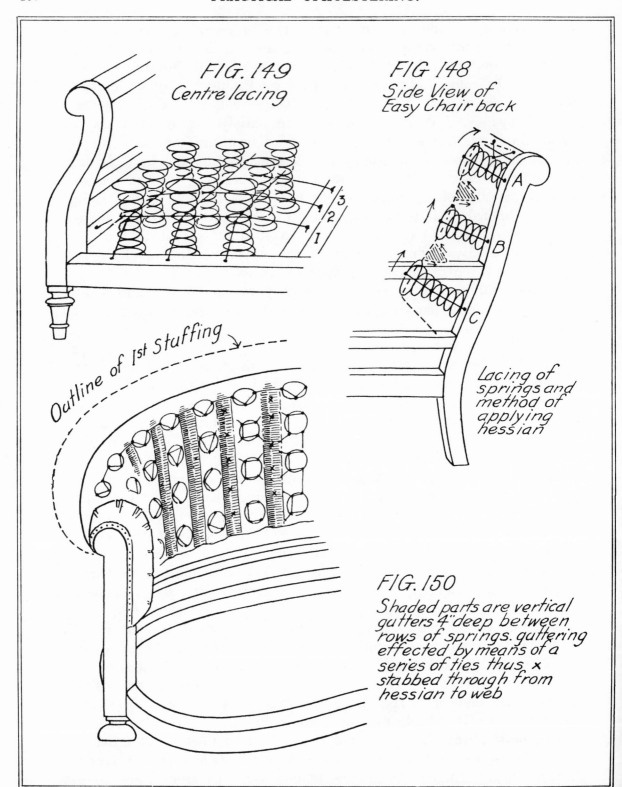

FIG. 149
Centre lacing

FIG 148
Side View of
Easy Chair back

3
2
1

A
B
C

Lacing of
springs and
method of
applying
hessian

Outline of 1st Stuffing

FIG. 150
Shaded parts are vertical
gutters 4" deep between
rows of springs. guttering
effected by means of a
series of ties thus x
stabbed through from
hessian to web

THE LACING OF SPRINGS
The Right and Wrong method compared

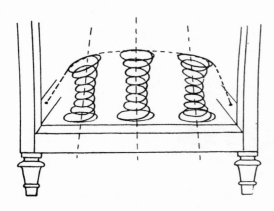

FIG. 151
The angle at which these springs are laced is incorrect

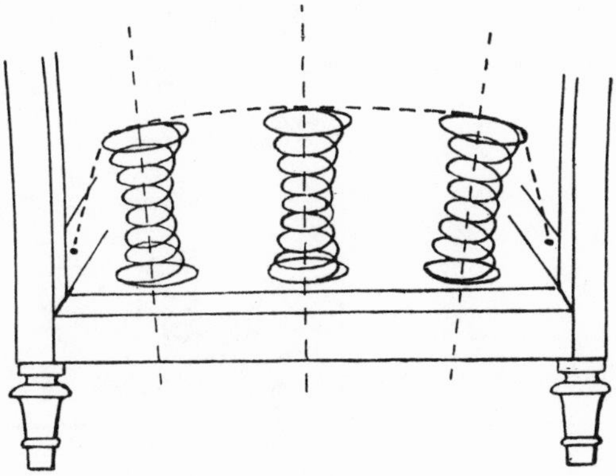

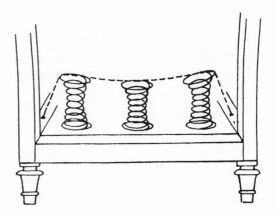

FIG. 153
Shewing springs correctly laced Fan shaped

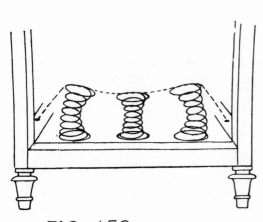

FIG. 152
When pressure is applied to the springs the waist bulges causing faulty seat

FIG. 154
When pressure is applied springs fall into vertical position

of 8in. springs the back row should be 7in., or if the front rows are 10in. springs the back rows should be 9in. (4) Before selecting and lacing springs the height of the front edge of the upholstery should be ascertained. (5) Commence from left to right; centre row of

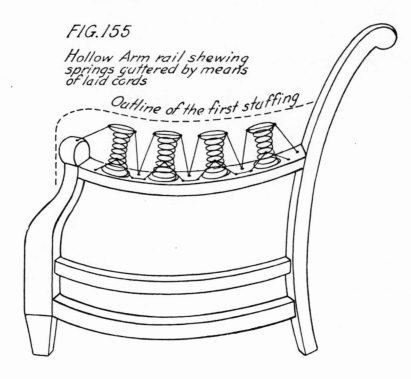

FIG. 155

Hollow Arm rail shewing springs guttered by means of laid cords

Outline of the first stuffing

springs should be laced first. (6) Avoid over straining; if the cord is subjected to severe tension it may break. (7) Work methodically, keep notes for reference, and avoid guesswork wherever possible.

CHAPTER 23.

FIRST STUFFING.

By first stuffing of upholstery is meant the proper disposition of the material placed on the foundation of webs, springs and hessian, already formed, as described. The process is not easy to acquire, and needs considerable practice even though the principles may be clearly understood. The beginner is frequently discouraged at this stage, as first stuffing is undoubtedly more complicated than the webbing and springing which he has already mastered.

When a chair is first stuffed it is implied that it is prepared ready for the second stuffing; that is to say, the shape has been moulded and the desired outlines formed by stitching or quilting. The stuffed edges of a chair are built up gradually by rows of twine stitching. The use of twine for this purpose occurs in many of the oldest examples of upholstered furniture. It should be noted, however, that some of the old examples from which present-day stuff-over work has been developed depended entirely upon wood outlines, and the making and shaping of the frames display great skill. The interior edges of the backs and wings were spoke-shaved to the exact outline of the subsequent stuffing, and the same remark applies to the arms also, which were shaped and tapered off gradually towards the back. On such frames as these the present-day upholsterer could produce stuffover chairs without any of the stitching or first stuffing required on frames of modern make. In a subsequent chapter the development of the styles and methods of stuffing will be described more fully.

For first stuffing the upholsterer requires a needle 8in. or 9in. long and a regulator. These regulators and needles may be purchased in various sizes from 6in. upwards. A needle that has a bayonet-shaped point is most serviceable, and is not so liable to break as the round-pointed needle. Regulators are made in various sizes, and have one end pointed and the other shaped as shown in FIG. 156. The regulator, though a simple instrument, is of much service to the upholsterer, as by its means hair may be passed from one portion of the seat to another, and an uneven surface can be made smooth and regular; edges, facings and scrolls may by its use be skilfully adjusted before the stitching process commences. In adjusting folds, pleats, fulness and button work in the final covering, a regulator is indispensable.

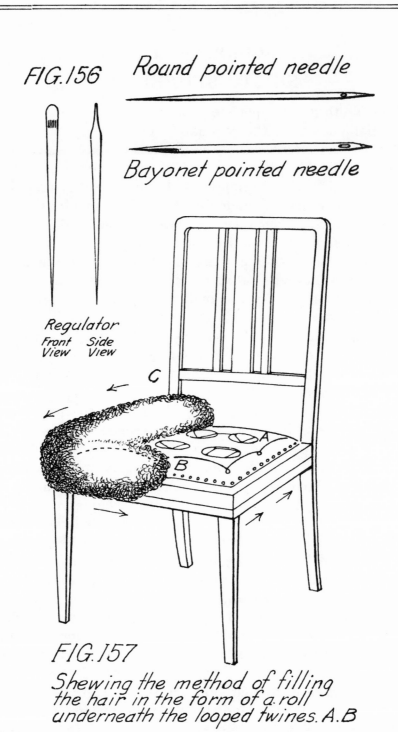

FIG.156

Round pointed needle

Bayonet pointed needle

Regulator
Front   Side
View   View

FIG.157

Shewing the method of filling
the hair in the form of a roll
underneath the looped twines. A.B

Hair is the ideal stuffing material, as already mentioned; its only disadvantage is its cost. Various qualities may be procured. A chair stuffed throughout with a low grade of hair does not differ very greatly from one stuffed with the best quality of Algerian fibre, which is used as a substitute for hair. The upholsterer will find it to his advantage to learn his trade on hair work, more especially in his attempts at first stuffing.

A start should be made with a small chair. First place hair twines on each of the four sides as shown in FIG. 157, commencing from the point C and following round in the direction of the arrows; the twine is looped 1½in. from the edges. This looped twine should be sufficiently loose to allow of the hand being freely passed through, see A and B. Hair generally requires a little opening or picking before being placed in position in the form of a roll. To effect this, take a small handful, pass underneath the twine commencing from C, shape up to the form of a roll, press back each handful with the left hand before placing successive layers; when finished the looped twine will be embedded in the hair. To aid the beginner in forming an opinion of the quantity required, it may be noted that an approximate amount for the first stuffing of an ordinary sized chair is 2½ lbs. The seat should now appear as in FIG. 158, the centre part being filled lightly on the springs to the level of the roll.

The canvas used for first stuffing must be pliable and not too harsh for working. "Scrim" is the name given to this class of canvas, though a superior material called cheese cloth is sometimes used by upholsterers for first-class work. To measure the amount of scrim required lay a tape measure over the hair from back to front, straining slightly to the top of moulding, and then from side to side at the widest part of the seat. 24in. to 26in. square is sufficient for an ordinary small chair. After folding to obtain the centre temporarily tack the scrim at the back, strain lightly towards the front and sides. In this operation the importance of keeping the threads of the canvas perfectly straight must be remembered. Also the roll formation of the hair must be pressed upwards and not dragged over, and if care is taken in this matter a clear space for the temporary tacks will be obtained. Beginners also are warned against the danger of tacking on mouldings or polished edges through carelessness. When this operation is complete the seat should appear as in FIG. 159 with the fulness of the scrim strained slightly to the corners, both back and front. ("Fulness" in upholstery is used to denote the folds, pleats, or slackness of any material that may be "cleaned" by

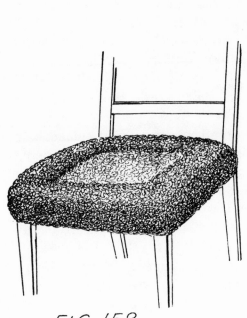

FIG. 158
Hair filled ready
for placing the scrim

FIG. 160
Method of placing
the hair twines

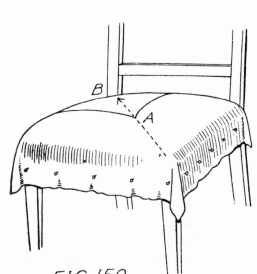

FIG. 159
Cutting Corners.
Fold canvas at right
angles & cut diagonally

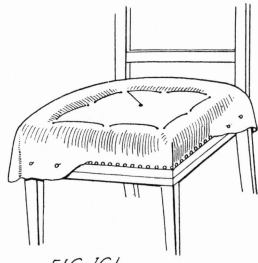

FIG. 161
Tacking down

straining taut). Examine the seat, release the tacks where any part appears over-strained. The back corners now require cutting ; to effect this, fold back the scrim, and set at right angles, FIG. 159. The beginner can hardly avoid making many bad cuts whilst learning, but the difficulty is minimised by not cutting close to the frame. Commence at A, cutting towards B, 1in. from frame. The hair must now be kept in position by means of a series of hair twines. To effect this, mark off and stab through the scrim with the point of the regulator about 4in. from the edge all round a series of holes, starting at A and back again to the same point, FIG. 160. With the needle threaded with a length of twine, thrust the eye end through at A until in position as shown at D. When the whole needle is clear of the scrim and hessian, push it upwards again at a distance of 1in. as shown at E. It is essential that a full inch of the hessian below as well as of the scrim above is taken up by the twine. The first loop at A is knotted. The twine is drawn moderately taut by gradation from B to A, C to B, etc., and finally knotted at the centre of seat G. In doing this care must be taken to see that neither twine nor needle becomes entangled in the springs or webbing. The seat is now partially shaped and prepared for the process of tacking down. The use of the hair twines described above is two-fold. (1) to keep the material used for stuffing permanently in position ; (2) in the process of tacking down, extra stuffing is required to obtain firm edges, and the hair twines act as a barrier, limiting the space for extra filling from the edge and preventing displacement of the hair.

CHAPTER 24.

TACKING DOWN FOR STITCHING.

There is no branch of the furniture trade in which poor materials and faulty construction are so completely hidden as in upholstery—especially in stuffover work. Poor material or bad workmanship may be detected in three ways (1) by a little judicious stripping of the outer covering; (2) by the critical eye and deft touch of an expert; (3) by wear and tear. Mention is made of this here, as there is naturally a tendency on the part of the beginner to think that although his work in one or more of the initial stages may not be quite up to standard, it will ultimately be well out of sight when the final covering is applied to the chair or settee.

Fig. 162 illustrates a seat tacked down, that is to say, the hair has been filled in, and the scrim tacked to a previously gauged line ready for the stitching process by which the exact contour will ultimately be formed. Stitching takes up a considerable amount of time, and it is absolutely essential to the comfort and wearing qualities of upholstery. To save trouble the thoroughly bad practice of substituting wood to take the place of stuffing and stitching is sometimes resorted to. It will be obvious, however, that the covering material is subjected to a much greater strain when the seat is compressed if the front is built up of wood, and therefore perfectly rigid, than if formed by means of a stitched edge that yields to pressure and returns to its original position. But to return to the proper method of tacking down for stitching. It will be recalled that the running through twines of first stuffing serve a twofold purpose (1) to compress slightly the hair on the seat and reduce the roundness; (2) to act as a barrier when extra stuffing is added from the edge to build up the contour. To commence tacking down first gauge the height of the seat. Measurements should be taken from the top of the stuffing either to the floor line or the moulding, that is to say, Fig. 162 from A to B, A to C, or A to the floor. The usual height from the top of the stuffing to the floor line is 18in., and the balance of that measurement from A to C will be the easiest method of reckoning.

First release the temporary tack in the centre, Fig. 161, add any hair that may be necessary to impart firmness and build up the correct contour, fold the scrim inwards and temporarily tack on the rasped edge of the frame as shown at Fig. 161. To obtain the

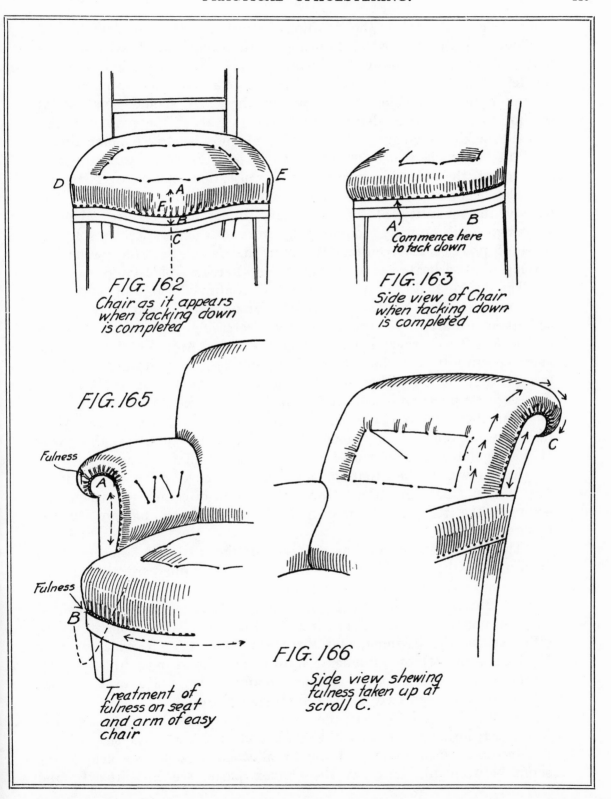

FIG. 162
Chair as it appears
when tacking down
is completed

FIG. 163
Side view of Chair
when tacking down
is completed

Commence here
to tack down

FIG. 165

Fulness

Fulness

Treatment of
fulness on seat
and arm of easy
chair

FIG. 166
Side view shewing
fulness taken up at
scroll C.

exact height compress the stuffing material with the thumb and forefinger at the top edge, drawing it slightly forward at the same time. Commencing from the centre repeat the operation towards the left, leaving 2in. at the corner, then continue in a similar way on the right hand side. The front of the chair should now appear as FIG. 162, the roll moderately firm, the threads of the scrim straight, and the tacking regular. The tacks should not be driven home finally until the exact height is obtained, as it may be necessary to release and adjust the scrim in parts of the work that appear overstrained.

The beginner will not be able to judge the firmness of the roll, namely the quantity of hair necessary to produce a firm edge by stitching, until actually commencing work with the needle; but by constant practice and continually laying hands on the stuffing he will develop that delicate sense of touch peculiar to upholsterers.

The tacking down should now be continued on the sides, see FIG. 163, starting at the point A. First work towards the front and then towards the back, slightly decreasing the height towards the back. The corners must now be treated. Any superfluous scrim must be cut off and the fulness that remains folded inwards to form two pleats, one on either side of the corner as shown at FIG. 162. The young upholsterer will find that he is unable to obtain a clean roll formation without the use of the regulator; parts of the work that are uneven can be moulded or shaped by inserting the point of the regulator as shown at FIG. 164. The regulator is used to draw the hair towards the front to form a firm edge prior to stitching. The dotted lines and the arrows show the direction in which the point of the regulator is moved to bring the hair forward to the required position.

The manipulation of the fulness of the material, especially at corners, and the keeping of the threads of the scrim perfectly straight is a stumbling block to learners at this process of the work. The term "fulness" at this stage infers a gathering of the scrim caused by the curves of the chair frame. Fulness always constitutes a difficulty for the beginner, and there are three ways in which it may be dealt with—(1) by forming it into a series of regular frills; (2) by pleating; (3) cutting out. At the tacking down stage of the work fulness is best regulated by the first-named method.

It will be noticed that the chair sketched at FIGS. 162 and 163 has a serpentine front, and the sides and back are also shaped. It is necessary when tacking down to allow fulness by slackening the scrim between the tacks at the convex parts, see FIG. 162 F, and

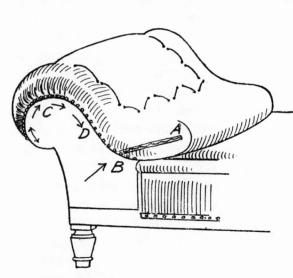

FIG. 167
How to treat fulness
in a large scroll

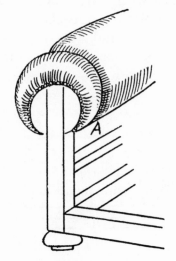

FIG. 170
Bolster arm settee
How to tack down
front facing

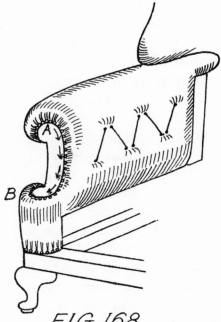

FIG. 168
Tacking down of
double scroll facing

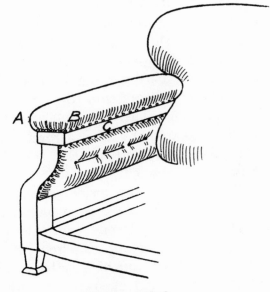

FIG. 169
Pad & panel arm.
Method of tacking down

FIG. 163 B. This fulness is necessary in order to obtain the proper shape when stitching. The regulation of such fulness requires careful manipulation, especially on large pieces of work such as are shown in FIGS. 165 and 166. At FIG. 165 B, the threads of the scrim are on the bias, and in order to obtain the firm roll formation and to get rid of or "clean" the fulness it is only necessary to tack closer than on the straight work indicated by the arrows. At FIGS. 165 A and 166 C are shown front and back scrolls. The fulness in these cases cannot be manipulated as at FIG. 165 B, because the threads are not on the bias (see outline indicated by arrows, FIG. 166) but straight, and the fulness is therefore gathered in a series of pleats or frills by closely tacking. FIG. 167 is an example of a large piece of work with the

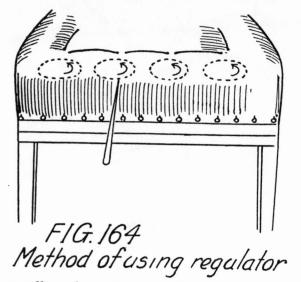

FIG. 164
Method of using regulator

scroll tacked down ready for stitching. To obtain the "swell" or bulge at A the fulness is folded inwards like a pocket and sewn from A to B. The fulness at C is regulated by a series of pleats and closely tacked. From D to B the scrim should be taut.

FIG. 168 represents the frame of a wing easy chair prepared for stitching. There is fulness at A and B, and a straight run where indicated by the arrows. FIG. 169 is a club easy with a large pad arm and panel. For the pad the requisite amount of scrim would be cut to size, and one edge when folded tacked the whole length of the inside of the rail C. The opposite edge (again folded) should be tacked on the outside of the rail thus forming an empty bolster with one end open at A—B. Hair is then crammed in and the fulness at the front regulated as already explained FIG. 170 is a bolster arm of a settee. The running-through twine is tacked at A, strained lightly over the canvas which it holds in position while the front is manipulated for tacking down. The fulness here would be treated as already described.

The following points should be remembered when tacking down :—
(1) To obtain good results the threads must be straight.

(2) Avoid overstraining the hair twines (or running through twines), FIG. 162.

(3) Wherever fulness is encountered closer tacking is necessary.

(4) When adjusting the work temporary tacking should be employed; the tacks are then more easily withdrawn without tearing the scrim.

(5) Tack on the rasped edge of the wood, otherwise the sharp edges of the tack heads will project and cut the coverings.

(6) Fulness is better regulated by a series of frills than by folding in pleats. On straight lines without fulness the scrim must be taut between all the tacks.

(7) Tacking down without employing the regulator is useless; the hair must be moulded into the requisite shape by frequent use of this tool.

CHAPTER 25.

STITCHING.

Though perhaps not quite so difficult as tacking down, the stitching of upholstery is complicated work, and, while the craftsman may understand the principles governing it, it is only by continual practice that he can become expert. Stitching, in addition to skill and judgment, requires an appreciation of good lines especially in the production of evenly-balanced scrolls, such as those shown on the fronts of settees and divan chairs in Chapter 14 of this series. In the style of upholstery which is associated with gilt furniture of French design, the stitching is very skilfully done, the different rows being placed herring-bone fashion, and the work quilted up into fine leather edges.

The beginner should, if possible, commence with small chairs, but he will get a good idea of the effect of the different rows of stitching by a study of FIG. 171. The number of rows of stitching depends upon the height of seat required. The general rule is three rows for a small chair. FIG. 171 shows four; C and D are called blind rows, B the second row, and A the top row. The various angles at which the needle is thrust through the work should be noticed, as this is important. The blind rows are so called because no stitches are visible on the top surface of the scrim. These blind rows serve the purpose of drawing the hair forward to the edge in order to form a firm bulge of stuffing for the subsequent rows. By the second row of stitching, B, FIG. 171, the hair is still further compressed in roll formation, the row of stitches in this case appearing on the seat as well as on the front edge of the work. The top row A is the final stitching, and on this the finished outline of the upholstery depends.

It must be remembered that when stitching a frequent use of the regulator is absolutely essential, and the upholsterer should so arrange the work that the stitched edges slightly overhang the frame, FIG. 172. Unless attention is paid to this, damage is frequently caused to the final covering, because it is liable to come into contact with the sharp edge of the wood frame at A, FIG. 173. Similar damage to the covering may also be caused in other ways, namely :—

(1) If the edges are insufficiently firm when stitched, see FIG. 173. In such a case the fault is at once apparent when pressure is applied to the seat.

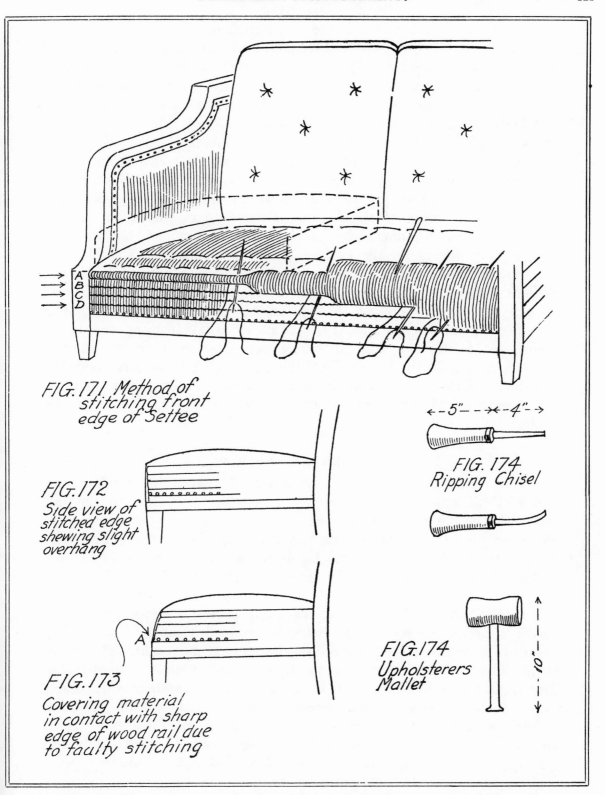

FIG. 171 Method of stitching front edge of Settee

FIG. 172 Side view of stitched edge shewing slight overhang

FIG. 173 Covering material in contact with sharp edge of wood rail due to faulty stitching

←- 5"- -→←-4"-→
FIG. 174 Ripping Chisel

FIG. 174 Upholsterers Mallet

10"

(2) If the number of stitches is insufficient.

(3) If, in stitching, the upholsterer finds he must juggle with the edge to rectify the tacking down, the final covering is again liable to the fault shown at A, FIG. 173. To explain this more clearly, let us assume that an edge is tacked down to measure 4in. when stitched. If after stitching the second row it is apparent that the proper height can only be obtained by sacrificing the correct position of the edge as shown at FIG. 172, it proves that insufficient scrim has been allowed. The remedy is to rip the work and adjust the scrim. It is very important that tacks should be well driven home on the rasped edges of the frame. Failure to do this is a common fault with the beginner, who should occasionally test his work by rubbing his fingers on the surface of a row of tacks. It will be to his ultimate advantage if he once or twice receives a painful reminder of any neglect in this respect, as the sharp edge of the head of a tack if left would soon cut through an expensive covering, FIG. 173A.

The ripping chisel, FIG. 174, is an essential tool for the upholsterer, for a stitched edge if wrong can only be properly adjusted as regards height by cutting out the stitches with scissors, removing the tacks with the ripping chisel, and taking in or letting out the scrim as required, and then retacking and commencing the work over again.

STITCHING A BLIND ROW.

The method of stitching a blind row is shown in the four diagrams, FIGS. 175—178. Commence at A, FIG. 175, close to the rail, insert the needle to B, draw the eye through in a circular movement as indicated by the dotted line, returning as shown at C, FIG. 176. The eye of the needle must not be drawn out at B for the blind row. A knot is tied at A, FIG. 177, and drawn tight. Insert the needle as before at B, drawing through at C, looping the twine twice, run the needle through A either to the right or left. After pulling the needle clear of the scrim, the twine is strained tight by compressing the canvas with the left hand, at the same time pulling the twine in the direction of the arrows at A, FIG. 178, with the right hand. The result of a blind row of stitching is the formation of invisible loops of twine which automatically draw the hair to the front, so forming a firm bulge of stuffing as shown at B, FIG. 178. It is advisable to commence with small stitches about 1in. in length and ¾in. apart. The needle must not be sloped too much, and the point

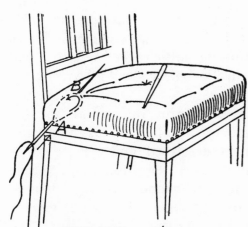

FIG.175   1st Operation
Upward movement
of the needle

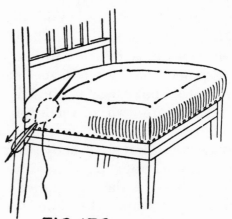

FIG.176
Downward movement
of the needle

Needle placed aside to allow free
use of the hands in tightening the
knot, by compressing the hair with
the left and
straining with
the right.

FIG.177   3rd Operation
Looping the twine
round needle

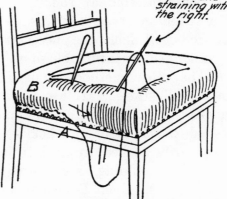

FIG. 178 4th Operation
Straining the
twine taut

when thrust through must be on the near side of the hair twines, otherwise more stuffing than is necessary will be caught up by the loops.

In many cases the stuffed backs of show-wood upholstery are prepared with a blind row of stitching only. In Chapter 12, Fig. 47, a panel back frame is shown so constructed that the covering material is placed in position first before stuffing commences. In such backs it is difficult to keep the stuffing sufficiently even to avoid ugly proportions, for as a general rule inside backs should be perfectly flat unless pin cushion stuffed.

There are two methods of placing the scrim to prepare for the blind row. The first is shown at Fig. 179. The hair is filled and twines run through exactly as previously described and illustrated at Fig. 160 (Chapter 23); a semi-circular needle, see Fig. 180, is then used instead of the straight one, both for the running through twines, Fig. 179 B, and the blind row, Fig. 179 A. The blind row is manipulated with the semi-circular needle, always working from left to right as described. A one-pointed semi-circular needle is more serviceable for this work than the double-pointed variety. The method of using it differs from the double-pointed needle, and both needle and twine must be drawn completely through the scrim and the point inserted at the same hole as shown at A and C, Fig. 179. The stitch must be kept as close to the tacks as possible, otherwise the roll will lack the necessary firmness. The second stuffing will be described in future chapters.

The other method of placing the scrim to prepare for the blind row is illustrated at Fig. 181. The quantity of scrim required is gauged by means of a tape measure, allowance being made for the desired thickness of the back. The scrim is laid on the hessian and temporarily tacked to hold it in position. Then mark off a line 3in. from the moulding, see A—B. With the semi-circular needle, commencing from C or D, make a series of running stitches as indicated by the arrows. A limited space is now left all round. This is filled with hair to bring it up to the required measurement and the scrim is tacked down. It is important that the upholsterer should leave sufficient space between the polished moulding and the tacks holding the scrim, in order that the subsequent covering material and trimmings may lie perfectly flat, see Chapter 12, Figs. 44 and 45.

Variations of blind stitching are shown at Fig. 182. On the wing at A tack stitching is illustrated, on the arm B there is an inverted blind row, at the scroll C an ordinary blind row with straight

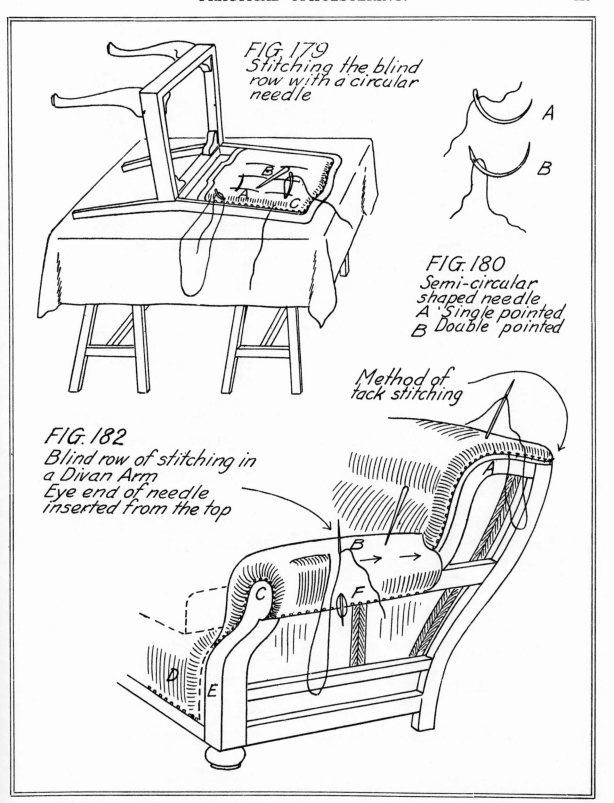

FIG. 179
Stitching the blind
row with a circular
needle

A

B

FIG. 180
Semi-circular
shaped needle
A 'Single pointed
B Double 'pointed

Method of
tack stitching

FIG. 182
Blind row of stitching in
a Divan Arm
Eye end of needle
inserted from the top

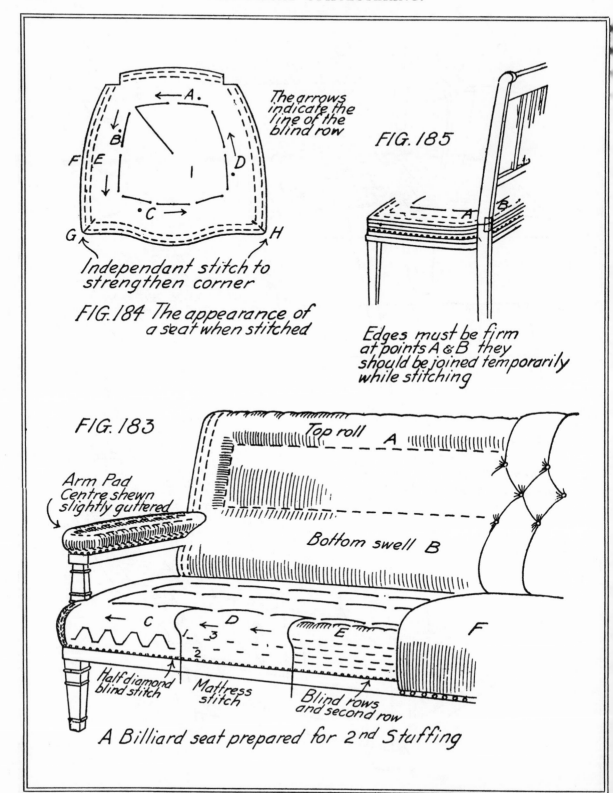

The arrows indicate the line of the blind row

FIG. 185

Independant stitch to strengthen corner

FIG. 184 The appearance of a seat when stitched

Edges must be firm at points A & B they should be joined temporarily while stitching

FIG. 183

Top roll A

Bottom swell B

Arm Pad Centre shewn slightly guttered

Half diamond blind stitch

Mattress stitch

Blind rows and second row

A Billiard seat prepared for 2nd Stuffing

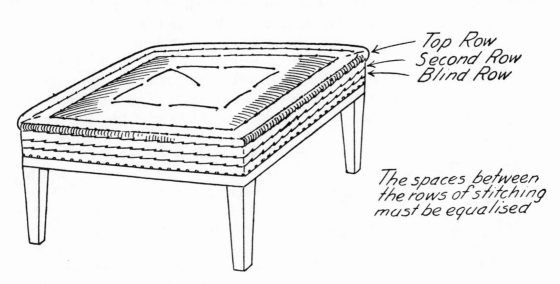

Top Row
Second Row
Blind Row

The spaces between
the rows of stitching
must be equalised

FIG. 186   Frame. First stuffed
Example of chain stitching

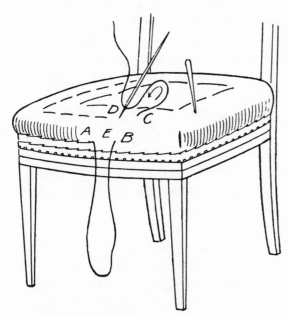

FIG. 187
Blind Row & Second Row
Method of stitching
the divided stitching

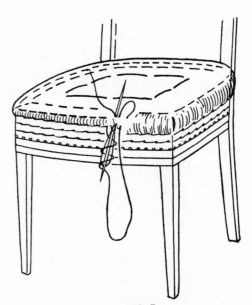

FIG. 188
The Top Row

needle, and at the knee D a blind row with a circular or spring needle. Tack stitching was much favoured by upholsterers of former times, and is to be found in the earliest examples of upholstered furniture. The process takes a little longer than the ordinary stitch, but the bulge of stuffing obtained in this way will retain its shape for a much longer period than in cases where the ordinary method is employed, and a much firmer edge is produced. In tack stitching the tacks are first driven in temporarily, the knot of the twine is strained on the outside of the tack, which is then driven home. It will be obvious that the twine tightly gripped by the tack cannot slacken to anything like the extent as is possible when tightened on the scrim itself. At the line indicated by the arrows at B on the arm, FIG. 182, it is necessary that the first stuffing should be firm. A blind row or second row of stitching is therefore formed. For this blind row the eye of the needle would be inserted at B to F and back again without completely withdrawing the needle, a method which has already been shown at FIG. 176.

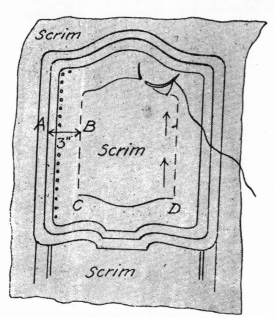

FIG. 181   Panel Back
Method of first stuffing

The backs of settees, divans and chesterfields are treated in this way, a bulge of hair being drawn to the top edge where the strain will be greatest in the subsequent covering. At C, FIG. 182, the scroll is tacked down and the blind row formed, as shown in FIG. 178. Owing to the proximity of the wood at the point E, a straight needle cannot be used. A semi-circular or spring needle is therefore required for the blind row at D.

Other forms of blind rows are indicated at FIG. 183, which represents a first stuffed billiard seat, which will be subsequently finished in the style of front known as the " pullover " or " round front " as at F. The half-diamond blind row shown at C is formed by carrying the stitch diagonally instead of horizontally. By this method a more rigid front is obtained, and at the same time fewer stitches are required. The blind row shown at D is called the mattress stitch. It is also made diagonally but without knots, and the line

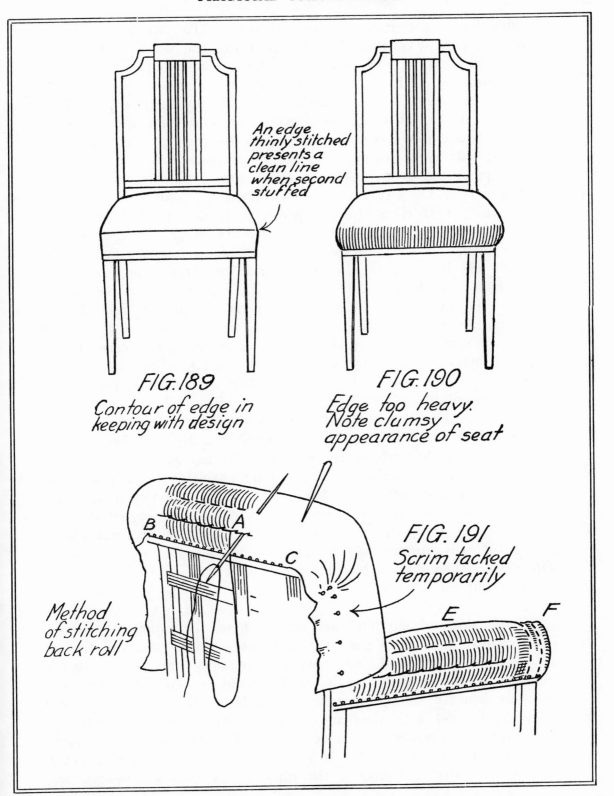

An edge thinly stitched presents a clean line when second stuffed

FIG. 189
Contour of edge in keeping with design

FIG. 190
Edge too heavy. Note clumsy appearance of seat

FIG. 191
Scrim tacked temporarily

Method of stitching back roll

of twine forms a continuous series of loops. To execute this stitch commence at 1 with ½in. blind stitch, insert the point at the same hole bringing the eye of the needle out at 2, withdraw the entire needle, inserting again at the same point to 3, and so on. As this stitch differs somewhat from the blind rows already described, it should be explained that at each stitch made not more than ½in. of scrim must be gathered up ; care must be taken also not to draw the twine too tight. It is necessary in stitching fronts in this way to resort to a frequent use of the regulator, which should be employed with an upward movement. At E are shown ordinary blind rows, and the second row of stitching. The bottom swell B, FIG. 183, may be either spring or top stuffed according to the design or depth of the seat required.

FIG. 184 is the plan of a small chair seat with the second and top rows of stitching. A, B, C, and D, together with the arrows, indicate the line of the blind row. E is the second row, F the top row. Independent stitches should be made angle-wise at G and H. They serve the two-fold purpose of shaping the corners and adding firmness to the edge, which is subjected to considerable strain when the covering material is fixed. Here it should be noted that the corners of all stitched edges must be firm. The beginner frequently finds pronounced difficulty with regard to this at the commencement and finishing points, see A and B, FIG. 185. A good plan is to join the ends of the scrim at the top as indicated. This will prevent any gathering of fulness and enables the stitches to be made in close proximity to the back of the chair. In joining the ends of the scrim care must be taken not to damage the polished wood when drawing the twine. To avoid this a piece of material placed beneath it will prevent any marking of the surface, see A and B, FIG. 185. When the stitching at the angle is completed, the temporary twine is cut out, and if correctly done, the corners should be quite firm.

Three rows of stitching are sufficient in the ordinary way for small chairs ; in some of the commoner grades three rows are stitched at the front only, and two rows at the sides and back. Before commencing the second row the work should be well regulated, and the hair beneath the scrim equally distributed in such a way that when compressed with the hand a smooth even surface is obtained. In stitching the second row a common fault with the beginner is to draw the stitches too tight. If he does so, a gutter and weak edge (see A, FIG. 192) is formed. The difficulty is overcome by practice,

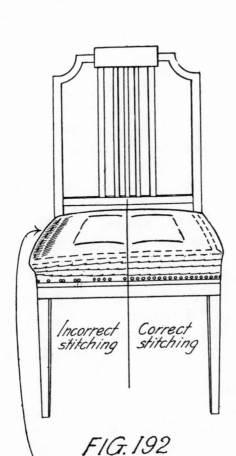

FIG. 192

Gutter formed by
straining the stitch
too tightly or insufficient
hair when tacking down

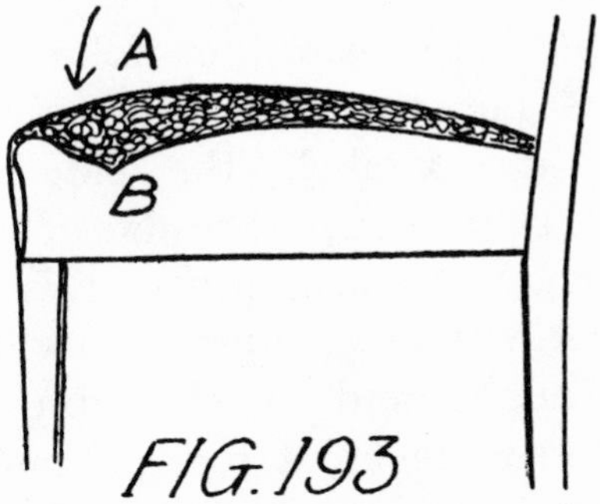

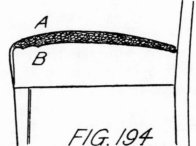

FIG. 193

Faulty foundation
of 1st stuffing

FIG. 194

Good foundation
of 1st stuffing

Fig. 193 shews the
extra hair required
in second stuffing
due to guttered stitches

but some time must necessarily elapse before the beginner is able to stitch skilfully and correctly. The chain stitch (FIG. 186) should be learnt first. This, though a slow, is a sure method of obtaining the necessary straight even line required for edges. FIG. 186 represents a square stool, the ideal shape of frame for beginners to use when practising tacking down and stitching, because on a rectangular frame of this kind the scrim is tacked down at right angles and the upholsterer can then follow the line of the threads when stitching. This is not the case in small chairs in which only the fronts and backs are parallel, the side rails converging slightly towards the back, causing the threads of the scrim to be on the bias. The beginner will soon prove this for himself, and will obtain uniform lines of stitching much more easily when the threads of the scrim are straight and so aid him in getting regular workmanlike lines.

When the blind row is completed the regulator must be vigorously applied before stitching the second row. FIG. 187 represents a second row commenced on a small chair front. The twine at A being drawn tight in readiness for the next stitch, thrust the point of the needle in at B, drawing it out completely at C, then insert the eye at D, drawing it out again at E. The twine from A is then folded twice round the needle and a knot formed and tightened as already described in connection with the blind row. To aid the upholsterer in drawing the stitch tight, the scrim is compressed at the top with the fingers and at the front with the thumb. The roll should be $1\frac{1}{2}$in. thick on the surface.

Small stitches about $\frac{3}{4}$in. should be used for the second row and $\frac{1}{2}$in. for the top row. The chain stitch, which is advocated for beginners, is shown at FIG. 186. Here the stitching appears continuous, each stitch being taken back to the same point on the scrim as the one immediately preceding it. The top stitching (FIG. 188) must be firm, for on the quality of workmanship in this row a good or bad edge depends. If too soft, it is useless for the purpose for which it is formed, namely, as an edge over which a covering material can be strained tightly without reducing its height. If the edge is too soft, the line will give and fall back, producing the fault shown at FIG. 193.

On straight edges, as shown at FIG. 186, the learner will find it best to follow the line of threads in the scrim after making the first stitch. Guttering the stitches can only be avoided by correct tacking down, frequent use of the regulator, and moderate straining of the twine; it is a difficulty which takes time and experience to surmount. The thickness of the top row that forms the edge is governed by two rules : (1) the weight of the fabric to be used for subsequent covering ; (2) the design of the particular work in hand. For example, the graceful lines of light Sheraton furniture would be entirely spoilt by a heavy roll edge on a second stuffing, which give the seat a bulky and clumsy appearance (see FIGS. 189 and 190). A thin stitched edge producing a sharp, clean outline, when covered, would be more consistent with the general proportions of this style of frame. A good rule to follow is to stitch thinly the edges of drawing-room furniture and small decorative work, and those of dining-room and library furniture slightly heavier. It must never be forgotten that it is the contours formed by the edges that regulate the finished appearance of all upholstery. A little experimental stitching is advisable for beginners, who are sometimes tempted to continue a piece of work, forming the stitches quite perfectly, but forgetting that their proportions are wrong, and the edge is either too large or too small, as the case may be. The scissors for cutting out mistakes must be used as freely, if necessary, as was the ripping chisel when tacking. The top row (FIG. 188) is manipulated exactly as the others, the only difference being that the stitch may be strained tightly without any fear of guttering the work. Correct and incorrect stitching is shown at FIG. 192. The gutter which is shown is due to two causes : (1) insufficient hair when tacking down ; (2) overstraining when stitching the second row.

It is important, in order to obtain a firm edge, to equalise the spaces between the various rows of stitching. At FIG. 192, the space between the blind row and the second row is too great, and when the top of the seat is compressed a bulge will form, which will eventually be apparent from the outside of the finished work.

Corners are subjected to much strain, as the fulness is dispensed with by straining at this point. The corner on the left (FIG. 192) is lower than the centre of the front edge. This may be due to one of three causes : (1) insufficient hair ; (2) the taking in of too much scrim ; (3) faulty stitching. Extra stuffing is needed to fill the gutter formed by faulty stitching, and a sagging front frequently results. The space between the top of seat, A to B (FIG. 193), requires more stuffing than the same space indicated by A and B (FIG. 194), which is correctly stitched. The foundation of first stuffing in the former case is faulty from the outset, and when second stuffed the covering is liable to sag, especially if heavy stuffing material, such as flock, is used. FIG. 191 shows the method of treating a stuffover easy chair

back.   After the scrim has been temporarily set, tacking down should
be commenced at the centre, and at this stage not completed, but
finished at B and C.   The stitching required at A is a second row
with or without a blind row.   The question as to whether one or two
rows are needed is governed by (1) the quality of the work; (2) the
covering used; (3) the stuffing material.   The arm E is shown first
stuffed; the facing, a side view of which is shown at F, is treated
with a second and top row of stitching.

After stitching horizontally as already described, the beginner
will experience some difficulty when attempting scrolls and facings.
In this work the needle is placed at a different angle; to obtain the
requisite contour, and the upholsterer has no line of threads in the
scrim to aid him in keeping a regular line as he has when stitching
straight work.   In spite of these difficulties equalisation of the rows
of stitching is of the greatest importance, as is also the skilful use of
the regulator.

Scrolls are generally stitched at the edges sharp and fine except
in the case of "under edge" work, a method of stitching that will
be described in detail later.   In the illustrations accompanying
chapters 14 and 24 a number of facings of different design are shown.
To obtain well-balanced curves for such facings it is wise to work
from patterns rather than set them out from measurements.   In a
properly organised workshop patterns of the different shapes for various
work are kept for reference, marked with a number or name to
identify them with a given frame, and essential details noted on them
as shown in the sketches at FIG. 196.   This system is recommended
for many reasons: (1) a new man in a workshop can readily see the
correct proportions of the upholstery from the pattern; (2) patterns
cut for a new design ensure correct measurements in repeats and a
saving of time is effected.   Buckram is the best material for such
patterns; a hole is usually made in them for the purpose of hanging
them on nails or pegs.

FIG. 195 shows a scroll arm stitched with three rows.   The needle
is held approximately at right angles to the work, as will be seen
at the various positions shown at A, B, and C.   Each row of
stitching commences from the point D, and they gradually converge
towards each other when nearing the point E.   All the work with
the regulator should be done before stitching commences, that is to say,
the regulator should be used from D to E; the outline can then be
criticised, and faults of tacking down re-adjusted if necessary.   Intermittent or sectional use of the regulator as from B to A is not advisable
in scrolls or shaped parts.

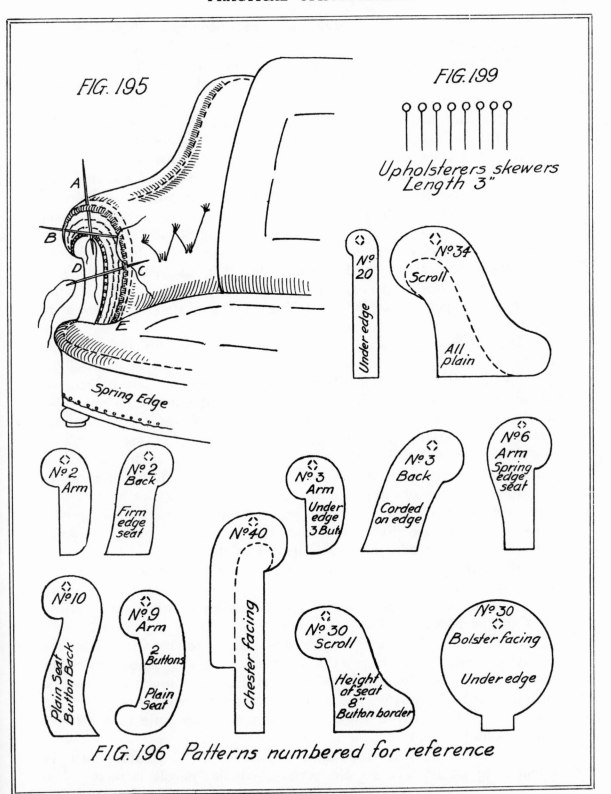

FIG. 195

FIG. 199

Upholsterers skewers
Length 3"

Nº 20 Under edge

Nº 34 Scroll All plain

Spring Edge

Nº 2 Arm

Nº 2 Back Firm edge seat

Nº 3 Arm Under edge 3 But

Nº 3 Back Corded on edge

Nº 6 Arm Spring edge seat

Nº 40 Chester facing

Nº 10 Plain Seat Button Back

Nº 9 Arm 2 Buttons Plain Seat

Nº 30 Scroll Height of seat 8" Button border

Nº 30 Bolster facing Under edge

FIG. 196 Patterns numbered for reference

It is not necessary to tack down or stitch the edges of scrolls and facings so firmly as seats. The material with which the work is to be covered governs this to some extent, leather, pegamoid, and other heavy coverings needing a firmer foundation than cretonnes, tapestries or linings.

If the hair has been crammed in the tacking down of the scrolls, it will not be easy to produce a regular edge. Care must be taken in this particular instance, as any such irregularities are more pronounced than in seats. In stitching scrolls and facings the edge of the upholstery should slightly overhang the wood as already described in the case of chair seats, FIG. 172. Care should be taken in respect of the following points when stitching scrolls: (1) the outline should be correctly formed by the regulator before stitching; (2) guttering of the canvas on the surface should be avoided; (3) the lines of stitching should taper gradually and evenly both at the starting and finishing points; (4) the stitching of the various rows must be equalised.

The stitching of scroll work presents many difficulties to the beginner. A skilful and painstaking man may stitch a scroll of such perfect shape as to call for eulogistic comment, but he receives a rude shock when he attempts to reproduce it exactly on the other arm of the chair or settee. The beginner is hampered by the necessity of working from left to right. On the left hand scroll he would commence stitching at the point D, but on the right hand scroll this would be reversed, and he would commence at E, finishing at D.

The stitching of spring edges shown at FIGS. 197 and 198 is more complicated than the stitching of firm edges. In spring edge work the cane, see FIGS. 136 and 142, takes the place of wood, and skewers, FIG. 199, are used instead of tacks.

Stitching a spring edge consists of five operations, which will now be briefly described. The first operation, FIG. 197, shows the scrim placed and temporarily set with skewers, which are stabbed through the hessian beneath the cane.

In the second operation the scrim is filled in with hair and skewered down to the cane; the scrim must be so gauged that when compressed by the hands a bulge of stuffing is obtained of such a size as to form above the cane a roll which will be either heavy or light according to the style of work; the scrim must be quite taut between the skewers.

Before commencing the third operation the regulator must be applied vigorously. To fix the scrim a circular needle is used. This

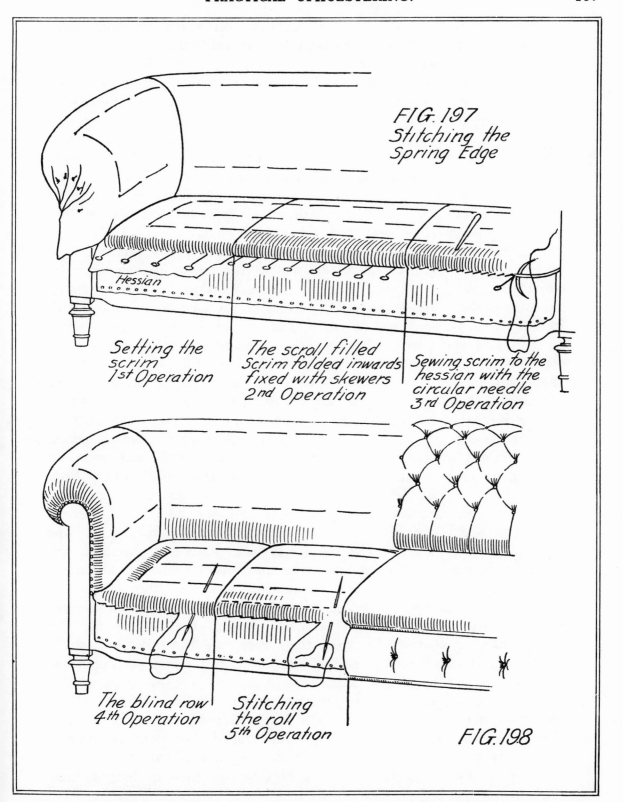

FIG. 197
Stitching the
Spring Edge

Hessian

Setting the
scrim
1st Operation

The scroll filled
Scrim folded inwards
fixed with skewers
2nd Operation

Sewing scrim to the
hessian with the
circular needle
3rd Operation

The blind row
4th Operation

Stitching
the roll
5th Operation

FIG. 198

is stabbed through the scrim and hessian, *not round the cane*. The stitches should be about 1in. apart, single knotted.

The fourth operation consists of forming the blind row, the method followed being exactly as that described for firm edges, but care must be exercised so that each stitch grips the threads of the spring hessian both in the upward and downward movement.

The final operation is the formation of the roll. The needle when forming this stitch should be nearly vertical, and care must be exercised to stab through the hessian as described for the blind row. The size of roll varies according to the particular style of work. The roll of a spring edge will always retain its original position if correctly stitched as described on opposite page.

In the ninth chapter diagrams illustrating iron back chairs were given. In first stuffing such chairs it is necessary to commence by forming a roll on the outside of the frame as a foundation for fixing the subsequent covering material. Many of the shapes associated with iron backs are also made in wood, but the principle of first stuffing is similar in each case. FIG. 199a is a shaped back, J the hessian tacked on the inside of rail, see arrows. A length of scrim not less than 12in. in width is now cut, the measurement being arrived at by placing the tape outside the rail of the back from scroll to scroll. A line is next pencilled on the hessian about 4in. deep, the distance being measured from K to L. The centre line of the scrim having been obtained by folding, it is placed in position at A, and sewing is commenced towards the left hand if working from the front. Running stitches about $\frac{3}{4}$in. apart are employed to join the scrim to the hessian, a circular needle is used, and for additional strength the scrim should be sewn on a double fold unless working on the selvedge. At A and B, also at D, E, and F, it will be necessary to allow fulness in the scrim owing to the convex shape of the frame, whilst from H to G the reverse is the case. At this position a cut about 3in. deep in the scrim will decrease the fulness at the concave part of the work. The hair to form the roll at the top is next filled in, commencing from the centre, and the scrim is brought over it and tacked to the rasped edge of the frame—it is important that the threads should be kept straight.

The line of stitching should run parallel to and directly above the outer line of the frame, so that the roll formed thereby projects the same distance all round. The roll I is stitched with or without a blind row. This process of stitching is one of much difficulty, and should not be attempted by a beginner on such a chair as that

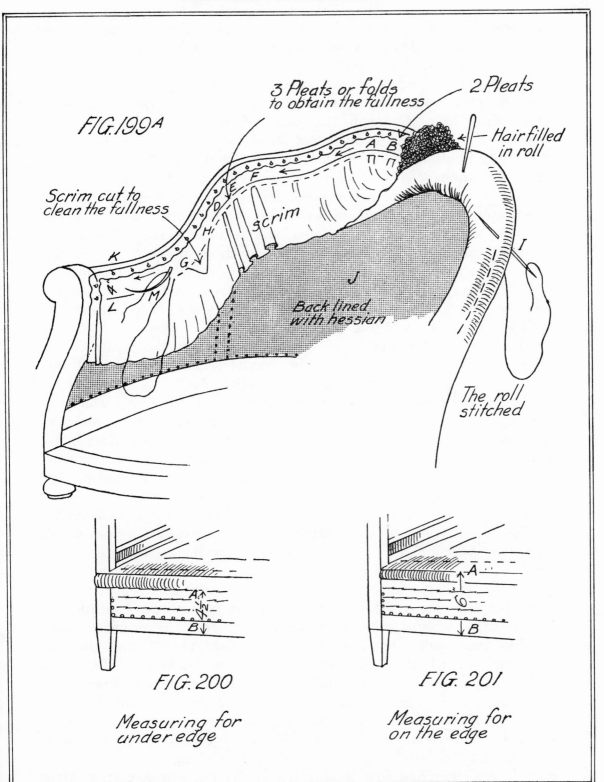

FIG. 199ᴬ

3 Pleats or folds to obtain the fullness

2 Pleats

Hair filled in roll

Scrim cut to clean the fullness

scrim

Back lined with hessian

The roll stitched

FIG. 200

Measuring for under edge

FIG. 201

Measuring for on the edge

sketched. To stitch well-balanced rolls and produce even lines on a shape such as this, especially on an iron back chair, requires all the skill of a first-class upholsterer.

The term "under edge" stitching implies that the trimming is to be sewn under the edge, as at FIG. 202, and not on the edge, as at FIG. 203. Although this form of stitching may be termed modern, it is in reality a revival of an old style, for many of Chippendale's sofa fronts of the type that are upholstered fully, without squabs, have the trimming placed under the edge, but not in quite so pronounced a manner as now obtains. This style possesses the following advantages : (1) a superior finish is given to the work ; (2) the trimming is under edge work, is less exposed, and retains its shape longer than if placed on those parts subjected to much wear, such as the tops of arms and the front edges of seats. Light stuffover upholstery of dainty design is much enhanced by under edge treatment, but this form of stitching requires much skill, as clumsy efforts completely spoil the appearance of the work.

For under edge work and on the edge work the measurements differ, see FIGS. 200 and 201. For example, in a seat to be tacked down for under edge, with a border $4\frac{1}{2}$in. deep, the measurement would be from the base B to the line of stitching A, while for ordinary or on the edge work the measurement of 6in. would be from the base B to the top of edge A. It should be further noted that under edge work is upholstered differently from the ordinary stitched edge, because the covering material in the former method is in two pieces, as shown at FIG. 206—the covering of the seat A being one piece and the border D another. In contradistinction to this the covering for an ordinary seat is generally cut and placed on in one picee unless a separate border is specified. (In the chapter on "Cutting" this is dealt with more fully.)

When tacking down for under edge work the beginner must remember (1) the difference in measurements already mentioned ; (2) the extra amount of scrim required compared with ordinary edges.

FIG. 204 shows the arm of a divan chair tacked down so that when upholstered the front would appear as shown at FIG. 202. The bulge of canvas at A should be well defined before commencing to stitch. It is wise to place the facing pattern on the front, as indicated by the dotted line, FIG. 204, as this ensures that sufficient scrim is allowed for the top stitch to project well forward when the work is finished. The scroll with the stitching finished is shown at FIG. 205, the front line of stitching of the top row A corresponding

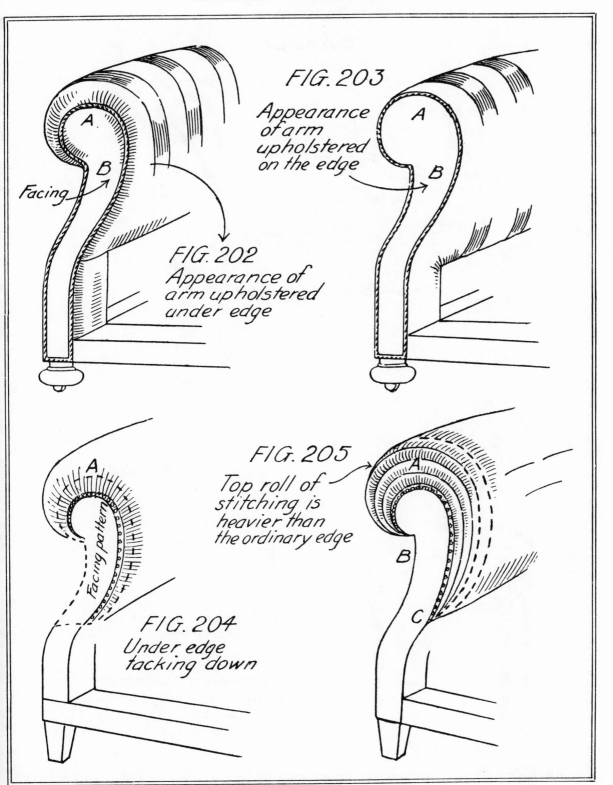

FIG. 203
Appearance of arm upholstered on the edge

A

B

Facing

FIG. 202
Appearance of arm upholstered under edge

FIG. 205
Top roll of stitching is heavier than the ordinary edge

A

B

C

FIG. 204
Under edge tacking down

A

Facing pattern

FIG. 206

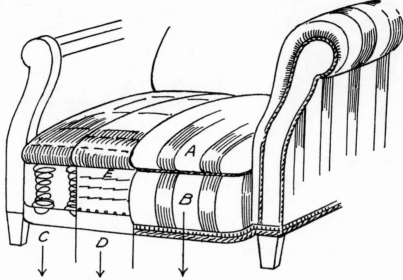

Spring
edge

Under
edge

Seat can be made
same in appearance
when second stuffed

FIG. 207

FIG. 208
Example of feather
edge stitching shewing
a cross stitch and
feather edge

to the cord line A of FIG. 202. It is essential that the top stitch is strained taut, as it forms the foundation for the fixing of the covering materials, which will be subsequently sewn to it ; if the scrim yields too easily at these parts, the sunken effect of the cord will be lost. The top roll for under edge work should be slightly larger than for on the edge work. The difference between the two styles is clearly seen at FIGS. 202 and 203. The superiority in finish given by the under edge facing is very marked—the general appearance is softer. It should be pointed out that under edge work necessitates greater expenditure of time by the upholsterer than ordinary or on the edge work.

Seat fronts stitched for under edge may be made closely to resemble spring edge work, see FIG. 206. Here at C and D the seat is shown first stuffed in two ways ; C, spring edge ; D, firm edge, stitched to a given height of 7in. under edge. When second stuffed and finished the appearance in both cases could be as A and B. It should, however, be understood that a spring edge as C is more buoyant than the firm edge at D.

This lengthy chapter on the complicated process of stitching would be incomplete without reference to the designs for show wood furniture of the Sheraton, Adam, and Empire styles, and French chairs of the Louis periods. In all these cases the outline of the upholstery must be well defined, as indicated in FIG. 207, as unless the contours are quite sharp and definite, the character of the chair is destroyed. French upholsterers are very skilful in this style of work. The plan for first stuffing such a chair is shown at FIG. 208. The row of stitching placed crosswise is called herring bone. On the top row an extra stitch is given which compresses the edge to a sharp thin line of stuffing. This stitch is called the feather stitch, and from the appearance of the work when covered the edge might be mistaken for a wood line. This style of stitching is only applied to decorative upholstery, and is generally associated with gilt furniture.

CHAPTER 26.

SECOND STUFFING.

The term "second stuffing" as applied to upholstery covers a wide field. After the foundation formed by first stuffing has been formed, the term "second stuffing" may refer to anything from a pin-cushion back 6in. square to the finishing of a double-sprung settee fully buttoned in morocco. Second stuffing, therefore, embraces a variety of different methods, and it is only by graduated experience in all these that the upholsterer can become proficient. The term second stuffing, as used in this series of articles, denotes the covering of the second stuffing of hair with calico or lining as distinct from the final covering of tapestry, leather or other material. In passing, however, it should be noted that in inexpensive work the final covering material is sometimes placed in .position without the use of any calico or lining, and upholstery treated cheaply in such a way is known in the trade as being finished "in the jacket."

The learner or apprentice when studying the different methods of second stuffing advocated here should clearly understand the difficulty of laying down a hard and fast rule for working. The various tackings used in the elementary stages will be set out, but to describe any one method as the best would be misleading ; the learner is advised to gain a thorough mastery of the principles under-lying the methods here described, and then follow his own judgment in order to obtain the best possible results.

Then again, different results are aimed at by different makers. For example, in finishing upholstery in morocco one maker will go to the greatest possible trouble to clean the fulness of a skin on the arms and back of a chair, though this result can only be obtained at the expense of making the work hard. On the other hand, another manufacturer of morocco work favours fulness and slackness of the leather in conjunction with softness. Thus the upholsterer in moving from one shop to another may be called upon to practise widely-opposed methods of second stuffing.

It is advisable for the learner to commence second stuffing on small work, such as loose seats, pin-cushion seats, and backs, before attempting chairs, and, if possible, in his first attempts, hair should be used as a second stuffing. When this material is used it is covered with calico or lining before the final covering is applied.

PINCUSHION STUFFING

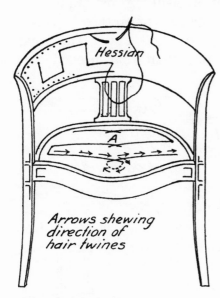

Hessian

A

Arrows shewing
direction of
hair twines

FIG. 209
Placing the hair twines

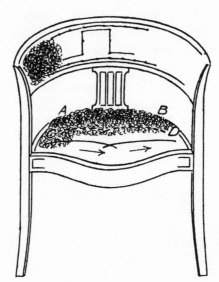

A   B
                    D

FIG. 210
Filling the hair

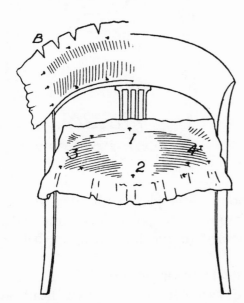

B

1
3   4
2

FIG. 211
Temporarily tacking
the calico

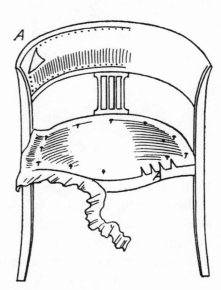

A

FIG. 212
Trimming off Calico

The correct contour of a seat is determined by the skill of the upholsterer when second stuffing. If the work is done as it should be, graceful curves are obtained, but over-filling or cramming of the hair results in uneven lines, and a poor appearance. This may be explained more clearly by referring to FIG. 214. The quantity of hair required at the centre A is greater than that needed at the side

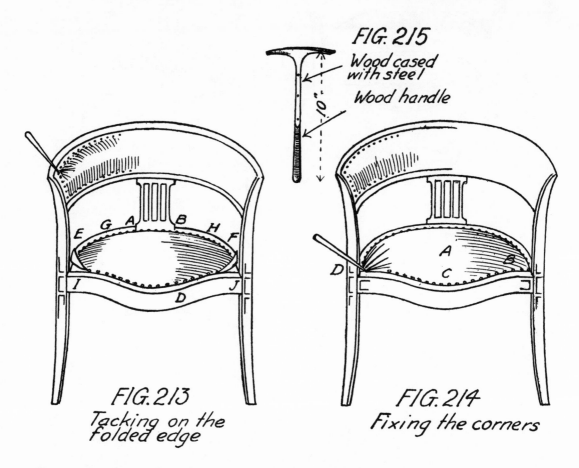

FIG. 215
Wood cased with steel
Wood handle

FIG. 213
Tacking on the folded edge

FIG. 214
Fixing the corners

B or the front C. If the same amount was placed all over the seat, the calico when strained would not graduate so well to the edges, because too much hair would be crammed in the limited space between the hessian and the calico.

For pin-cushion work a cabriole hammer is needed for tacking close to the mouldings. A cabriole hammer has a small head and is of light weight, and does not possess the heavy fall of the ordinary hammer. The French pattern illustrated at FIG. 215 is preferable to the English type. The slender part of the handle is strengthened and cased with steel.

Pin-cushion upholstery—the simplest form of second stuffing—is illustrated at FIGS. 209-214. This form of work usually consists of a webbed seat over which is tacked a layer of hessian without any first stuffing. As this forms the only foundation for the second stuffing, it is important that great care should be exercised when fixing the webs; frames associated with pin-cushion work are generally light in weight (see Chapter 17). Loose seats for chairs, such as are shown in Chapter 9, FIG. 30, are second stuffed in the pin-cushion style, so also are small chair backs; occasional chairs, arm pads, etc.

At FIG. 209 the hair twines are shown. These should be sewn either from side to side or from back to front. If hair is used, the former method is the better because the stuffing materials in seats always have a tendency to become displaced at the front owing to compression. This danger is lessened somewhat when the twines are placed from side to side. It is important that the hair twines should overlap at the centre, to facilitate close fitting at that point. The filling has already been described at FIG. 157. When flock is used as a stuffing material it is not generally strung in, although the wearing qualities of a seat would be improved if this method were followed. FIG. 210 shows a seat with the hair partly filled both on the back and seat. When placing the hair in position use small rather than large handfuls, and work from A to B until that row is complete, and then follow on from C to D, etc., till the seat is finished. The hair should be well picked or opened both before and after it is placed beneath the twine so that the surface is free from lumps. When all the hair is placed in position its contour should be similar to that of the finished outline. The back of such a design as that illustrated only requires a very thin layer of hair, otherwise it will appear clumsy.

The difficulty experienced by all beginners in pin-cushion work is that they make the seats too round or full, and thus destroy the subtle, graceful curves upon which the beauty of this class of upholstery depends.

It should also be remembered that it is useless to aim at softness; sufficient hair must be used to ensure that the seat is firm to the touch after the covering is strained on. In high-class work unbleached calico is the material used as a first covering over the hair. The first covering is shown tacked temporarily at FIG. 211, the measurements having been obtained by placing the tape measure over the hair and allowing sufficient for folding in. A good plan is to tack first at 1, strain the calico and tack at 2, repeating the process from 3 to 4, and so on all round the seat until the whole surface is taut. The greatest pressure must be applied at the corners, which should taper gradually to the edge, and it is at these parts that fulness or slackness of the material must be· drawn tightly and " cleaned," as it is termed in the trade.

The principles on which insistence has been laid when referring to the hessian and scrim must be adhered to, notably in regard to the keeping of the threads of the calico straight. Before trimming off, a process which is illustrated at FIG. 212, the threads should be examined, and if they are on the bias, the tacks should be lifted and the calico adjusted to its proper position. When trimming off the superfluous edges of the material, allow about 1in. all round for turning. At the concave part of the seat at A, FIG. 212, and at the back B, FIG. 211, a series of cuts should be made with the scissors up to the edge of the moulding. This will facilitate the folding of the calico when it is firmly fixed. At FIG. 213 the calico is shown folded at the edges and tacked. This should be accomplished in sections at right angles, so that the threads each way are straight before the corners are strained. Commence tacking a few inches from A to B, then continue from C to D. The folding of the calico inwards is ·a matter of some difficulty for the beginner, as it must be strained tight at the same time. This is best accomplished by using both hands to draw the folded edge into position for tacking, then releasing the material with the right hand and tacking as closely as possible to the left hand. In doing this care must be taken by the upholsterer (1) to see that his hammer is within easy reach ; (2) that the calico held in position by the left hand is so placed as to leave a margin of wood clear for the tacking down of the outer covering and subsequent trimming. The operation is repeated in the same manner from E to F. The curves G and H are next treated, some skill being needed to manipulate the fulness equally so that the material lies naturally and does not drag. The two corners at the front are left until the last and then drawn into position by means of the regulator as shown at FIG. 214.

The regulator is a very useful tool for pin-cushion work. By its use the calico may be drawn and held firmly by pressing the point into the wood, and when this method is followed, the danger of the material slipping, as sometimes happens when it is grasped with the fingers, is obviated. There is another danger which must be pointed out, unfortunately one which it is difficult to master. The learner is very liable to damage the polished mouldings with

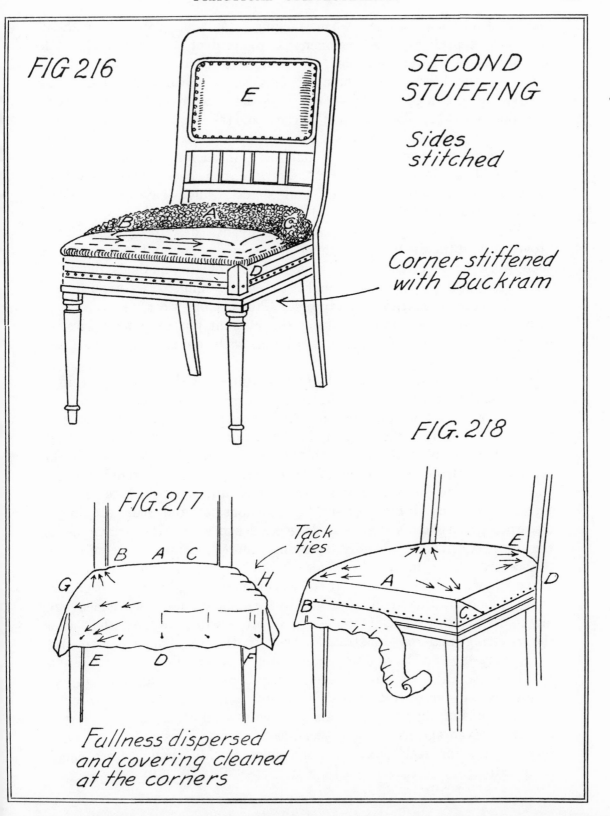

FIG 216

SECOND STUFFING

Sides stitched

Corner stiffened with Buckram

FIG. 218

FIG. 217

Tack ties

Fullness dispersed and covering cleaned at the corners

the head of his hammer when tacking. A safe plan, although it may not appeal to the beginner, is to protect the moulding with his fingers wherever possible. If owing to carelessness or lack of judgment the head of the hammer falls on his own nail rather than the one he intended to strike, the blow he receives will serve a two-fold purpose:—(1) The polished surface of the moulding will be protected; (2) the beginner will learn by painful experience that great care is needed when using the hammer for tacking down.

The chair illustrated in Figs. 209-214 has been chosen specially to embrace the various corners and shapes which have to be dealt with in occasional chairs treated with pin-cushion stuffing.

The pin-cushion second stuffing already described should not prove very difficult for a beginner if he has opportunities to observe such work in progress; failing this a study of the methods described and some necessary practice ought to enable him to accomplish this class of second stuffing creditably. Pin-cushion work is sometimes termed " skate " or " flat " stuffing, the different phases being suggestive of thin and light upholstery associated with dainty occasional and show-wood chairs.

Fig. 216 shows a small chair first stuffed with a second stuffing of hair partly filled at A. The hair twines are run crosswise, just as in pin-cushion seats, and for the same reason. The size of the seat determines whether there shall be three or four rows. The filling of the hair should commence at the back, and the work should be accomplished from left to right. The hair should be carefully picked and opened, and small handfuls used. The aim is to produce an even surface, and any lumpy or knotty portions of the hair should be discarded. The quantity used largely depends on the character of the first stuffing. Generally speaking, more stuffing is required at the centre, A, than at the sides, B and C, to obtain the crescent shape shown at Fig. 218. It is a common mistake with beginners when second stuffing to fill too heavily with hair, and when endeavour-ing to rectify this extreme too much is often withdrawn, so that when the covering material is strained over it, the seat appears too flat. It is only by much practice and careful observation of the results of his work that the upholsterer gains a matured judgment of the quantities of filling required. In many large factories a specified quantity of stuffing and materials per chair is allotted, and this system is very advantageous to the beginner, and teaches him the exact requirements for each piece of work more quickly than a freer choice of quantities.

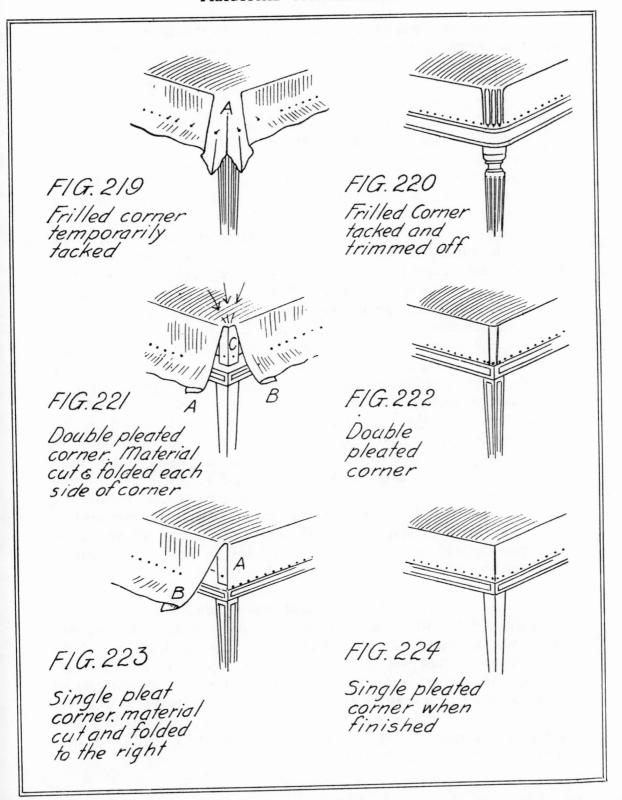

FIG. 219
Frilled corner
temporarily
tacked

FIG. 220
Frilled Corner
tacked and
trimmed off

FIG. 221
Double pleated
corner. Material
cut & folded each
side of corner

FIG. 222
Double
pleated
corner

FIG. 223
Single pleat
corner. material
cut and folded
to the right

FIG. 224
Single pleated
corner when
finished

After the hair has been placed in position satisfactorily the next operation is to cover it with calico or lining—for a small chair a piece of 24in. square is generally sufficient. The work should be commenced by temporarily tacking at the centre of the back at A (FIG. 217) and continuing at B and C, not too close to the corners. Observe and adjust if necessary the threads of the calico to ensure that they are perfectly straight, then strain and tack temporarily at D. In this operation the difference between straining and pulling must be noted. If the calico is pulled over and tacked, what are known as "tack ties" in the seat will quickly become apparent as shown at H (FIG. 217). The term "tack ties" implies that a well-defined drag of the threads of the material is visible from either the side or the surface of the seat. The appearance of a seat incorrectly strained, and consequently tack tied, is very ugly, and especially so when the subsequent outer covering is fixed. To avoid this the calico, instead of being pulled, must be strained correctly with the left hand with the assistance of the right until it is in position for tacking, and the upholsterer must make quite sure that the second-stuffing hair is clear of the stitched edge, on which the contour of the seat depends. When straining from the centre D to E (FIG. 217) the upholsterer is assisted and tack ties avoided by pressing the surface of the seat with the right hand in the direction indicated by the arrows while straining with the left. Tack ties can be avoided by this process, and their occurrence is an evidence of careless workmanship.

Next proceed to tack at the sides G and H (FIG. 217), working toward the front corners, and leaving sufficient space to fold the calico for cutting diagonally at the back corners, as indicated at FIG. 159. At this stage the work should be taken off the board or trestles, placed on the floor, and well sat on, in order to slacken the materials as much as possible while in this temporary stage of tacking. This operation will also serve to indicate if any extra material is required, and is one that should always be adopted by beginners. It is further a good test for faulty work. The weakness of springs incorrectly placed is detected, and springs laced too closely together will "talk"—that is to say, the top coils will meet and overlap, and a grating noise result when the seat is compressed. In large pieces of upholstery that have plain seats this initial treatment by compression is important and should never be omitted. It is specially necessary if flock is the stuffing material used and when a calico underlining is dispensed with.

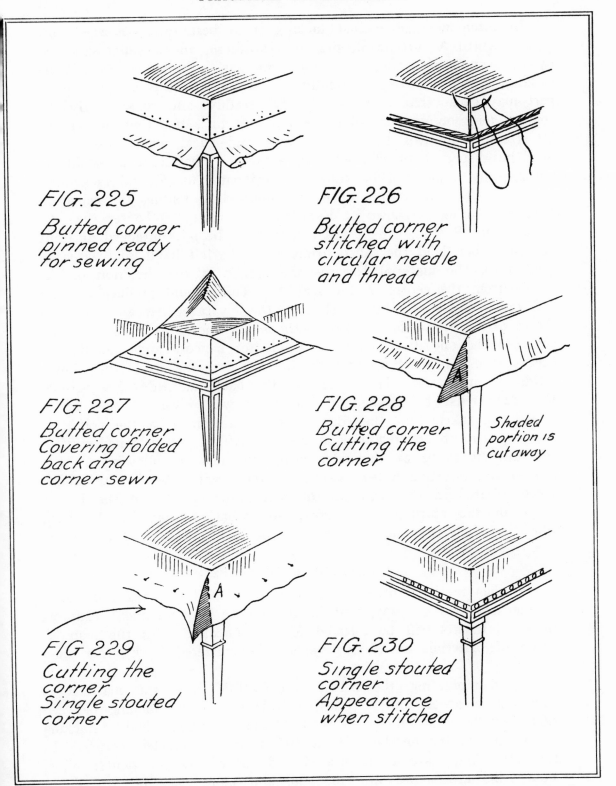

FIG. 225
Butted corner
pinned ready
for sewing

FIG. 226
Butted corner
stitched with
circular needle
and thread

FIG. 227
Butted corner
Covering folded
back and
corner sewn

FIG. 228
Butted corner
Cutting the
corner

Shaded
portion is
cut away

FIG 229
Cutting the
corner
Single stouted
corner

FIG. 230
Single stouted
corner
Appearance
when stitched

In commencing the final tacking it is best to commence work at the centre A (FIG. 218), first well straining all the fulness caused by the compression to which the seat has been subjected. While tacking, watch the edge carefully, as weak stitching at any given part may cause that part to yield too readily, and consequently the contour may become irregular. Avoid any tack ties that may occur by straining towards the corners front and back, where the fulness may be dispersed or cleaned (see arrows). The corners should be stiffened by a piece of buckram, or cardboard, folded and tacked on either side D (FIG. 216). The best method of folding the calico to clean the corner is shown at FIGS. 218 C and 238. To set the left-hand corner B (FIG. 218), a few inches must be left untacked at front and side, then hold the calico firmly with the left hand, and with the right work the material towards the corner in the direction of the arrows from the centre of the seat A. This should produce a clean and taut surface. Without releasing the leverage fold and tack, as shown at C (FIG. 218). Other methods are shown at FIGS. 220 and 222, but the one described is advisable for calicoes and underlinings, because the danger of spoiling the line by dragging the corner downwards is eliminated. The fulness at the back and sides (see arrows, FIG. 218) must be cleaned in the same way towards the corners, care being taken that the edge is not overstrained at the points D and E. The upholstered back at E (FIG. 216) is pin-cushioned stuffed, the crescent shape at the sides being obtained by allowing a little fulness and inserting a few mattress stitches with the circular needle. Backs treated in this way are of good appearance, and the hollow shape of the stuffing gives great additional comfort to the back when the chair is in use.

TREATMENT OF CORNERS.

Various methods of treating corners in final covering are shown in the diagrams 219/237, and in the course of subsequent chapters these treatments will be referred to in connection with the manipulation of materials at various parts of upholstered work other than corners.

In manipulating the frilled corner (FIG. 219) the material is equalised as at A, and a series of frills formed by tacking between each fold, but not on the folds (FIG. 220). This method of tacking forms the distinction between a frilled and a pleated corner. In the latter the material is pleated and tacked on the double folds. Four frills are shown at FIG. 220, and more may be formed in

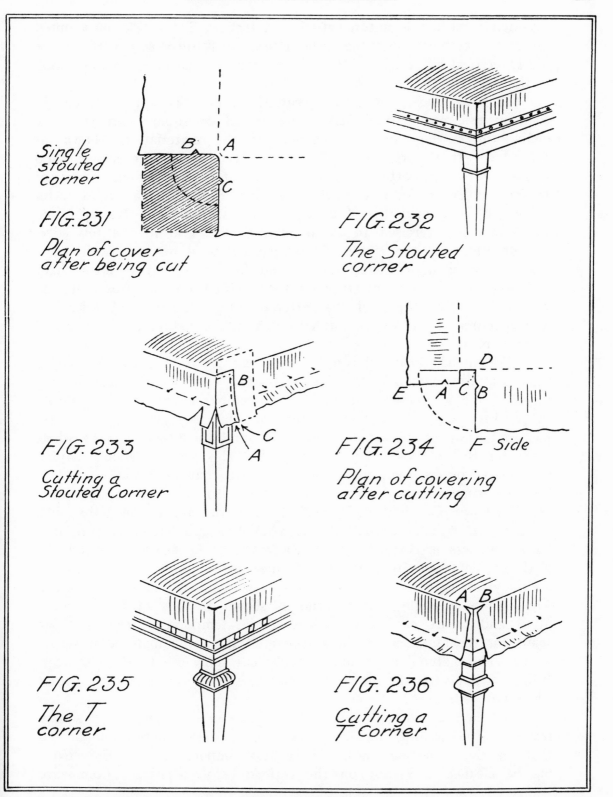

Single stouted corner

FIG. 231

Plan of cover after being cut

FIG. 232

The Stouted corner

FIG. 233

Cutting a Stouted Corner

FIG. 234

Plan of covering after cutting

FIG. 235

The T corner

FIG. 236

Cutting a T Corner

accordance with the nature of the material. This style is adopted for round corners, and the frills must be formed so as to lie as nearly vertical as possible. If they are oblique, the effect is unpleasing to the eye.

FIG. 222 shows a double-pleated corner. This is a style in common use, and suitable either for round or square corners. The method of cutting away a portion of the material is shown at FIG. 221. It is first strained in the direction of the arrows, and tacked at C. A portion is then cut on either side leaving sufficient to fold under to form a pleat at A and B. The material C after being cut is termed the " tongue." In carrying out this operation care must be exercised to avoid cutting too close to the top edge.

At FIG. 224 the single pleated corner is shown. This is more suitable for square-cornered frames and for work that requires sharp and fine edges. The pleats should be folded on the front, see B, FIG. 223, and a tongue of the material cut as shown at A. Corners are sometimes sewn by the upholsteress if the nature of the material permits of it.

The butted corner shown at FIG. 226 is first pleated on either side as at FIG. 222, but the edges instead of being apart meet or butt together, and a greater amount may therefore be cut away, as shown at A, FIG. 228. If leather is the material used, it can be folded back and sewn as indicated at FIG. 227, and the taking off the whole cover for this purpose may be avoided. This style is more adapted for square corners than for those which are rounded.

The single-stouted corner, shown at FIG. 229, is generally associated with leather work, and the material is cut on either side, as indicated by the dotted line A after the upholsterer is sure that all the fulness is cleaned. Such corners may be sewn either on the work or detached from it, the former being preferable, as greater accuracy as regards the position of the seam is thereby obtained. The plan of a single-stouted corner is shown at FIG. 231. The nicks at B and C are cut before releasing the temporary tacks, and are made for the guidance of the upholsteress after the material is folded back. The material at A must not be cut too close to the top edge. FIG. 230 indicates the finished appearance of a single-stouted corner when stitched.

The stouted corner, FIG. 232, is specially adapted for square frames. The cutting for this style is a little more complicated than in the preceding ones. It is most important that the covering be cleaned and taut on the surface before cutting. Commence

at the dotted line A, FIG. 233, 1in. from the corner, making a
perpendicular cut not quite to the top line of edge. Another cut
not less than ½in. at right angles will give the piece B. Cut out
the rectangular piece B as marked by the black line (FIG. 233), the
plan of the material when cut is shown at FIG. 234. The nicks at
A and B are not always necessary. When joined together the
stouted corner appears as at FIG. 232, and care must be exercised
to allow sufficient material for sewing.

FIG. 235 indicates the T corner which is suitable either for
square or rounded frames. The method of cutting is clearly shown
at FIG. 236. A first cut is made as at A, FIG. 228, and on either
side a small cut about ½in. at right angles, the top portion of the

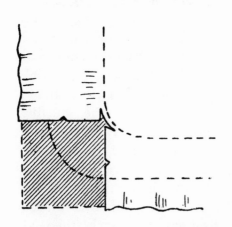

FIG. 237   T Corner
Plan of covering
when cut

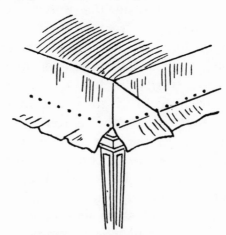

FIG. 238
Treatment of corner
in Calico. to avoid
overstraining

material being cut according to the shape required. FIG. 237 is the
plan of a seat cut for a round corner as indicated at A.

Stouted corners applied to leather work generally wear better
than those that are pleated, in addition to possessing a much neater
appearance when cut and fitted correctly. The projections caused
by pleating, see FIG. 222, are sometimes very pronounced, especially
if thick leather is used, and will begin to show signs of wear much
more quickly than a stouted corner. If again the pleats are not
drawn sufficiently tight, they commence to sag, and the corner becomes
clumsy in appearance. Faults at the corners of leather work, especially
in small chairs, are of frequent occurrence. They are generally attri-
buted to the fact that these parts are subject to much wear. The

practical man, however, realises that the upholsterer in cleaning the fulness both at the sides and front subjects the leather at the corner to extra straining, and renders the surface more sensitive to friction by opening the grain. In future chapters dealing with leather work this question will be dealt with more fully.

There are many kinds of stuffover chairs in which the seats, as regards measurements, differ but slightly from those of ordinary full-size small chairs, but because they have a stitched edge at the front only, and the contour of the sides and back is governed by the second stuffing, this second stuffing at once becomes a complicated operation. FIG. 239 is a light stuffover chair illustrated in two ways—on the left as an ordinary pull-over seat, and on the right finished in the under-edge fashion. In commencing the second stuffing of the seat of such a chair it is necessary to form a foundation of stuffing all round on which to strain the calico at the sides and back. This foundation is made as follows :—After placing the hair twines small handfuls of hair are inserted between the seat and back as from G to H to I, see line of arrows. In doing this care should be taken that the material does not protrude through the stuffing rails at J; the hair is then filled over the entire seat. By frequently laying the hands on the surface and compressing slightly, a sense of touch will be acquired and inequalities and disproportions will at once become apparent. The importance of filling hair firmly at the front edge of seats has already been insisted on. The calico is placed as on a small chair, temporarily tacking first at the back, then at the front, following on at the sides until the whole is set. Some upholsterers favour the plan of securing the front first, but the former method is advisable for learners. The treatment of the backs is described in the following chapters.

At the uprights of the frame, K and L, it is necessary to cut the calico. This is a more difficult operation than on a small chair, because the woodwork is hidden by the first stuffing, and there is a greater danger of making bad cuts. To cut at the upright K first fold the calico at right angles, as shown at FIG. 158, and cut in the direction of the dotted line B. To avoid mistakes, the space between the fold of the calico and the block is ascertained with the left hand whilst cutting with the right. The calico, when pulled through, should fit closely on either side of the upright. A similar cut is made at L. Care must be exercised to allow for stretching ; if the calico is not taut, the positions of the cuts become displaced, and recutting is necessary to obtain the direct strain required at the

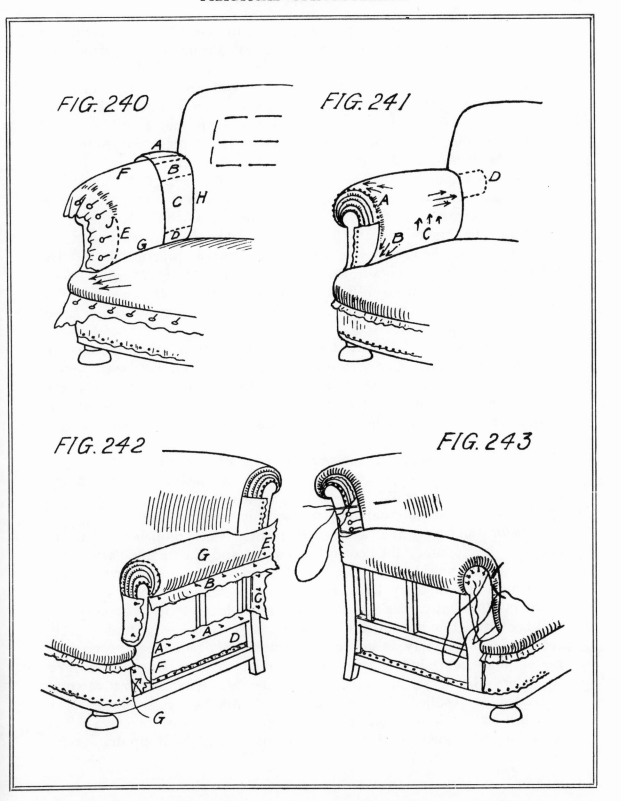

FIG. 240

FIG. 241

FIG. 242

FIG. 243

uprights. The method described for small chair seats should be followed, and the seat well compressed by sitting on it, whilst the calico is temporarily tacked. By this test faults due to bad workmanship are discovered and the hair is pressed into position. In the example shown (FIG. 239) the width of the wood is about 1½in., and the width of the cut should not exceed 1in. at K and L.

In tacking down permanently work is commenced from the centre, M, releasing the temporary tacks, straining the calico, and tacking in sections of 3in. to 4in., leaving the corner N untacked. Repeat at centre of back at H, also tacking a few inches right and left of the centre and complete at the sides G and J. It should be noted at this juncture that the contour of the seat entirely depends upon equal straining of the calico, and much practice is needed before a learner can obtain the clean sight line necessary to a good job. The reasons why difficulties occur in producing an even line of stuffing are set out below, and should be carefully studied, as they apply to any seat :—

1. The contour of a first-stuffed seat with a stitched edge on all sides is already partly formed, but in a stuffover seat, where the edge is stitched at the front only, the contour of the back and sides is governed by the strain at each tacking : from L to H the outline can be broken by unequal straining of the calico at any part.

2. The operation of tacking down stuffover work is rendered more difficult because the contour cannot be observed while straining and tacking so readily as on a small chair.

It is only by alternatively temporarily tacking and viewing the seat before finishing the work permanently that proficiency can be attained in forming the correct contour and in manipulating the various tackings which are in awkward positions to deal with. The importance of temporary tacking at this stage cannot be over estimated. Learners frequently neglect it until reminded of its necessity by the need for the use of the ripping chisel to remedy faults. The above remarks apply also to upholsterers of maturer experience. Better lines are always produced if temporary tacking is resorted to before the tacks are driven permanently. The amount of time expended is justified, because subsequent ripping up is unnecessary, and because, as a rule, one alteration leads to another in cases where work has been guessed at and not graduated and built up by careful methods.

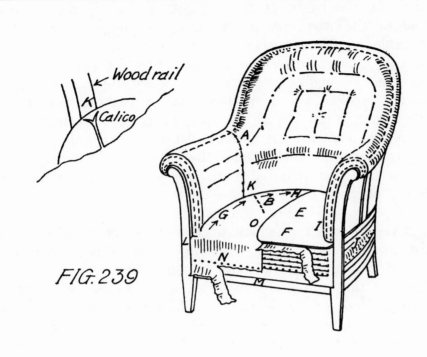

FIG. 239

FIG. 244

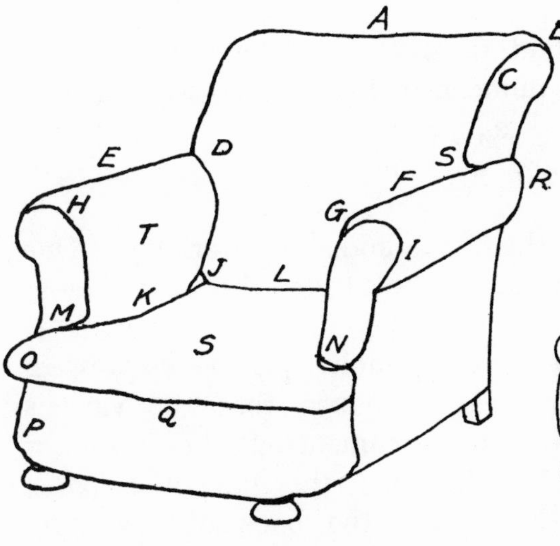

FIG. 245

Stuffover Chair with
faults emphasised. See list.

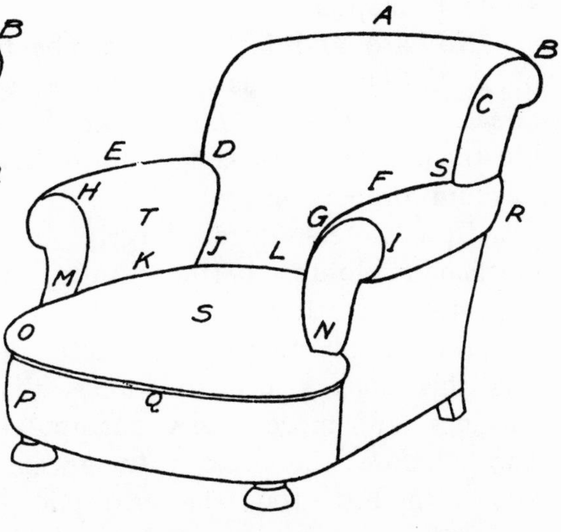

Stuffover Chair with
correctly formed contours

When straining the calico at the uprights L and K the material must fit close to the wood on either side. Although no difference may be noticeable in the appearance of the seat, it is advisable to form the habit of cutting correctly, as this makes for that additional neatness which is so highly important to successful upholstery at all stages of the work. The fact that another covering has to be applied to the work is no excuse for bad or careless cutting. The upholsterer who has practised the correct cutting of the scrim, hessian, and calico is far more likely to master the cutting of expensive outer coverings of silk or other material than one who is careless in connection with the cheaper stuffs because they will not be visible when the work is completed. The seat that is first covered with an underlining in the style described (the pull over) can be temporarily tacked all round without any detriment to the work before driving the tacks permanently, and beginners are advised to follow this method. From a cursory glance at the examples shown the correct tacking of the back may appear a difficult task, but the upholsterer will soon adapt himself to the varied and sometimes awkward positions. Sufficient space for the subsequent tackings of the final covering must be allowed between N and the moulding M. It is a good plan to leave the stuffing rails clean, placing the tacks on the upper surface J.

The under-edge style of upholstery will be referred to in a subsequent chapter.

No hard and fast rule can be laid down as to whether the arms of a first-stuffed chair should be commenced before the seat or *vice versa*. The chair sketched at Figs. 240/243 has been selected for illustration as possessing the ordinary cuts necessary in a chair of medium proportions.

Upholsterers differ largely in their methods of working. One craftsman obtains better results by second stuffing the seat before the arms, another reverses this procedure, and so on. When it is a question of morocco a more decisive opinion can be expressed, and this applies also to frames that are so shaped that the various tackings are more easily manipulated by commencing the arms or back before the seat. Instances of this are the pad and panel shown in FIG. 169, the arm pad (FIG. 183), the back of FIG. 179, and others. The hair twines of the arm (FIG. 240) are placed from back to front, and should be closer than those of a seat, care being taken to ensure that one row is directly in the centre of the arm F, also at the side G (FIG. 242) Hair is inserted between the seat and arm, also at H (FIG. 240) before commencing to use the hair twines. The appearance of the hair when filled in should closely resemble the shape of the arm when finished. The size of the calico required is obtained by the use of the tape measure, and sufficient must be allowed to tack over the stitched edge on the front. The material is shown temporarily set at FIG. 242. It is first tacked on the rail A, strained upwards and over the top of the arm, and tacked underneath the rail B. At J (FIG. 240) the calico is fixed temporarily on the edge by means of skewers. The arrows at A, B, and C (FIG. 241) indicate where the greatest strain is required to clean the fulness. To return to FIG. 240, fold back the calico and cut at dotted lines. The piece thus formed at B is called a " tongue," which is strained and tacked at the back D (FIG. 241). C (FIG. 240) is shown pulled through at C (FIG. 242). The tongue G (FIG. 242) is best obtained from the outside at F (FIG. 242). When the various cuts have been made and the calico once more carefully set, the scroll will appear as at FIG. 240. Next cut horizontally, as shown at FIGS. 241 and 242. The lower half of the calico is tacked in position, and the upper portion cut away with scissors, leaving sufficient material to fold in and pin for subsequent sewing. The removal of the upper portion as shown does away with the difficulties which would arise if the upholsterer had to disperse the fulness at this point. The arrows A, B, C (FIG. 241) indicate where most strain is required to obtain the best results.

At this stage the learner should acquaint himself with the points that correct upholstery work should possess, and a study of the two sketches (FIGS. 244 and 245) should at once demonstrate the value of line in upholstery. Arms and backs appear hard and clumsy if strained too flat, and should appear bow shaped, as shown at Fig. 245. The insides of the arms at T should be flat, as it is always advisable to allow plenty of seat room.

A LIST OF FAULTS AND THEIR CAUSES.

(The Letters refer to FIG. 244.)

FAULT.	CAUSE.
A.—Covering drawn too tight at the centre.	Absence of springs, insufficient stuffing, or covering incorrectly cut.
B.—Second stuffing too full at the edge, giving clumsy effect.	Bad judgment as regards quantity of stuffing required.

FAULT.	CAUSE.
C.—Scroll out of proportion.	Overstraining of material, edge not firm enough. Contour badly formed when tacking down.
D.—Contour out of proportion to front scroll, and consequent common appearance.	Insufficient second stuffing.
E. & F.—Repetition of the fault.	As indicated at A.
G. & H.—Too much fulness at edge.	Second stuffing not thinned sufficiently to give the necessary tapering line.
I.—Edge hanging back.	Incorrectly stitched or not enough scrim allowed when tacking down.
J.—Corners devoid of stuffing liable to show extensions that are placed on covering material to increase size.	Overstraining; insufficient stuffing, neglect of the use of regulator. Covering material cut too small.
K.—Bad contour at side of seat.	Covering strained too tightly.
L.—Bad contour at back of seat.	Bad judgment as to quantity of second stuffing required. Springs incorrectly placed.
M. and N.—Edge stitched too wide. Lessens the seat space.	Too much scrim allowed for stitching in the tacking down.
O.—Front roll overhanging—a bad point in spring edge work.	Cane fixed incorrectly or too much scrim allowed for stitching the roll.
P.—Stuffing in borders has always a tendency to sag, and should taper near seat rail.	Too much stuffing or cane incorrectly placed.
Q.—Front line uneven.	Guess work when placing the cane instead of using rule. Incorrect setting of border.
R.—Bad shape of arm at back.	Too much second stuffing, preventing tapering effect when straining the covering.
S.—Seat too flat at centre.	Wrong size springs used; insufficient number of springs used; bad judgment in placing springs; insufficient second stuffing.
T.—Convexity inside arms limiting seat space.	Too much second stuffing.

CHAPTER 27.

SECOND STUFFING, CUTS AND COLLARS.

The covering of upholstery with calico or some kind of underlining material prior to the subsequent outer covering applies as a general rule only to seats or work that is to be finished plain. Upholstery of the best class, hair-stuffed throughout, is entirely covered with an underlining before finishing; this is also most essential for leather work.

The advantages gained by following this course are as follows :—

1. In order to obtain the required shape of a seat or back it is necessary to strain the material at some parts very taut, and this straining is best accomplished by graduation in temporary tacking; in a calico these strains, cuts and tackings are made without danger of damage as would be the case if a covering of silk or other fine material were subjected to the same treatment.

2. It is frequently necessary to reduce or add to the quantity of stuffing. This fault is more easily rectified in an underlining than in a fixed outer covering.

3. The danger of incorrect cutting of the outer covering material is eliminated because the stuffing has been first compressed into position by the calico; in show-wood work, or where many cuts are necessary, this is a great advantage.

4. The outer covering is protected by the calico from direct contact with the stuffing material. Friction caused by compression is thus lessened, and the outer covering wears longer.

5. An underlining acts as a support to the outer cover, and the danger of the fabric sagging and fulness forming is lessened.

For the beginner in the craft of upholstery the use of an underlining is an advanatge, as it is an exact duplicate of the outer covering, and when manipulating it he becomes acquainted with the cuts to be made and those parts where most strain has been found necessary to obtain the required contour. The beginner naturally cuts a calico underlining with more confidence than an outer covering of expensive material.

Faults in connection with bad cutting are frequent, and if they are not apparent at once, they become pronounced after the seat is subjected to much compression. The upholsterer may be quite conversant with the method of cutting, but much depends on the nature of the material used; some fabrics stretch or give more than others, and this must be taken into consideration. The satisfactory outward appearance of upholstery is no sure indication that the workmanship is good, and before a decisive opinion can be expressed, those parts of the work where cuts have been necessary should be examined. Inspectors of upholstery purchased for the Government are fully alive to the importance of cuts, as they affect the wear of a fabric, and often stipulate that coverings must be " welted " or " collared " at certain parts as a preventive against faulty work arising from bad cutting. Welting or collaring will be described in a subsequent chapter.

The beginner cannot always avoid bad cuts, but a study of the diagrams and directions given here should give him confidence in dealing with them. The chair shown at FIG. 246 would be too complicated an example for a beginner to start on, embracing as it does seven distinct cuts. There are various means of manipulating materials to fit tightly round blocks, or, as they are sometimes termed, "stiles." The formation of a tongue is the most general method, and these again are sub-divided into long tongues (FIG. 251), or the small triangle (FIG. 247). The collar shown at FIGS. 254-256, sometimes called a pocket, is the most complicated method, but it gives a neat and superior finish, and eliminates the danger of bad cutting.

The triangle cut will now be described, and the reader is referred to FIG. 247. The width of the splats is assumed to be 3in. First cut in a direct line towards the centre of the splat as from E to B, which is $1\frac{1}{2}$in. from the splat A. Now make cross cuts on either side from B to C and B to D. The tongue piece so formed is shown at A, FIG. 248. This may be manipulated in two ways, either by means of the regulator or by passing down between the seat and the frame by means of a twine sewn to the tongue, which is subsequently fixed by tacking underneath the frame as shown at FIG. 252.

FIG. 249, by means of a dotted line, shows the triangular tongue inserted between the seat and the frame and B and C butting together at FIG. 250. FIG. 251 shows the long tongue ready to be passed through between the seat and the frame by means of the regulator and tacked, as shown at FIG. 252. The uprights are cut as already described (see FIG. 159).

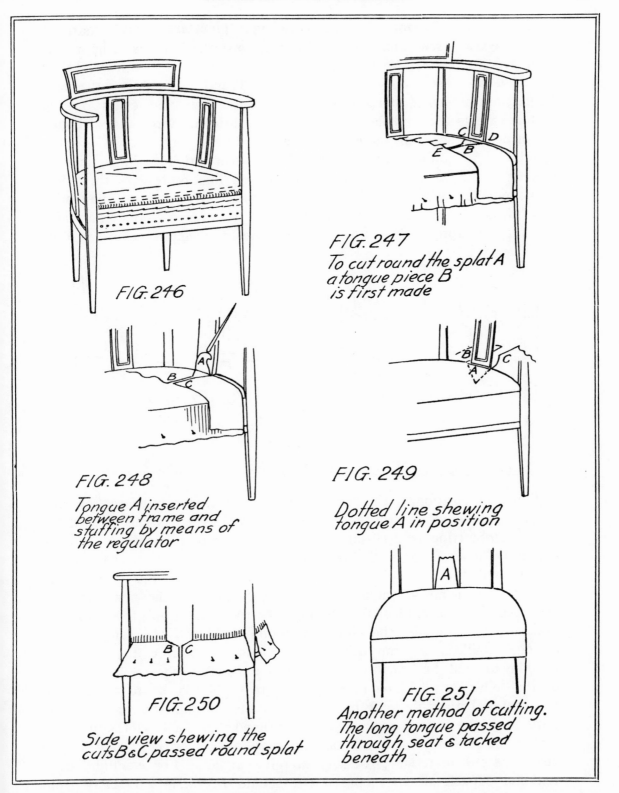

FIG. 246

FIG. 247
To cut round the splat A
a tongue piece B
is first made

FIG. 248
Tongue A inserted
between frame and
stuffing by means of
the regulator

FIG. 249
Dotted line shewing
tongue A in position

FIG. 250
Side view shewing the
cuts B & C passed round splat

FIG. 251
Another method of cutting.
The long tongue passed
through seat & tacked
beneath

To cut a collar for an upright or splat a section of the material is cut away (see FIG. 253). In this operation it is important, when cutting soft fabrics, that the measurement between C to D should be at least 1in. less than between A and B. In a subsquent chapter dealing with morocco work it will be seen that collar cutting in that case is accomplished in an entirely different way, and although the principles are the same, the method differs considerably in that material. A ground plan of the calico, when cut for the collars or pockets, is shown at FIG. 254. The dotted line represents the edge, A and C the splats, B and D the uprights. At FIG. 255 the collar piece C is shown sewn into position to fit round a splat, as also that for the upright D. FIG. 256 indicates the collars reversed prior

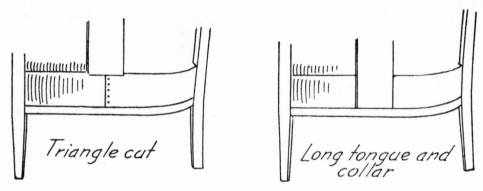

Triangle cut   Long tongue and collar

FIG. 258
Side views of Tongue & Collar cuts when finished

to fixing in position. The dotted lines in FIG. 257 indicate how the collar is inserted by the regulator, and unless it is cut too deep, no further cutting is necessary. In this diagram, in order to demonstrate the method more clearly, the collar is shown wider than would be required for the splat in the chair sketched at FIG. 246. The learner, after some attempts at cutting according to the methods here described in some kind of underlining material, will be able to distinguish between the value of the collar cut compared with the tongue. He is most unlikely at the outset to produce a perfect fit, but the experiment will be worth while to prove conclusively the superiority of the collar cut. When cutting, the great point is so to manipulate the material that it shall fit close and taut round the frame. The nature of the material must be considered, as some cloths give or stretch more easily than others, and may be cut with greater liberty than a stout material possessing no give at all. For example, in a material capable of stretching a cut should be made $\frac{1}{2}$in. away from

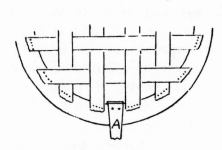

FIG. 252

Shewing tongue passed
through seat & tacked
on to frame

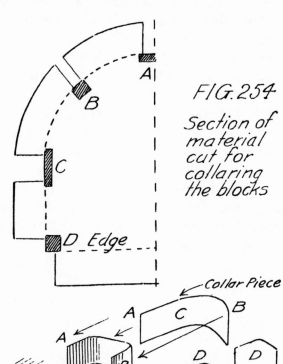

FIG. 254

Section of
material
cut for
collaring
the blocks

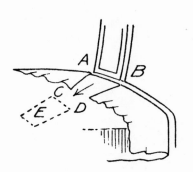

FIG. 253

The Collar method of
manipulating the cut

Collar Piece

FIG. 255

Collar pieces
sewn in position

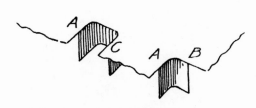

FIG. 256

Collar pieces reversed
ready to place on seat

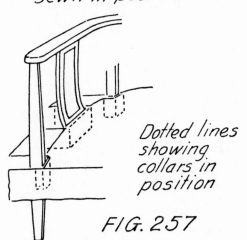

Dotted lines
showing
collars in
position

FIG. 257

the block, and the material would make up the deficiency, but to follow this course with a material which will not give would spell failure.   In dealing with the independent collar pieces C and D (FIG. 255) the work of a machinist is necessary.   A sewing machine is really part of the equipment required by an upholsterer.   In stuffover work especially there is a considerable amount of sewing in connection with the various extension pieces and seams of a covering after it is cut.   An upholsterer should be able to use a machine with as much facility as he uses needle and twine, but few are enterprising enough to learn.

No upholsterer is master of his craft until he is able to use a machine, trim with cord, fix castors, and cut loose covers, and it should be the aim of every ambitious youth to fit himself to undertake all these branches of the trade.

CHAPTER 28.

SECOND STUFFING, SEATS OF VARIOUS STYLES.

There was a time when in the workshops a distinction was made between stuffover work and show-wood or suite work. The craftsman who was skilled in the upholstering of suites of show-wood furniture could not, as a rule, undertake the more complicated stuffover upholstering on large chesterfields and divans. Even at the present day advertisements for upholsterers frequently contain the phrase, "Men used to stuffover work preferred." To-day the work is not specialised to so great an extent, and it is therefore desirable for a man who is learning the trade to make himself proficient in both stuffover and show-wood work. A great deal of skill is, for instance, needed to obtain the correct lines and proportions in an example such as is shown at FIG. 207, and unless the improver has some opportunity for working at both branches of the trade, he will ultimately find himself at a disadvantage. The man who has done little but stuffover work has had no opportunity of making himself proficient with the cabriole hammer which would necessarily be employed in fixing the outer cover of the seat and back in an example such as is shown at FIG. 207. The learner becomes more accurate when using the hammer if he has to tack in close proximity to polished mouldings. He does not gain experience of this kind in stuffover work.

The ambitious young upholsterer generally aspires to become a good stuffover worker, but in this connection he must remember that the term is loosely applied, and in modern usage refers to what may be termed imitation stuffover work as well as the real article. This will be clear from a comparison of the frames shown in Chapter 7 with such pieces as are sketched at FIGS. 167, 170, and 182. In the latter cases the lines so necessary to the finish of a piece of work are moulded and built up with stuffing, whilst in the former the essential contours are formed of wood, and do not call for the same amount of skill on the part of the upholsterer.

Some genuine stuffover work is very complicated, and often presents well-nigh insuperable difficulties to the jobbing upholsterer when taken to pieces for the purpose of re-upholstering. On the other hand such chairs as are shown in Chapter 7, though classed as stuffovers, are by comparison simple to manipulate. The uphol-

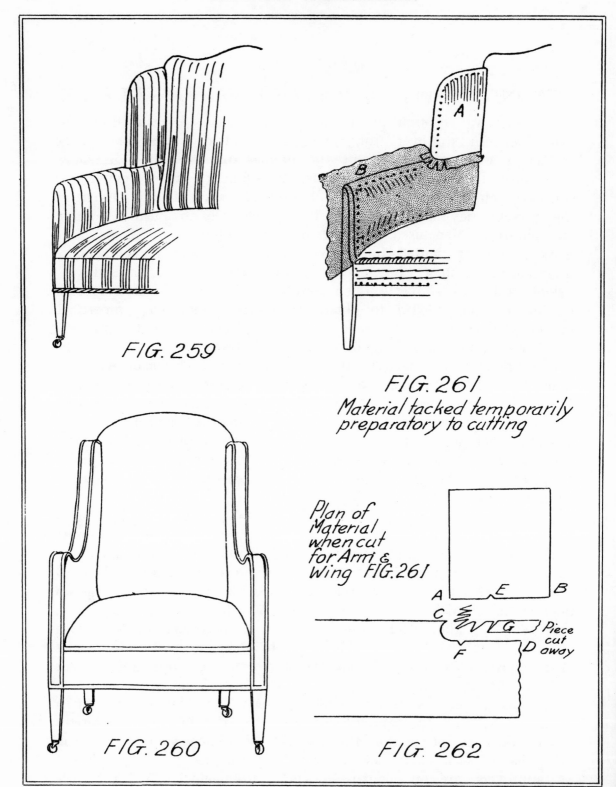

FIG. 259

FIG. 261
Material tacked temporarily
preparatory to cutting

Plan of
Material
when cut
for Arm &
Wing FIG.261

Piece
cut
away

FIG. 260

FIG. 262

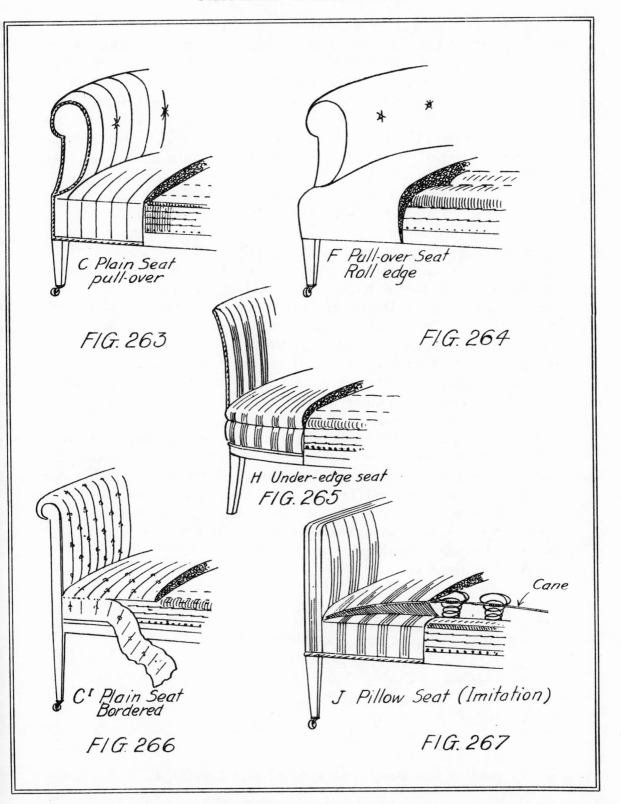

C Plain Seat pull-over

FIG. 263

F Pull-over Seat Roll edge

FIG. 264

H Under-edge seat

FIG. 265

C' Plain Seat Bordered

FIG. 266

Cane

J Pillow Seat (Imitation)

FIG. 267

stering of such designs as were shown in Chapter 7 provides excellent practice for a beginner, although a first covering in calico is not generally associated with these styles. If he is able to first and second stuff a small chair seat correctly, he should also be able to cover in tapestry or cretonne without underlining the designs shown in FIGS. 259 and 260. The backs and arms are treated in the same manner as the pin-cushion seats, described in Chapter 26, that is without any first stuffing. There is no first stuffing in such chairs except in the seats, and the placing of the final covering material on the stuffing of arms and backs is really less complicated than working on a foundation of first stuffing, especially if the covering is prepared and cut out by a competent cutter. The beginner who is able to accomplish this style of medium-class work to the satisfaction of his foreman should again be reminded that it is purely repetition work, varying only in the different cuts required at concave or convex portions of the wood that forms the frame, and although such work as this is correctly termed stuffover on account of the absence of any show-wood except the legs, the difference between FIGS. 259 and 260 and the genuine stuffover such as is shown at FIG. 182 is very great. The further treatment of such a chair as is shown at FIG. 259 will be dealt with in the chapter on cutting.

There are many varieties of treatments in stuffover work, and before proceeding further with the manipulation of second stuffing the upholsterer should acquaint himself with the various styles and their nomenclature. He should also study, as far as he is able, the proper relationship of first stuffing to second stuffing in the various styles of seats. A list of the names applied to various styles of seats (some of which have been previously described) is given below.

A.   The pin-cushion seat.
B.   The loose seat.
C.   Plain seat (pullover) ; C¹ (bordered).
D.   Button seat (pullover or bordered).
E.   Pullover seat (stitched edge).
F.   Pullover seat (rolled edge).
G.   Pullover seat (spring edge).
H.   Under-edge seat.
J.   Pillow seat (imitation).
K.   Pillow seat (fixed).
L.   Squab seat (imitation).
M.   Squab seat (loose).
N.   Cushion seat (loose) and stitched edge foundation.

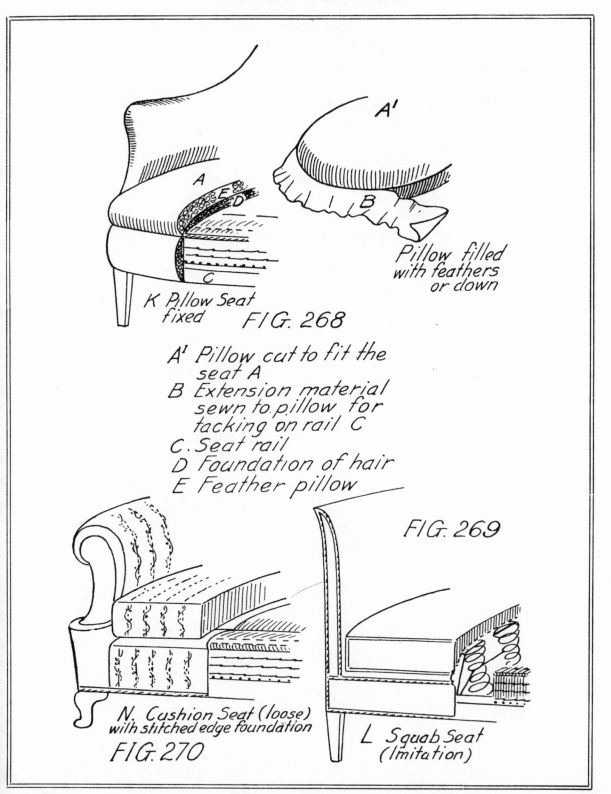

K Pillow Seat fixed

FIG. 268

Pillow filled with feathers or down

A' Pillow cut to fit the seat A
B Extension material sewn to pillow for tacking on rail C
C. Seat rail
D Foundation of hair
E Feather pillow

FIG. 269

N. Cushion Seat (loose) with stitched edge foundation

FIG. 270

L Squab Seat (Imitation)

O. Cushion seat (loose) and spring edge foundation.
P. Spring edge (single border).
Q. Spring edge (double border).
R. The double spring.
S. Bible front (plain or buttoned).
T. Double-cushioned seat.
U. Mock-edge seat.
V. Mock spring-edge seat.
W. The loose spring cushion seat.
X. Independent seat.
Y. The cradle spring seat.
Z. Decorative seats (plumed, buttoned, or frilled).

CHAPTER 29.

SECOND STUFFING OF WINGS.

Before commencing the second stuffing of any piece of upholstery as it stands in the first-stuffed stage there are many points which the craftsman must consider. The manipulation of the stuffing material requires considerable practice, and only experience can teach the quantity needed to give the necessary firmness. The treatment is similar for arms, back, and seats, varying only according to the design, size, and shape of cuts. Below the reader will find a summary of the points which call for his special attention when second stuffing.

When too much stuffing material is used and the seat is stuffed too full, the surplus stuffing frequently sags and gives fulness to the covering material.

Wherever possible second stuffing should be strung—that is, filled beneath twines, as indicated at FIG. 209. Flock can be laid on with greater ease than hair, although on scrolls, fronts of seats, and arms flock also should be strung.

The testing of upholstery by sitting on the work while it is in the temporary tacked stage has already been referred to in connection with hair stuffing. It is quite as important, if not more so, when flock is used. If seats are well tested in this way when temporarily tacked, the danger of fulness is eliminated, as this practical expedient shows whether too great or too small a quantity of stuffing has been employed. Correct proportion in stuffing arms, backs, and seats is very important. This is a point that presents considerable difficulty to the beginner. He is apt to concentrate on one part of the work at the expense of others, and before commencing second stuffing he should endeavour to form a mental picture of the work as it will appear when completed. Comparison with work of a similar character, if he has access to it, will also be an advantage.

Ample seat space in a chair is a prime consideration. However comfortable a chair may appear, it is unsatisfactory if the sitter cannot move freely.

The stuffing of the insides of arms must be kept flat and vertical. Compression at the top of the arm always renders it liable to bulge, and thus diminish the seat space.

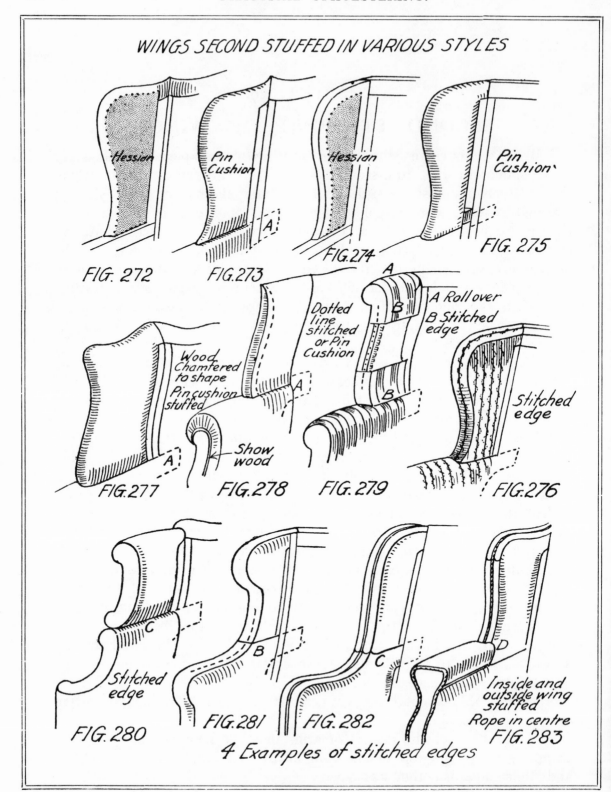

WINGS SECOND STUFFED IN VARIOUS STYLES

Hessian

Pin Cushion

FIG. 272

FIG. 273

A

Hessian

FIG. 274

Pin Cushion

FIG. 275

Wood Chamfered to shape

Pin cushion stuffed

A

Dotted line stitched or Pin Cushion

A

Show wood

FIG. 277

FIG. 278

A Roll over

B Stitched edge

A

B

B

FIG. 279

Stitched edge

FIG. 276

C

Stitched edge

FIG. 280

B

FIG. 281

C

FIG. 282

D

Inside and outside wing stuffed Rope in centre

FIG. 283

4 Examples of stitched edges

Cramming should be avoided. If additional stuffing is required at any part of the work, more satisfactory results are obtained by lifting the material and adding extra stuffing on the surface.

It is difficult to gauge the quantity of stuffing required at the front of a seat, because the gutter caused by the stitching forms a hollow space, and generally needs more stuffing than the centre. In any case it is wise to fill the front well, as much straining is required to clean the fulness of the material at this part.

In stuffover work it is skill in the formation of the contours that makes a good piece of work, and great care should be taken with the lines where the arms and back meet the seat. Beautiful lines are obtained by placing the stuffing correctly and straining the material adequately.

In positions where a number of materials meet at the corners, for example, at J (FIG. 245), second stuffing may be added with advantage from the sides or back by inserting it between the stuffing rails without displacing the covering at the front part.

Intermittent cutting is the best mode of procedure for a beginner. This, combined with temporary tacking until the desired outline and requisite firmness are obtained, is the safest method. To make a first cut and a perfect fit in one operation would tax the skill of the most competent workman.

The quantity of second stuffing material required is regulated by its nature and quality. If loose common hair is used as a second stuffing, more is needed than if good hair is employed. The former, being more easily compressed than the better quality hair, should be used with greater liberality. The same rule applies in regard to a seedy flock: more is needed than is the case when a full, rich quality is employed.

A mistake not uncommon among young upholsterers is the placing of second stuffing over the edges. The edges are built up carefully to form the contour of the work, and if the second stuffing is dragged over them by the straining of the material, an uneven outline is the inevitable result. In order to avoid this, stuffing that has become displaced should be put back into its proper position by placing the hand underneath the material before straining.

If the seat of a chair or settee is stuffed soft and yields easily when compressed, the arms must not be stuffed high. If they are, the elbow of the sitter will be thrust upwards, because the arms of the chair do not yield to pressure in the same degree as the seat.

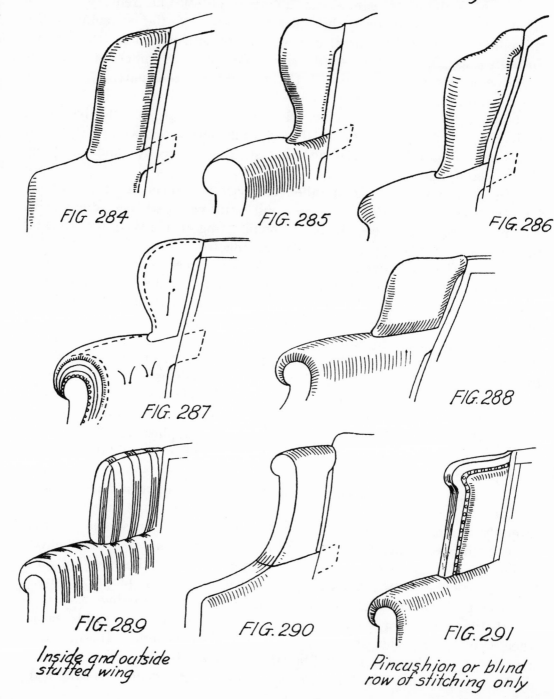

WINGS SECOND STUFFED IN VARIOUS STYLES

FIGS. 284 to 289 are examples with stitched roll edges

FIG 284

FIG. 285

FIG. 286

FIG. 287

FIG. 288

FIG. 289

Inside and outside
stuffed wing

FIG. 290

FIG. 291

Pincushion or blind
row of stitching only

The convex portion, or swell, at the bottom of a back (see FIG. 183), if stuffed too full, will prevent the sitter from resting the head in a natural and comfortable position.

Seats should always slope down towards the back. Attention was called in the chapter dealing with springing to the use of smaller springs at the back. The second stuffing should be filled in proportion; a sloping seat, if not too pronounced, is more comfortable than one that is level.

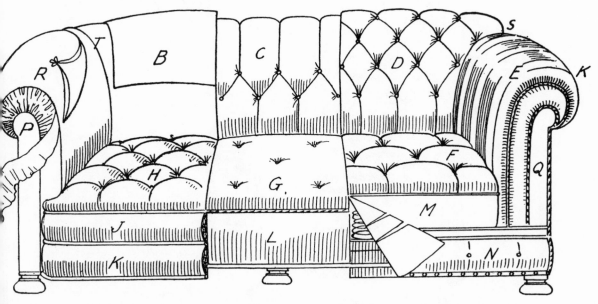

FIG. 271 Various styles in stuffover finish

B Fixed pillow back
C Semi buttoned ,,
D Ordinary buttoned
E ,, ,, Plain arm
F Squab seat (deep tufted

G. Plain seat (starred)
H. Ordinary buttoned seat
J. Double border finish
L. Single border
M Squab border

N. Independent button border
P. Double facing (frilled)
Q. Double facing (plain)
R. Pillow arm (fixed)
S & T The mitre point of seam

Arm-chairs that have wings or head rests are generally known as grandfather chairs. Care must be taken in the stuffing of the wings, otherwise they are clumsy in appearance. Examples of wings of various styles are shown at FIGS. 272 to 296. Lightly stuffed wings are more satisfactory than those treated more heavily. Winged chairs, unless carefully designed, are deceptive as regards comfort. If the lower part of the wing is too wide (back to front), a sitter cannot rest his elbow comfortably on the arm of the chair. Wings that slope well back, or that are concave at the lower part, are free from this defect.

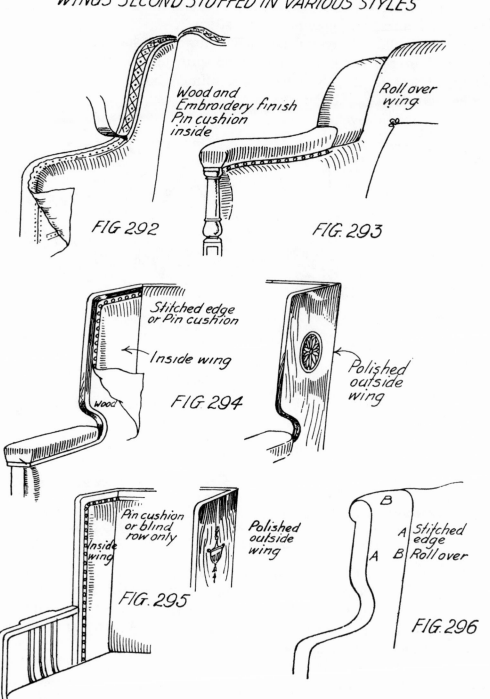

WINGS SECOND STUFFED IN VARIOUS STYLES

Wood and Embroidery finish Pin cushion inside

FIG. 292

Roll over wing

FIG. 293

Stitched edge or Pin cushion

Inside wing

Wood

FIG. 294

Polished outside wing

Pin cushion or blind row only

Inside wing

Polished outside wing

FIG. 295

B

A Stitched edge

A

B Roll over

FIG. 296

There are certain minimum dimensions (finished sizes) which should be observed in stuffover easy chairs if they are to be comfortable in use, viz., depth of seat back to front, 23in.; between arms at the front, 19in.; height of seat from the floor, 15in. Much, of course, depends on the design, especially as regards the seat; for example, if a seat is upholstered very soft, liberty can be taken with the height.

CHAPTER 30.

CUTTING AND COVERING.

For the planning and cutting of upholstery materials a cutting board such as is shown at Fig. 297 is necessary. Its dimensions should be adapted to the amount of space available, but it should not be less than 7ft. long by 4ft. 6in. wide. The top should be of hardwood to stand the continual hammerings of the pritchawl occasioned by the marking out of various materials. The upholstery cutter needs but few tools. The chief of these is the shears, which should be a well-made pair of French pattern, slightly larger than those used by the upholsterer. Hammer, yard stick, tape measure, pritchawl, straight edge, a large square, French chalks of various colours, blue pencil, and pins, complete the list. An upholsterer cannot be regarded as a master of his craft unless he is able to plan and cut covering materials. In large factories where much repetition work is done the learner has little opportunity of gaining experience in measuring and cutting, and may even attain the status of a journeyman without much knowledge of this side of his craft.

Upholstery fabrics are, as a rule, expensive, and to use a piece of material 3 yards in length when by skilful cutting $2\frac{3}{4}$ yards would suffice makes a considerable difference in cost. Even when an exact estimate of the yardage of material required has been obtained waste may occur on account of incorrect planning.

Much depends on the material, a small conventional spot pattern being easier to plan and cut than a bolder design with a large medallion centre or evenly-balanced floral motif which makes it necessary for each cut to be treated with due regard to the nature of the pattern. Figured fabrics are more wasteful in cutting than plain or self-coloured materials, because the pattern requires matching. Centre patterns on some designs are repeated at inconvenient distances so that waste is unavoidable. Much practice is necessary to become a skilled cutter, and it is a safe rule to plan out the various pieces carefully before commencing to cut, but as has been pointed out, plain materials, small powdered or spot patterns, require less planning than floral or figured fabrics.

If the upholsterer starts to cut before planning failure is usually the result, and to this must be added waste of time and unnecessary seaming. Before making calculations the cutter must be conver-

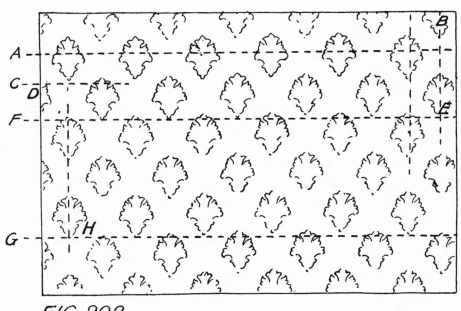

FIG. 298

FIG. 299

sant with the width of the material he is using, as accurate quantities and estimates cannot be given unless the width of the material to be used is known.

Various upholstery fabrics are now generally made in definite widths, and in specifying cretonne (single or double width), tapestry, velvet, moquette or brocade it would hardly be necessary to detail the exact number of inches in the width. Fabrics for upholstery are now woven in a convenient size for cutting, and vary from 48in. to 52in. wide. Velvets are largely used, and the inconvenient 24in. width has become old-fashioned. Single width cretonne generally measures 30in. wide, while double width cretonne is woven the same width as tapestry. Moquettes, brocades, silks, damasks and various kinds of artificial leather are all made in widths to suit the convenience of the upholsterer. Corduroys follow cretonne as regards width, both single and double, and there are numerous other materials obtainable in tapestry widths. It should be noted that a double width material usually cuts up more economically than single width.

Seams constitute a bugbear both to the upholsterer and customer if they are too numerous or placed in such positions as to offend the eye, and seams which are objectionable in appearance or indiscriminately placed give rise to many complaints. The aim of the cutter, therefore, should be to reduce the number of seams to a minimum. In some materials the joins show very distinctly, while in others they are scarcely visible. In patterned fabrics of small set design or foliage the joins are not so conspicuous as in those where the fabric is plain. Velvets need great care in planning, especially self-coloured weaves. Moquettes also present difficulties, as they are of a stiffer nature than velvet, and unless the join is to some extent hidden by the pattern, it is difficult to prevent a clumsy appearance however carefully they are sewn and pressed. In stuff-over work seams are unavoidable, but the skill of the cutter lies in so planning the work that they are neither numerous nor conspicuous.

An insufficient quantity of material is the general cause of too many seams : a lesser quantity may suffice, though this economy is practised to the ultimate detriment of the work and at the risk of complaints from customers, while the upholsterer himself is hampered through a lack of pieces for joining and making up. It is true that the fabric for covering a piece of upholstery is a most expensive item, and economy is necessary ; but it is folly when finishing the work to spoil its appearance by not allowing enough material. Another argument against undue economy as regards material is that it causes

FIG. 300

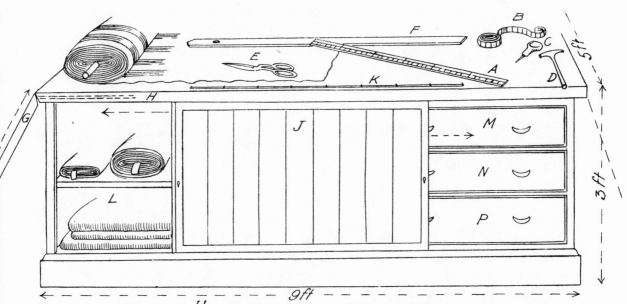

FIG. 297 UPHOLSTERERS CUTTING BOARD

A The yard measure
B The tape measure
C Pritchawl D. Hammer
E French pattern scissors

F. Straight edge or leveller (5ft)
G. Extension leaf
H. Sliding rod to support
    extension leaf

J. Sliding door
K. Sunk brass measure
L. Shelves for covering materials
M. N. P. Drawers for patterns.
    gimps. cuttings. etc.

tight coverings which, from the upholsterer's point of view, are difficult to deal with and require much skill and care in planning out ; this means that additional time is required, and when the work has to be finished in a given number of hours, the period set apart for the actual covering of the piece is curtailed, to the detriment of this most essential process.   Seams are not so prominent when they are matched, and the skilful upholsterer can take advantage of the pattern to hide the seams or camouflage them—to use a modern word.   In high-class work the joins are always matched, and the quantity of material allowed is governed by the pattern.   The length of a repeat in a patterned material may vary from a few inches to about a yard, and it is frequently a matter of great difficulty to obtain matches for all parts of the work.   In such cases the inside of the work should be studied first where the seams to be matched are more conspicuous than those on the outside.   At FIGS. 298, 299 and 300 are shown three designs.   FIG. 298 is a small conventional pattern, FIG. 299 a damask with a medallion centre, FIG. 300 a foliage pattern.   To plan out a three yard length of FIG. 298 would be less complicated than either FIGS. 299 or 300, because the length of the repeat in the larger designs increases the difficulty of finding a match.   Such a fabric as FIG. 298 may be planned without difficulty ; a first cut made haphazard at the line A would find a match at the line C. The match would be made at B and D.   A measurement taken from B to E could be matched at the next cut as from F to G.   The match would meet at E and H.

To attempt cutting haphazard on such fabrics as are shown at FIGS. 299 and 300 would be to ask for disaster.   Such a design as FIG. 299 to be used to advantage and with the best effect must be carefully planned before cutting.   The positions which the medallions will ultimately occupy are important and best obtained while the work is on the floor level.   In an ordinary divan a medallion would be necessary for the centre of the back, another for the seat, and two more for the arms.   The cutting of this particular design will be described in a subsequent chapter.

FIG. 300 is a foliage pattern, and one that, generally speaking, allows the cutter plenty of liberty.   The design being of an all-over character, the failure to match exactly is not so apparent.   For instance, it would be possible to join the part A to D on account of the similarity of the leaves ; also by piecing the material the reverse way, such parts as C and E might be joined, also B and F.   Foliage designs are economical in cutting, but more suitable in style for massive, heavy stuffovers than for light, graceful work.

CHAPTER 31.

CUTTING AND COVERING *(continued)*.

Extensions or straining pieces are portions of material other than the covering joined to it at various parts to increase the size (FIG. 301). Much saving can be effected by this method, but upholsterers must not overdo it. Economy must not be carried to the length of giving a maximum of extension and a minimum of covering material. If it is, it becomes a source of complaint on the part of customers. The use and abuse of extensions will now be explained.

For such a chair as is shown at FIG. 245 the approximate amount of double-width material needed would be 3½ yards, but without extension pieces this quantity would not be enough, and the various pieces are extended by adding strips of another material, as shown at FIG. 301. To dispense with extension pieces would considerably increase the cost of upholstery, and there is no disadvantage in their use if they are placed in the correct positions and strongly sewn. Extensions should be formed of a strong thin material according to, the nature of the covering used. For tapestry ordinary calico strips may be used ; for morocco or imitation leather black linen is preferable; but whatever the substitute it must be remembered that is has to bear a large amount of strain and pull, and that this is greater on plain work than buttoned work. Extensions should be placed in such a way that they are not visible at any part of the work.

In cases where economy has been carried too far—that is to say, where there is too little covering material and too much extension —the extension is liable to become visible and unsightly in compression, and as the purchaser is not generally aware of this device for economising material complaints frequently arise when it is found that a different fabric has been used. Thus the use of extensions, though perfectly legitimate, becomes a source of annoyance when the practice is abused. The pieces of velvet which surround rugs and carpet squares (*i.e.*, saddle-bags) are also termed extensions.

Plain velvets and self-coloured materials, when accurately measured and skilfully planned, are most economical, because no matching is required. Velvets are now woven double width, following tapestry measurements, and replacing the old-fashioned 24in. widths, which necessitated many joins. Joins or seams in plain velvets are very

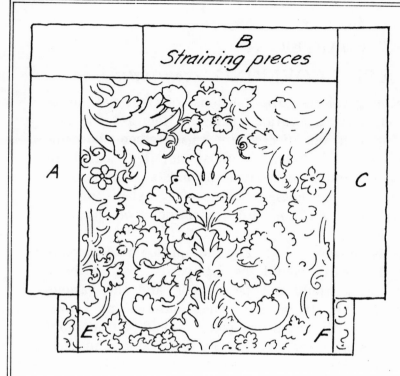

B
Straining pieces

A

C

E   **F**

FIG. 301

Method of increasing the size of covering by extensions
A.B.C = Calico
E.F. = Covering

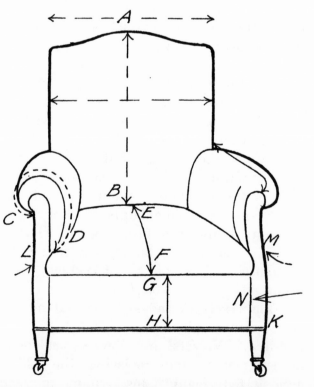

FIG. 302

Seat meas: 26"x 29" back to front
Inside arms 24"x 27 "   "
Inside back 25"across x 31"
Border 8"x 28"
Outside arms 15"x 27"
Outside back 22½" x 29"
Front facings 5"x 20" (2)
Back "   "   5"x 14" (2)

noticeable, but figured velvets can be matched with ease, and in some designs they can hardly be detected unless pointed out. It is important when cutting velvet to lay the various pieces over the work, so that the shading tones correctly. As a general rule, the darkest shade of a velvet is more pleasing than the lighter ones. In cutting lengths of covering material for an ordinary stuffover chair eight or nine pieces are required, apart from those for joining. A great saving of time is effected when these are marked with chalk, commencing from a first cut, either top or bottom. Some varieties of velvets are very difficult to shade correctly, and often appear to better advantage when placed in the opposite way to which they have been cut. The cutting and shading of velvets by artificial light should be avoided. Good natural light is absolutely necessary for plain velvets, but in figured varieties not so essential, because the pattern forms a guide to correct cutting.

The beginner who is fortunate enough to learn his trade in a shop in which a variety of work is done should constantly make notes. He will find these invaluable when the opportunity arises for him to cut his own materials. Many useful hints in connection with cutting can only be gained by observation. Some upholsterers waste a deal of time through planning out carelessly or not planning out at all. The beginner should form the habit and strictly adhere to the rule not to commence cutting until quite sure that he has sufficient material. Careful planning creates confidence when cutting, because the upholsterer has made sure of his ground and has left nothing to chance.

The best method of obtaining measurements from a double-width material is to calculate by half-widths. In cutting for small chairs, loose seats, and stuffover work, calculations are best made from the half-width. For example, the measurement of a small chair would be taken from back to front, and sufficient for two obtained from the full width. In easy chairs the half-width rule applies, and the width is increased by matched extensions of the same material when necessary. Figured designs of a set pattern in tapestries and brocades are generally duplicated in the double width, so that by cutting in the centre the pattern is the same on either side. The example shown at FIG. 302 is a simple stuffover chair for which eight distinct pieces of material are required independent of those for facings and extensions. The names of the cuts are: inside arms, outside arms, seat, inside back, outside back, and border. To measure for the inside arms insert the tape between the arms and seat to a depth of 4in. at D and measure, following the line of arrow, to C underneath the arm.

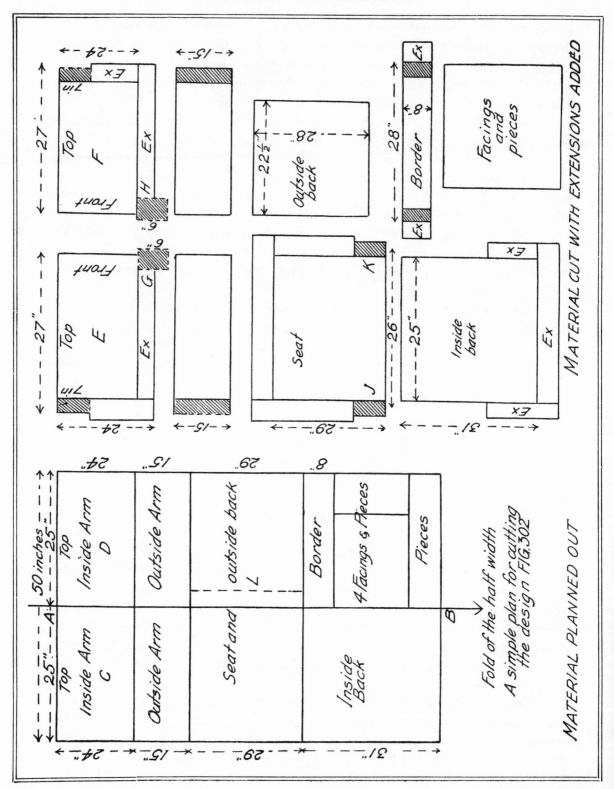

MATERIAL CUT WITH EXTENSIONS ADDED

MATERIAL PLANNED OUT

A simple plan for cutting
the design FIG.302

Fold of the half width

The seat and back sizes are obtained in the same manner, B to A for the back, E to F for the seat, the tape being inserted at E to the depth of 6in. instead of 4in. The border, G to H, requires an additional 3in. on the net measurement. For the outside arms, L and M, and outside back, A, sufficient material must be allowed to fold at the top, also 1in. to tack underneath the frame. The planning of the material for a chair already second stuffed in a calico or underlining is less complicated than when the calculations must be obtained from the first stuffed stage. This is the chief difficulty experienced by a beginner in his first attempts at cutting out, and it is necessary for success that he should be able to visualise the work as it will appear when finished. The 4in. and 6in. mentioned above at D and E between the seat and upper parts of a stuffover chair, while sufficient for such an example as that shown, must not be taken as the general rule, but a safe plan to eliminate the danger of faulty extensions is to allow as much as possible at these parts. By careful planning the upholsterer should be able to see exactly how much material he has at his disposal over and above the net measurements, but to plan carelessly or make first cuts because the quantity of material allowed appears ample is to court failure. The beginner must leave nothing to chance, and it is only by practice that he will be able to form a correct judgment of the number of inches to allow beyond the net measurements. A simple method of planning the covering for the chair (FIG. 302) is shown at FIG. 303. A to B represents a 2¾ yard length of a double-width material, the vertical line, A—B, indicating the centre fold. The width being 50in., the measurements are calculated by 25in. This method of cutting cannot be applied to all covering materials. For instance, with a centre pattern, such as FIG. 299, it would be necessary, after obtaining the measurements of the pieces required, to mark each cut with chalk or pins and place in position on the work. It will then be seen if the various pieces are planned to the best advantage and any alterations marked before cutting. The tapestry extensions (see shaded portions) added to increase the size, also straining extensions, are shown on the right (FIG. 303). The pieces G and H of the inside arms E and F are continuation pieces carried down between the seat border at N (FIG. 302) because the edge is independent (see FIG. 134). This piece would not be required on a fixed edge (as FIG. 135). The extensions J and K could be dispensed with by cutting at the dotted line L, leaving sufficient for the outside back. There are several ways in which the material can be planned, but the one shown is simple and should not present much difficulty to a beginner.

CHAPTER 32.

CUTTING AND COVERING (concluded).

As an introduction to the final covering of upholstery with tapestry, moquette, leather or other material, simple work such as small chairs and loose seats should be first attempted. These should present no great difficulty if the manipulation of the second stuffing in calico has been mastered (FIGS. 217-218). For such an example as is shown at FIGS. 304-309 cut a piece of the material 25in. square. If the chair has been second stuffed in hair, a layer of wadding must be used before the covering material is placed in position. In the final covering first centre the front and back of the material, and make corresponding marks on the chair to ensure that the threads of the material are kept straight: at FIG. 304 the covering is shown set, with the back corners folded and cut.

FIG. 305. Commence from the centre A, fold covering inwards if not too thick, and work right and left, leaving a few inches at each corner.

FIG. 306. The sides should be commenced at the point A, and the work should proceed to B.

FIG. 307. The material should first be cut at A and tacked raw edge for the following reasons :—(1) Much straining being necessary to clean the fulness at this part, the tacking is more easily done on the raw edge than when turned in. (2) Tacking on the folded edge is liable to cause unsightly projections at this part of the work.

FIG. 308. Back covers are treated like those in front, the superflous material is cut away, the fulness cleaned, and the material folded inwards close up to the woodwork A. Tack on the raw edge from B to the back leg.

FIG. 309. Trim off with a sharp knife the pieces left raw edge and the seat is ready for the trimming.

FIG. 310. In covering a loose seat the procedure is much the same as in the case of a small. Temporary tacks may be placed on the sides of the frame if the nature of the material permits, but this practice must not be followed with velvet, leather and leather cloths, as in these coverings the marks remain visible and become a source of complaint.

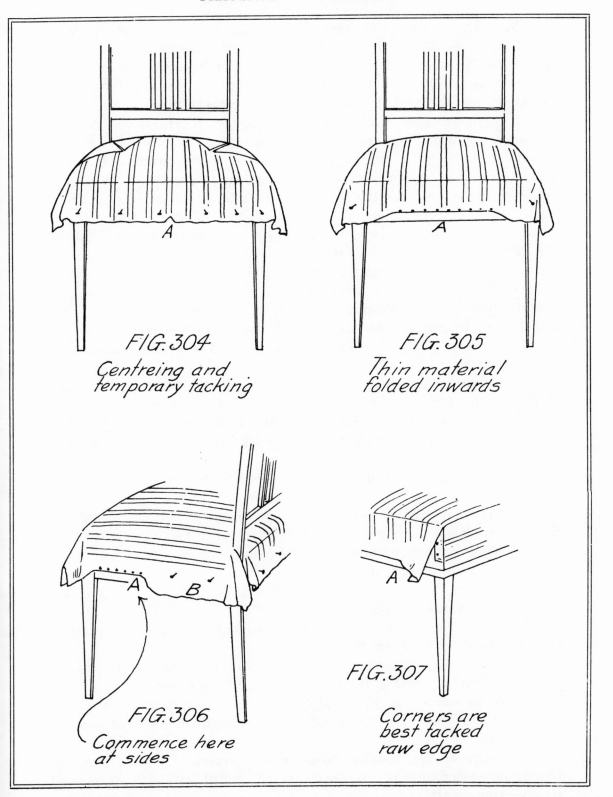

FIG. 304
Centreing and
temporary tacking

FIG. 305
Thin material
folded inwards

FIG. 306
Commence here
at sides

FIG. 307
Corners are
best tacked
raw edge

FIG. 311. Shows the underside of the seat with the covering tacked inwards about 1in. and trimmed off neatly. The corners are treated like those of a small chair, but it is important to cut away as much as possible of the superfluous material because unnecessary fulness causes the seat to fit too tightly, especially when the frame is not quite true, as shown at FIGS. 30-31. There is no definite system of measurement when calculating the quantity of covering material needed for upholstery, and it is only by practice that the upholsterer may become competent. Absolute accuracy is, of course, the ideal thing, but as this only comes with experience, it is better when calculating to allow a little more than a little less than is necessary, because an insufficiency entails a number of complications and difficulties in making ends meet.

To calculate the quantity of material needed for a chair when it is in the first stuffed stage is more difficult than one which is second stuffed in an underlining; this is because of the extra over and above the net measurement which must be allowed for.

The following points should be remembered when measuring a first stuffed chair:—

(a) Correct calculations cannot be made without a knowledge of the width of the material to be used (see Chapter 30).

(b) Double width materials are best calculated by the $\frac{1}{2}$ width.

(c) Visualise the proportions of the work; this is helpful in making a decision.

(d) The quantities should be checked either mentally or, preferably, in writing.

(e) Extension pieces serve their purposes as straining pieces; they are useless as a remedy for a tight cover (Chapter 31).

(f) When making calculations first allow not less than 4in. in a small easy chair or 6in. in a large one for the material hidden below the junction of seat and back, then judge the amount by the proportion of the first stuffing.

(g) As a general rule, the larger the work, the greater the quantity of material required from the sight line.

(h) Study the appearance of the front of the work—more liberty may be taken as regards seams, pattern, etc., with outsides.

(j) When making up the total be sure that the balance of material, if any, is sufficient for the smaller pieces required, such as facings, arm extensions, etc.

(k) Tight covers usually mean tight corners, faulty extensions, unnecessary straining of the material, a multiplicity of seams, and finally—complaints.

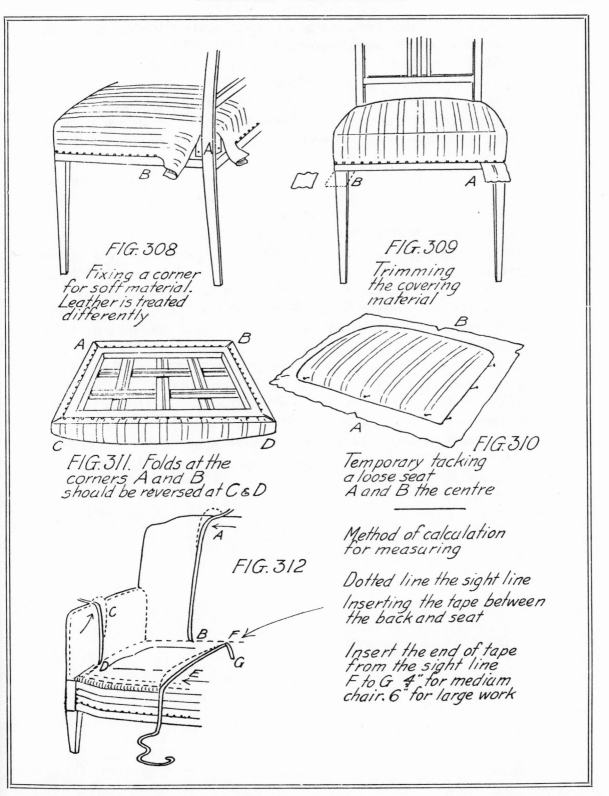

FIG. 308

Fixing a corner
for soft material.
Leather is treated
differently

FIG. 309

Trimming
the covering
material

FIG. 311. Folds at the
corners A and B
should be reversed at C & D

FIG. 310

Temporary tacking
a loose seat
A and B the centre

FIG. 312

Method of calculation
for measuring

Dotted line the sight line

Inserting the tape between
the back and seat

Insert the end of tape
from the sight line
F to G 4" for medium
chair. 6" for large work

(*l*) Careful, correct measurements mean good work, and save both time and temper when covering.

(*m*) When in doubt as to a measurement, the beginner should err by allowing too much rather than too little material.

Below is set out the method of calculation with a tape measure from a first stuffed chair. The additional number of inches required over the net measurement is governed by the proportions of the first stuffing (See Fig. 312).

(1) At D, B and F insert the tape 4in. beyond the sight line.

(2) If the hand be placed beneath the measure at the parts A, C and E, by raising it slightly above the required proportion a good idea of the gross measurement is obtained.

(3) When noting the various calculations the different cuts should be indicated, viz. : I.A. = inside arm, S. =seat, O.A. = outside arm, O.B.=outside back, F.=facing, B.O.R.=borders, and so on.

(4) Having cut the material for the various parts, the top edge should be indicated with chalk in order to avoid the pattern being placed upside down.

In calculating, the inches should be reduced to yards, any balance of inches being increased to a simple fractional part rather than decreased. For example : 2 yds. 7in. = $2\frac{1}{4}$ yds. ; 3 yds. 11in. = $3\frac{1}{3}$ yds. ; 3 yds. 20in. = $3\frac{5}{8}$ yds. ; 4 yds. 21in. = $4\frac{2}{3}$ yds. A beginner should note any faults in calculation which become apparent when covering, comparing his estimates with the results in practice. He will in this way gain confidence, and his notes will be of value in the event of repetition work.

CHAPTER 33.

CUTTING AND COVERING FOR TAPED-IN BACKS.

Coverings for chairs, the backs of which are semi-circular in shape, are more complicated to cut than those in which the backs and arms are independent of each other, and may consequently be cut separately. An example of a semi-circular backed chair is shown at FIG. 256, and the back and arms would need to be planned and cut on the work and afterwards joined together in one piece. In dealing with imitation leathers, morocco or hide, the greatest care must be exercised in cutting to ensure that the fulness created by the hollow of the back shall be reduced to a minimum. This style of back is sometimes cut with advantage on the first stuffing. FIGS. 313/317 show the method of cutting for a chair shown at FIG. 261, a first stuffed semi-circular back in soft fabric collared and taped. The term " taped " or " taped-in " implies that the covering as from A to B, FIG. 313, is fixed by means of a piece of strong tape about 1in. wide sewn by hand to the threads of the fabric on the reverse side. This tape is afterwards sewn through the first stuffing and a defined sunk line without any stitches visible from the front is thus obtained. Backs treated in this way have a superior appearance and if the line is carefully placed—neither drawn too tight nor left too loose—it prevents the covering from sagging in the hollow of the back. This operation will be dealt with when describing cutting for the present example.

It is first necessary to plan out the line for tape A to B, FIG. 313, also line C to D where the arm and back meet. The lines should be indicated by means of a blue pencil rather than by chalk. The line C to D should be set well back, FIG. 315, as when it is so, the fulness may be cleaned more easily. It is unnecessary to mark the tape line on the first stuffing, but it may be indicated on the covering itself by means of pins or skewers.

First measure the length of the material required, FIG. 313, E to F, and increase it in width, if necessary, by matched extension pieces. Mark the centre E to F, fold the material in half and fix with skewers at E, G, and F. Next draw the cover to the position of C to D, and by a series of cuts as H, also from D to F, the fulness will be released; then pin to the marked line and trim off. This operation is best done by gradation. The material should be cut

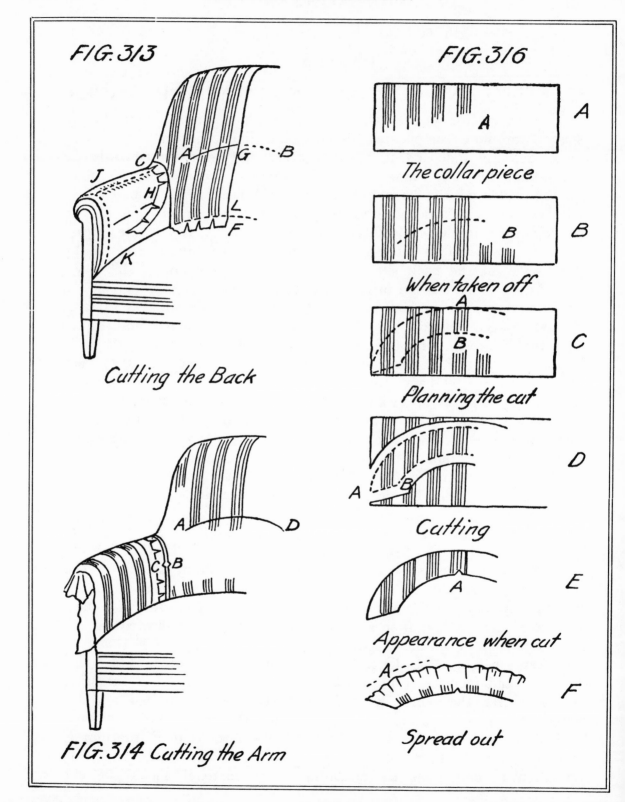

FIG. 313

Cutting the Back

FIG. 314 Cutting the Arm

FIG. 316

A — The collar piece

B — When taken off

C — Planning the cut

D — Cutting

E — Appearance when cut

F — Spread out

on the underneath fold and the shape duplicated on the upper fold when taken off. At the cuts, D to F, care must be taken to allow sufficient for the seam to be made slightly under rather than above the dotted line. The armpiece should now be dealt with. First obtain the measurement from J to K, making allowance for the second stuffing, compare FIG. 312. Place the material in position, release fulness exactly as described when dealing with the back, until the two edges of the material butt together. Now mark the material with pencil or by notching at the points C and B, FIG. 314, for the guidance of the upholstress when making the seam. The line for the tape A to D, FIG. 314, is best obtained by a series of pins or skewers stabbed through the covering, duplicated on the opposite half of the material. This line should be short rather than long for reasons which will be subsequently explained.

The method of cutting a collar is the same for a large or small piece of work and varies only as regards the width and length of the material. The length of the collar piece is found by measuring from D to E, FIG. 315, across the seat with an allowance of 3in. or 4in. on either side, the width from centre G to H, with an allowance of 4in. or 5in. Set the material over the seat in front of the points D and E rather than behind. As this is to form a continuation of the back, care must be taken that the material is placed in position the reverse side up. With the collar piece thus spread in place, mark a line close up to, and the exact shape of, the sight line of back, see dotted line J, FIG. 315. FIG. 316, A to F, shows the method of marking out and cutting the collar.

A. Is the piece of material cut ready for fixing on the seat.

B. The marked line corresponding with the contour of the back.

C. Superfluous material marked off by a second line to the width A B.

D. Material cut away. It is important that the line A to B should not be cut horizontally.

E. The collar cut. The notch A will meet the centre of back L, FIG. 313.

F. The collar is shown spread out, the fulness at the dotted line A caused by the material being cut on the bias.

At FIG. 317 the material for the back is shown pinned on the cutting board. A to B are pins marking the line of tape, and at C the half cut is duplicated. FIG. 318 is an enlarged view of the back sewn together ready for permanent fixing. When placing

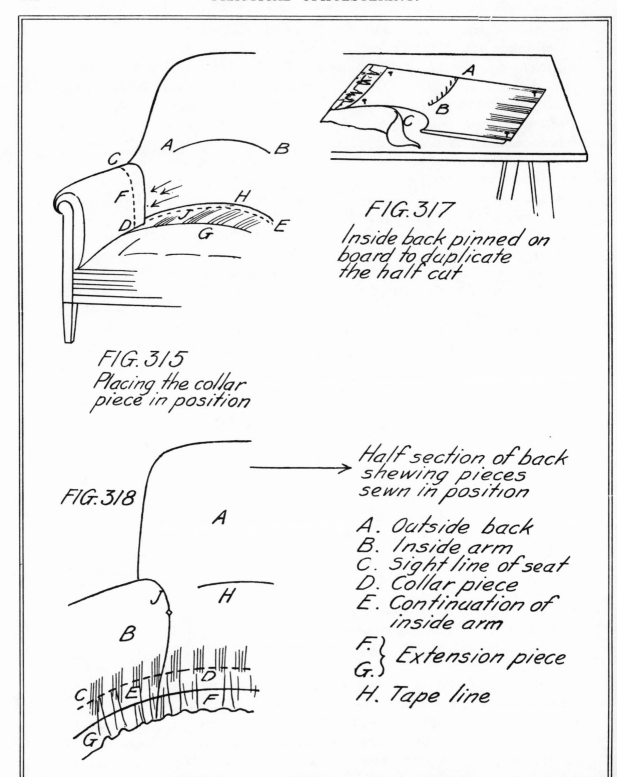

FIG. 317
Inside back pinned on
board to duplicate
the half cut

FIG. 315
Placing the collar
piece in position

FIG. 318

Half section of back
shewing pieces
sewn in position

A. Outside back
B. Inside arm
C. Sight line of seat
D. Collar piece
E. Continuation of
     inside arm
F. ⎫
   ⎬ Extension piece
G. ⎭
H. Tape line

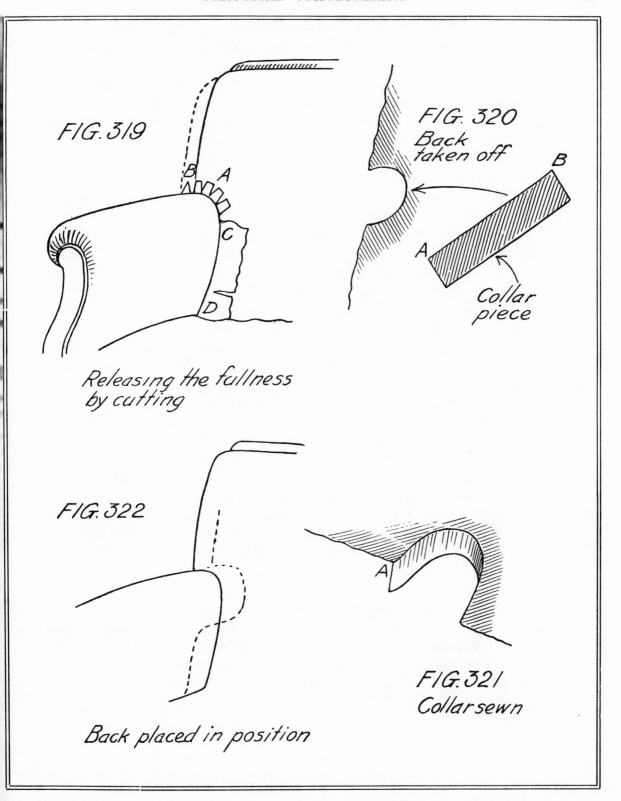

FIG. 319

B A
C
D

Releasing the fullness
by cutting

FIG. 320
Back
taken off

B

A

Collar
piece

FIG. 322

Back placed in position

FIG. 321
Collar sewn

A

a covering such as this it is important that the line of seam J and the taped line H fall directly on the marking made on the first stuffing. The tape must first be sewn in position with a straight needle taking small stitches about ½in. long and ½in. apart, and care being taken that all the knots of the twine are made on the back hessian. The tape must not be drawn tight until the whole back is set. If at first the desired clean effect cannot be obtained a series of temporary tackings must be given, the tacks released, and the material strained a little harder each time until the fulness is dispersed. Backs such as these, when cut correctly, should fit like a glove, and the superior appearance of this style of upholstery will amply repay the pains taken in planning and cutting.

For the backs of large pieces of stuffover work the cutting of collars is most essential. Such examples as FIGS. 165, 169, 241 and 245 are cases in point. In order to obtain a correct circular shape a series of cuts is needed to release the fulness. Collars in backs are treated differently to those for seats because the material need not be cut on the bias. FIG. 319 shows how to cut a back covering for a collar. A indicates a series of first cuts to release the fulness, B to C, the length of the collar in a soft material, but in leather work the joining of the material being welted and visible from the outside a better effect is obtained by forming a collar from B to D. FIG. 220 shows the material cut and prepared for placing the collar piece A to B, and FIG. 321 the collar sewn in position. FIG. 322 indicates the back and collar when fixed. It will be seen that the danger incidental to bad cuts is eliminated because no cuts are necessary. The formation of collars in this way should be the rule rather than the exception, for very little extra time need be expended on it and the appearance of the work is considerably enhanced. As described when dealing with the semi-circular shaped chair, the covering may be cut on the single or double width and the importance of keeping the threads perfectly straight at both angles must be observed to obtain the best results. It must not be expected that perfection will be reached at the first attempt, as fulness of the material in the hollow of the back is often very difficult to manipulate, failing to respond to the pull unless the cutting has been done skilfully.

CHAPTER 34.

MOROCCO AND IMITATION LEATHER WORK.

The young upholsterer who has formed the habit of making notes for future reference will find the practice very necessary when first attempting leather work. There is no branch of upholstering in which accumulated workshop experience is so valuable as in the manipulation of leather. Indeed, a volume might be written on the devices, means and methods of producing good work and of saving labour in the working of leather, either real or artificial, as distinct from the treatment of other upholstering fabrics.

Covering with leather calls for a high degree of skill and there are many upholsterers who are quite competent in other branches of the craft who never thoroughly master leather work. In spite of the fact that so few upholsterers are first-class leather hands (the manager of a firm employing great numbers has placed it at 5 per cent.) there is a growing demand for men skilled in this work. This is occasioned by the development of the motor and aircraft industries and the high-class furniture required for large hotels, clubs and ocean-going liners.

The reader is referred to FIG. 150, which represents a kidney-shaped settee. To upholster such a piece of work in crimson morocco with buttoned back, loose down cushions on a spring edge foundation, calls for a high degree of skill. The same remark applies to such a chesterfield as is shown at FIG. 198, which might be specified apple green morocco, buttoned all over, double sprung seat, or all plain in a hide. The upholsterer who has followed these articles so far might also question himself as to his ability to upholster a billiard seat such as is shown at FIG. 183 in dice-grained morocco or all buttoned in a straight grained morocco. Let him also question his skill in dealing with such a piece as is shown at FIG. 245 under edge, wood facing, and with monogram in centre of back. Or again, FIG. 271, finished in morocco.

Artificial leathers are extensively used for upholstery work as substitutes for morocco (goatskin) and roan (sheepskin). Artificial leather is somewhat more difficult to work than real leather because it is less pliable, and therefore harder to manipulate. It should, however, be pointed out that many varieties of artificial leather have been so improved in manufacture that they possess a certain "give" which is a great aid to the craftsman. The makers have put on the markets special grades suitable for different classes of work,—*i.e.*, buttoned, plain, and so on. The American cloth at one time so largely used presented no difficulty to the upholsterer in making up. It was, in fact, quite as easy to manipulate as an ordinary soft fabric, and in some cases more so.

The obtaining of a good appearance with artificial leathers depends on the skill of the upholsterer, especially in stuffover work, and it is futile to expect satisfactory results from an upholsterer who is inexperienced with this material. Many large manufacturing firms set apart certain men for dealing with leather work only, because it is realised that a leather hand can only become really competent by continual practice. Some upholsterers show no inclination to become specialists in leather work, possibly because its use entails more physical labour than softer fabrics, and also on account of the difficulties occasioned in rectifying mistakes and faulty workmanship. On the other hand, if such work appeals to the craftsman he may be unfitted for it in other ways. It is, for instance, essential that the upholsterer who is working in leather should possess a dry hand, because the continual rubbing and straining the surface of a skin with a hand that is moist with perspiration produces marks which it is impossible to remove. Certain dyes are very sensitive, and the skin is easily damaged, and when the surface has once been stained in any way it is almost impossible to treat it successfully, and a new skin is often necessary. The young upholsterer generally has an ambition to become a leather worker, but after a few attempts many are content to remain unskilled in this respect, and to take the line of least resistance by working in soft fabrics instead of in leather if they are given any choice in the matter.

The upholsterer who aspires to be a good leather worker should first learn to appreciate the qualities of the different skins, and should be able to distinguish by the sense of touch their relative value for any given part of a piece of work in connection with which they are to be used. He should also develop as far as possible his colour sense in order to be able to match the skins. A morocco is seldom, if ever, of uniform colour, and where two or three skins are used side by side, such as in FIGS. 183 and 198, much skill is required so to choose the skins that the shades or tones are agreeable to the eye. He should also learn to discern the differences between skins in respect of their strength and durability and so be able to

MOROCCOS & ROANS. CHARACTERISTICS OF SKINS, AND USES OF VARIOUS PARTS

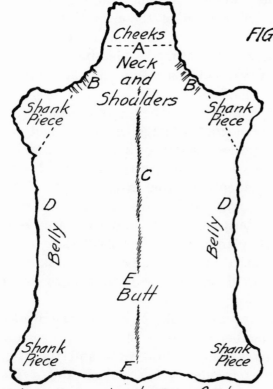

FIG. 323

Cheeks
A
Neck
and
Shoulders
B
B
Shank Piece
Shank Piece
C
D
Belly
D
Belly
E
Butt
Shank Piece
Shank Piece
F

Approximate shape of Skin
Terms used to describe various parts

A. The extreme upper part of the skin generally cut away.
B.B. Fullness sometimes very pronounced here.
C. The backbone mark forms a centre line for seats & backs, but not arms
D.D. Belly portion usually inclined to fullness. This portion adapted for sides rather than fronts of chairs.
E. Butts are generally clear and free from marks. are best placed at the fronts and prominent parts of a chair.
F. This portion of the butt can be used the whole width of a good clear skin with a minimum of waste

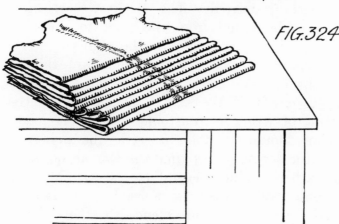

FIG. 324

Method of selection of the different shades. The skins are folded as shown, placed in a natural light (not artificial.)

The various shades can be toned and blended together.

choose the most suitable morocco for positions where fulness is likely to be pronounced. Fulness in leather is quite a different matter from fulness in a soft material; while a soft, pliable material is amenable to treatment, leather frequently presents almost insuperable difficulties. A critical customer would describe fulness as "those nasty wrinkles," and it is the manipulation of these wrinkles that calls for much judgment and skill on the part of the upholsterer. Fulness in morocco work treated skilfully can be made pleasing to the eye. On the other hand, its faulty treatment may ruin the appearance of the work.

Moroccos vary considerably in size. They are usually sorted by the merchants and sold in three grades—large, medium, and small; in addition there are further grades denoting qualities suitable for plain or buttoned work. Some skins are faulty, having blemishes on the surface resulting from accidents to the animal while alive, or from defects caused by the dressing. Such skins though not suitable for plain work might be used for buttoned work, and they are therefore graded accordingly. By careful planning a blemished skin may be used without cutting much to waste, and in many cases a skin which presents difficulties may be worked in to good advantage by dint of a little careful thought.

In dealing with skins which are too small, or to use the workshop term "tight," it should be remembered that a morocco or roan may be said to possess two sets of sizes—the natural sizes and the stretching sizes. This is a point which is frequently overlooked, and it should also be remembered that for plain work a tight skin generally produces the best results. At FIG. 323, a morocco is shown spread out with the names of the various parts indicated. The thickest part of a morocco or roan is generally to be found from the neck to the butt on either side of the centre. The outer edges of the skin are more likely to cause fulness on account of the fact that they are thinner than the centre part. The back bone mark on some skins is more or less pronounced the whole length of the skin. This is not detrimental from the point of view of wear, but customers sometimes complain about it. The salesman should be able to settle the point by explaining that this is one of the surest proofs that the skin in question is of real and not artificial leather. When several pieces of upholstery are to be used together in one room great care must be exercised in selecting the different shades to tone and blend together. The sketch at FIG. 324 shows the method of arranging the skins. In strong daylight the shades are clearly seen in the outer folds of the skin. For large work it is necessary to assort the shades in this manner because they will be joined together by vandyking (button work) or welted seams (plain work) in order to make up the necessary dimensions. More liberty may be taken with the skins for small chairs provided the difference in shade is not so marked as to be conspicuous.

CHAPTER 35.

METHOD OF WELTING IN LEATHER.

When manipulating the fulness of a scroll or seat upholstered in leather much depends on the nature of the skin. Some are " papery " in substance and need careful handling, especially when cutting the corners ; others are coarse although at the same time they may be pliable. Turkey grain moroccos are easier to work than straight grain, the fulness of the skin in the latter variety being very difficult to treat. Fulness which is so detrimental to the finished appearance is often disposed of by the upholsterer at the expense of the surface of the skin. Although there is always a certain amount of " give " or " stretch " in leather too much advantage must not be taken of this, as there is always a danger of the grained surface cracking and breaking, producing a fault which it is extremely difficult to remedy. In buttoned work, no straining being necessary, the danger is eliminated and the natural beauty of the skin retained. Upholsterers of the old school were not so particular on this question of fulness though they were quite alive to the superior appearance of a piece of work when the fulness was properly cleaned. Evidence of this is to be found when stripping old leather work in which tacks are frequently found to be actually touching each other. Fulness in a leather-covered chair is not always attributable to faulty workmanship for reasons already stated, but careful attention to the instructions given below will reduce fulness to a minimum.

It is most essential to remember that the foundation of the work must be prepared specially for a leather covering. For example, in a small chair the stitched edge must be extra firm to retain its position while straining and temporarily tacking the leather. At the corners both front and back fulness is generally pronounced, see FIG. 326, A, B, C. If the edge is too weak it will not bear the strain and falls back, which is a bad fault. The next point is that a seat to be covered with leather must not be too round when second stuffed. It gives them a common appearance, and this fault also necessitates undue stretching of the skin. The front of a small chair is less difficult to clean than the sides or back.

The method of covering a small chair in leather will now be described. To begin with, it should be noted that a skin is easier

FIG 325

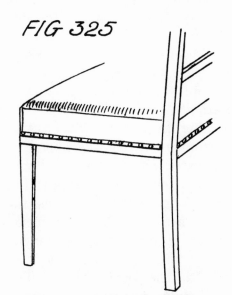

Appearance of a leather
seat cleaned of fulness

FIG. 326

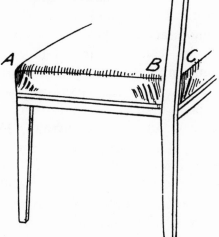

Fullness at sides and
back, caused by
incorrect straining,
a tender "papery" skin,
or bad judgment
in temporary tacking

FIG. 327

A & B. The
tongues
are strained
and tacked
one on either
side of the
back rail

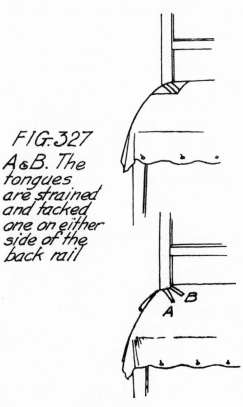

FIG. 328

The fulness is best
disposed of at the corners

to manipulate when the line of the backbone is placed directly in the centre of the seat. When using temporary tacks make sure that they are placed close to the moulding. The point of a tack breaks the surface of a skin, and the puncture if carelessly placed cannot always be hidden by the subsequent banding and studding of the chair. Tack temporarily from front to back or *vice versa* (some upholsterers favour the former method, some the latter), but a beginner is advised after setting the leather in the correct position to tack first at the back and strain to the front, repeating the operation at the sides. The arrows, FIG. 328, indicate where the maximum strain is required, the object being to obtain a clean, taut appearance at C and D when tacked. After a series of temporary tackings the fulness can be finally disposed of at the corners, A, B. The pleats are best treated last. After completing at E and F, the tongue method, FIG. 327, helps greatly in cleaning fulness at the side and allows of the leather being finished close to the back rail. When the nature of the skin will not permit of fulness being cleaned the next best plan is to equalise it in the tacking. It will be clear to the upholsterer who has studied this series of articles that a seat which is too round naturally creates more fulness of the leather than if it is of normal proportions. The fault may be remedied by running through the seat with twines in the manner indicated at FIGS. 329 and 330. Care must be exercised in doing this, as if the twines are drawn too tight when they are released the edge will not assume its original position but hang back instead of slightly forward. Artificial leathers are treated in the same way as real leathers. Some brands are so skilfully manufactured that from the upholsterer's point of view they are quite as easy to work as some soft fabrics. Others are often more difficult than real leather when fulness is encountered.

Considerable skill is required to cover in leather, either plain or buttoned, such examples of upholstery as are shown at FIGS. 198 and 242. Owing to the limited size of a skin many joins are necessary. These are shaped and cut on the work, then taken off, and the seams welted and finally replaced in the same position. Seams in artificial leathers are reduced to a minimum because of the width available for cutting, and in seats and backs of great length this is an advantage. Welted joints give a superior finish to leather work, but quite apart from this they are considerably stronger than ordinary plain seams. They are, however, best placed under-edge, being protected in this position and less subject to wear and tear than on the edge.

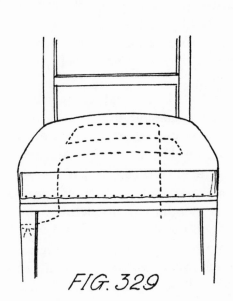

FIG. 329

A seat when too round
gives fulness to leather
at the front and side

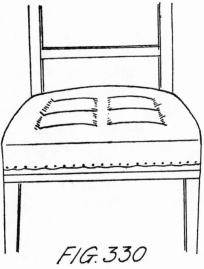

FIG. 330

A seat tied down

METHOD OF TYING SEAT TO THE WEBS

The twines are removed when seat is finished

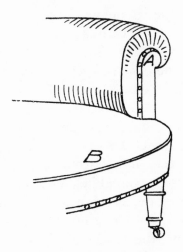

FIG. 331
Tacked-in Arm

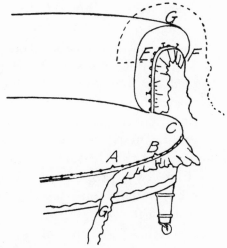

FIG. 332
Leather pinned on edge of seat

The preparation of the seats and arms of stuff-overs in leather is so complicated that a beginner would hardly attempt it without a practical demonstration to enable him to understand more clearly how to set about it. Though theory is helpful, a great deal must be learnt from actual observation at this stage.

The leather may be cut on a first or second stuffed foundation, but the former method is not advisable unless undertaken by a skilled workman. In a leather-covered chair of simple design as shown at Fig. 331 the seat is finished with a welted border, and the arms have pullover or tacked-in facings as they are termed in the trade. In leather-covered upholstery welted seams play an important part. The various contours and evenly balanced scrolls when defined by the projection of the welts have a very attractive appearance. A welt in leather upholstery work may be described as a seam with an edging. In connection with them very much depends on the skill of the upholstress, as a skin may have been cut with the utmost care and then spoiled by an inexperienced worker.

The first operation in connection with a welted seam and border is shown at Fig. 332. The skin is strained tightly on all sides, but as tacks cannot be used on the edge A, strong pins are employed. Skewers are too clumsy. A little fulness will be encountered from B to C, but this is generally disposed of easily when the welt is to be finished on the edge. After making sure that the seat is correctly placed and that any unsightly fulness has been cleaned, proceed to cut about $\frac{1}{8}$in. outside the pins; the detached strip is seen at G. A sharp knife such as is used by a shoemaker is the variety best suited for this purpose. A seat such as this may be welted either on or off the work. The one here described is intended to be taken off and replaced when finished. It is of the utmost importance that the leather shall be replaced exactly in the same position as when temporarily pinned. To ensure this a pencil or chalk mark is necessary on the underlining with a corresponding mark on the leather. For the guidance of the upholstress when welting two pieces of leather together, a small triangular cut or notch is made on the extreme edge of the leather as shown at C and D, Fig. 333. Fig. 334 shows a facing and border pinned with the notches cut to correspond with notches on the seat and arm. D is an extension piece of leather, needed when the required width cannot be obtained from a skin or when it has been found necessary to cut away a faulty part and thus shorten the length. The join between the leather and the extension piece need only be plain seamed.

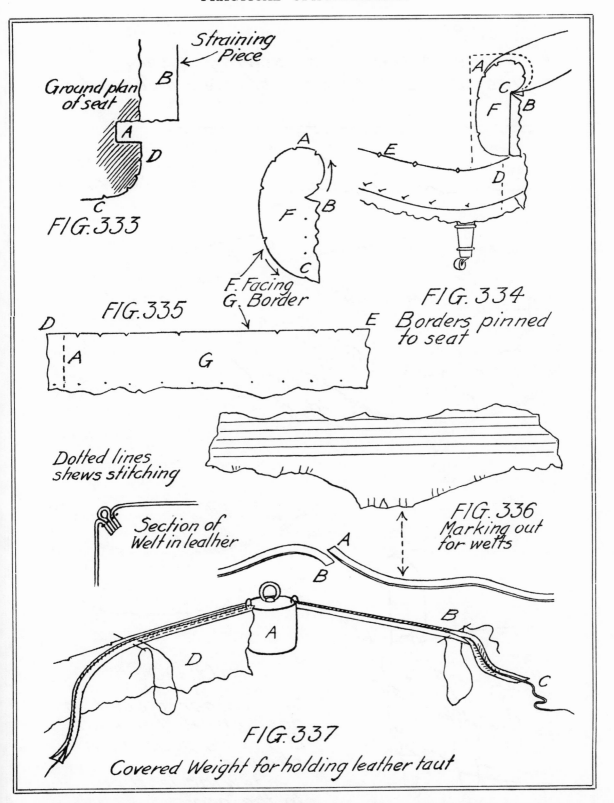

Straining Piece

Ground plan of seat

B

A

D

C

FIG. 333

A

F

B

C

F. Facing
G. Border

FIG. 335

A

C

F

B

E

D

FIG. 334
Borders pinned to seat

D

A

G

E

Dotted lines shews stitching

FIG. 336
Marking out for welts

Section of Welt in leather

A

B

B

D

A

C

FIG. 337
Covered Weight for holding leather taut

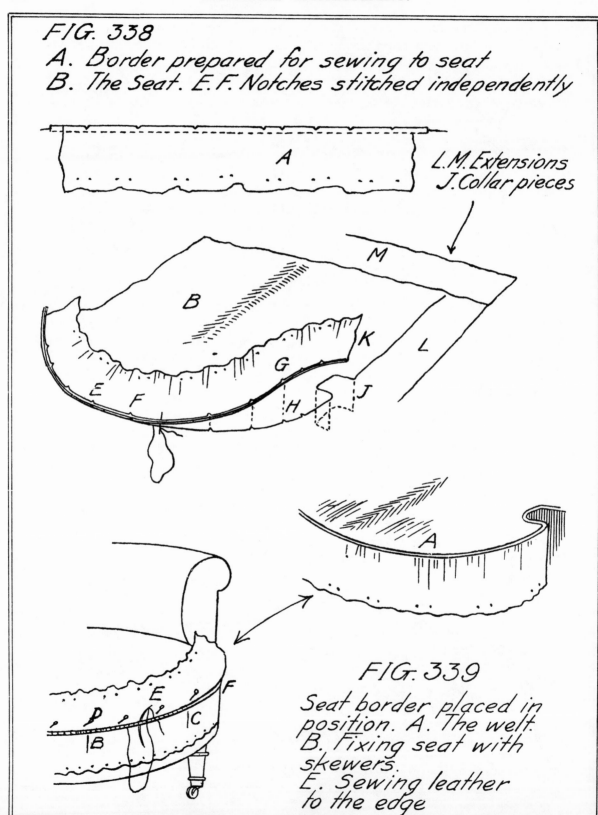

FIG. 338
A. Border prepared for sewing to seat
B. The Seat. E.F. Notches stitched independently

A

L.M. Extensions
J. Collar pieces

M

B

K

L

E   F   G

H   J

A

FIG. 339

Seat border placed in position. A. The welt.
B. Fixing seat with skewers.
E. Sewing leather to the edge

P   E   F

B   C

Superfluous leather as from the facing A may be trimmed on the work or a line scratched from pin to pin and cut subsequently on the board. To obtain the shape a cut is made at C. The leather at B is left on for a two-fold purpose. (1) To set the facing in position when finally covering. (2) For tacking on the outside arm. The diagram at FIG. 335 shows the facing and border removed and prepared for a welt to be sewn from B to C, and D to E.

FIG. 336 indicates a piece of leather marked out to be cut into strips ¾in. wide. The required length of a welt is generally made up of odd pieces, the ends are chamfered to a skiver edge on and under the face of two ends A, B, and afterwards pasted together. Shoemaker's paste is the best for this purpose, as glue will sometimes crack and the join becomes ineffective. A piece of twine is inserted in the strip of leather to give firmness to the welt. This is then oversewn, FIG. 337, to keep it in position whilst stitching to the facing or border. FIG. 338 A shows a border stitched on a seat, B. The notches are first stitched together, E and F, the notches on the border and seat corresponding, see G and H. A few independent stitches may be put in before commencing to stitch finally. FIG. 339 shows the border stitched and reversed, A, the welt, B, C, marks corresponding with those on the seat and skewers for fixing the leather in position. E is a circular needle for sewing the leather to the edge. Welting for leather work is generally stitched entirely by hand, although some straight parts can be machined, though by the latter method there is always a danger of the skin being cut. Only a very skilful machinist should attempt it.

Before placing it on the work, the welt, which will now consist of four thicknesses of leather, should be hammered out on the reverse side to compress it as much as possible. If the leather is at all thick a difficulty is met when sewing, E, FIG. 339. A good plan is to drill the holes with a pritchawl on the board, but care must be taken to avoid breaking the stitches or making the holes too large. FIG. 332 shows how to deal with the arm. A twine is fixed at E, the leather at G is held in a horizontal position and drawn gradually to F. A, B, and C represent the leather pinned on the edge of the seat.

CHAPTER 36.

BUTTONED WORK IN LEATHER.

Buttons in leather work are usually placed in rows, so many inches apart, according to the work, and set diamond fashion. Half diamond implies 2 rows or lines of buttons placed horizontally, FIG. 340; 1 diamond, 3 rows, FIG. 341; 1½ diamond, 4 rows, FIG. 342; 5 rows would be termed 2 diamonds, FIGS. 343 and 344. The size of the diamond depends on the style of work, and the number of *buttons* is calculated from the width, not the depth; for example, 3 buttons 5½in. by 7in. and 1 diamond would equal a total of 8 buttons (see FIG. 341).

Whatever the length of a piece of work, the number of *diamonds* is reckoned from the depth, *i.e.*, from top to bottom in a back, or front to back in a seat. For example, a 12ft. billiard seat with 3 horizontal rows of buttons in the back would be spoken of having 1 diamond (3 rows of buttons). A Chesterfield seat with 5 rows of buttons would imply 2 diamonds (see FIG. 344).

Diamonds of equal dimensions are superior to the old-fashioned long-shaped diamonds. Also large size diamonds are preferable to small; buttons that are too close give a common appearance to a piece of work, and the limited space between the buttons makes the work hard and firm.

In buttoned work, whether in leather or a soft fabric, the covering being fixed and held in position by the buttons, no strain or pull on the material is needed. In leather especially this is a great advantage; the grained surface retains its natural appearance and is more durable than when used in plain work. Buttons should be placed in positions pleasing to the eye; if set too close or at too great a distance from the edge the appearance is clumsy. It is important for buttoned work that the groundwork of a seat should be flat, or nearly so; if too round, or if the springs are placed too high, or too much hair on the first stuffing, the buttons cannot be strained down sufficiently, causing them to float, a bad fault in buttoned work. In small chairs and show-wood upholstery the seats are prepared specially for buttoning, and the springs are laced down to a lower position than for plain work.

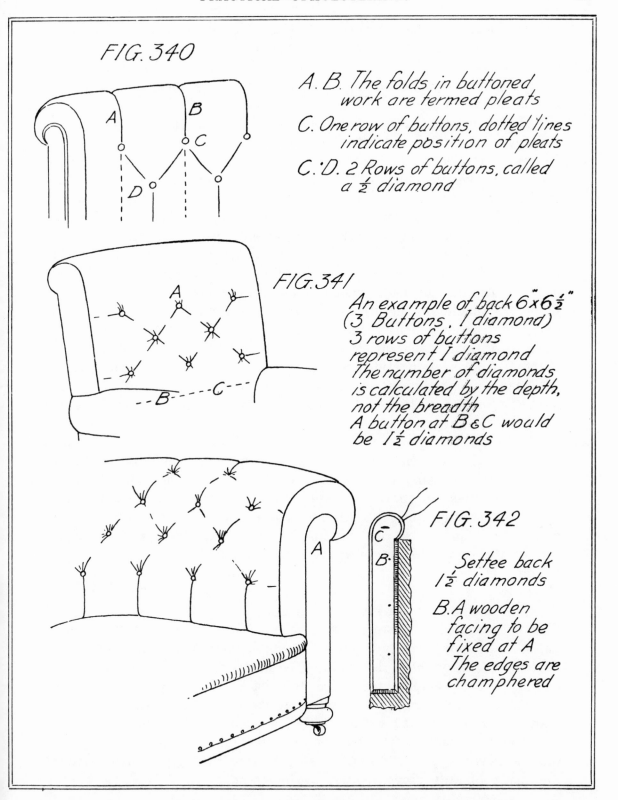

FIG. 340

A. B. The folds in buttoned
work are termed pleats

C. One row of buttons, dotted lines
indicate position of pleats

C. D. 2 Rows of buttons, called
a ½ diamond

FIG. 341

An example of back 6″×6½″
(3 Buttons. 1 diamond)
3 rows of buttons
represent 1 diamond
the number of diamonds
is calculated by the depth,
not the breadth
A button at B & C would
be 1½ diamonds

FIG. 342

Settee back
1½ diamonds

B. A wooden
facing to be
fixed at A
The edges are
champhered

To calculate the number of buttons required for a seat it is necessary to mark the centre of the work by drawing a vertical line from back to front (see FIG. 343), then place tacks in the scrim to represent buttons, changing them to various positions, until a definite size is decided upon.

If, for example, a seat with plan such as FIG. 344 is to be marked, 7in. by 7in., 3 buttons at the front, and 2 diamonds, proceed as follows. (1) Mark the centre line A to B. (2) From the front edge B strike the line B—C the first row of buttons. (3) Mark off 7in. for the line D—E, repeat for line F—G. (4) From the centres K, J, H, mark off 7in. on both sides. (5) The remainder of marks are obtained by striking diagonal lines each way, as at L.

The distance of a first row of buttons from the front edge or the top row of a back is governed by the size of the diamond, about half the length, not less. The marks for the position of the buttons should be made in the first instance by stabbing through the scrim only, with the pencil point, afterwards cutting it diagonally and forming a small hole with the finger about $\frac{1}{2}$in. in diameter for the purpose of ascertaining the position of the buttons in the final covering, FIG. 345. It is important in this operation to work the hair away from the surface of the scrim and, at the same time, to avoid making the hole too large.

Take an example with 1 diamond, 4 buttons. To strike out a diamond $5\frac{1}{2}$in. by 6in. for the back (FIG. 346) the size would be obtained in the same manner (i.e., by setting out tacks in the scrim to the number of buttons required). (1) Strike the vertical line AB; (2) the top line C at right angles; (3) from the line C at a distance of 6in. mark off the line D; (4) mark off $2\frac{3}{4}$in. on either side of the centre to obtain E, G, and $5\frac{1}{2}$in. from E to F; (5) repeat at line D, striking a line crossways to find the centre markings, H, J, K.

The method of striking the size of a diamond applies to any kind of buttoned upholstery work, whether of leather or soft material, unless the dimensions are known beforehand. When the size of a buttoned seat or back is given, the numbers are calculated in the length. For example, to mark the back (FIG. 341), 1 diamond, 3 buttons, would imply 1 button on either side of centre A, or 1 diamond, 4 buttons, as FIG. 346, i.e., 2 each side of centre.

The next step is the cutting and planning of the leather. The most economical way is to cut from patterns (FIG. 348). The patterns are made of stiff brown paper, or buckram.

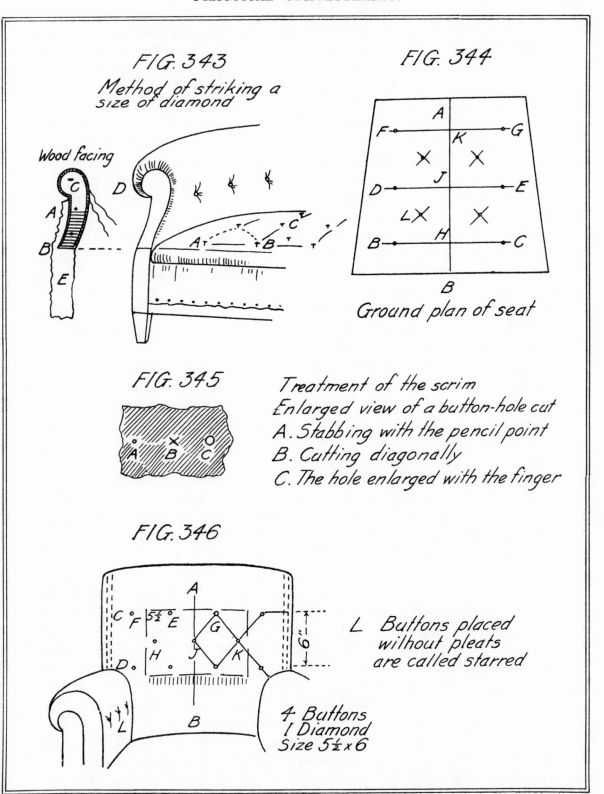

FIG. 343
Method of striking a
size of diamond

Wood facing

FIG. 344

Ground plan of seat

FIG. 345

Treatment of the scrim
Enlarged view of a button-hole cut
A. Stabbing with the pencil point
B. Cutting diagonally
C. The hole enlarged with the finger

FIG. 346

L Buttons placed
without pleats
are called starred

4 Buttons
1 Diamond
Size 5½ x 6

Figs. 347 and 348 show the marking out of a small chair seat as Fig. 216, the size of diamond 6in. by 7in., 1½ diamond, 3 buttons, at the front.   To obtain the shape and rise of the seat it is necessary to increase the size of the diamond; this is termed fulness.   1½in. each way enlarges the diamond to 7½in. by 8½in. on the pattern (Fig. 348), plus the measurement to the top of moulding E to C front, B to A back, F to G, and J to H, the sides.   An additional 1½in. or 2in. should be given to these outside measurements, to allow for the rise caused by the stuffing.   The skin is spread out, and the pattern placed on the surface when adjusted, so that any marks in the skin will not appear in a conspicuous position; fix the pattern at the corners with tacks, and stab the holes with the pritchawl. Useful pieces such as the butt K should be selected when arranging the pattern; the holes in the leather should be strengthened by pasting or glueing small pieces of scrim or linen about 1in. in diameter over each on the reverse side of the leather.   Much pressure when straining a button down will sometimes cause the leather to break away, a very difficult fault to remedy.

Fulness in buttoned work can be gauged to a nicety by a skilled workman; incorrect or bad judgment in this respect will spoil the entire appearance of a job.   As a general rule leather does not require so much as a soft fabric, because the former, being a firmer material, retains its position better than a pliable one such as tapestry or brocade.

A good plan to obtain a fulness calculation from a marking on a first stuffed ground work is to place the tape from one button hole to another, raising to the desired height by placing the hand beneath.   A note should be kept of the fulness given to different sizes of diamonds, also of different kinds of materials; these will be found very useful for comparison and reference, and will often result in the saving of considerable time, especially in repetition work.

To facilitate the working of the leather when manipulating the pleats or folds caused by the fulness, the skin must be creased or ironed, before placing on the work; this may be done in two ways, (1) hammering out, or (2) rubbing the skin on the reverse side with the flat edge of the scissors.   The line of creases is shewn on the pattern, Fig. 348, and the method of creasing, Fig. 349.

At Figs. 342 and 343 a method of finish for a front or side facing is shown.   The facing is cut from white wood or bass wood about ½in. thick, with the edges chamfered; ¼in. tacks should be used when covering.   Facings to fit a concave shape of front, as Fig. 343, are

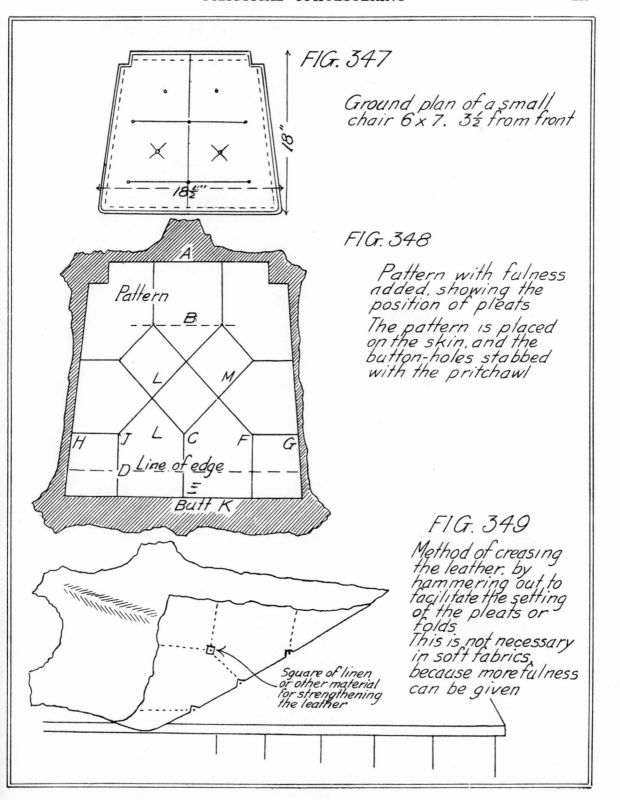

FIG. 347

Ground plan of a small chair 6 x 7. 3½ from front

18"

18½"

FIG. 348

Pattern with fulness added, showing the position of pleats

The pattern is placed on the skin, and the button-holes stabbed with the pritchawl

Pattern

A

B

L   M

H   J   L   C   F   G

Line of edge

D

E

Butt K

FIG. 349

Method of creasing the leather. by hammering out to facilitate the setting of the pleats or folds

This is not necessary in soft fabrics, because more fulness can be given

Square of linen or other material for strengthening the leather

best obtained by a series of saw kerfs, A to B, temporarily nailed on the work, and strengthened by glueing a strip of linen or canvas over the cuts. If the concavity is pronounced, a safer method is to soak the facing for a few hours in water, before fixing. It is sometimes necessary to support the top portion of a facing; this may be done by threading a stout cord through at B, passing through the stuffing and fixing on the underside of arm rail, D. Facings can be generally held in position by means of nails carefully placed on the front, A, B, before tacking finally.

The shaped facing, before it is fixed finally, is covered with leather extending from C to E, a process which will be described later.

CHAPTER 37.

VANDYKING IN LEATHER WORK.

The tools required for the manipulation of buttoned work are few in number. Long, thin needles are necessary in order to allow of a firm grip by the hands after the needle has been passed through the work; the most useful sizes are 10in., 12in., 14in., and 16in. Both large and small regulators are needed, and a pritchawl for stabbing the material after marking out. A T-square and straight edge are also essential.

In large pieces of work, such as chesterfields, settees, etc., the hair frequently becomes displaced while the upholsterer is finding on the groundwork the holes corresponding to those in the covering. A large regulator about 18in. long with a 6in. handle instead of the flat end will be found useful for replacing the stuffing in its original position.

In buttoned work in leather, to a greater extent than in soft fabrics, the main object aimed at is to clean the fulness of the material between the buttons. This fulness is disposed of to some extent when the buttons are slightly strained down ("floating" as it is termed in the trade) by the use of the smooth, flat end of the regulator which is utilised to gather the fulness into a set position forming a pleat or fold, FIG. 356. Before the buttons are drawn down into their permanent positions fulness is visible, and by the use of the large regulator the sunken parts can be filled with stuffing. The careful cleaning of the fulness in diamonds in leather work is essential because slackness surrounding the buttons gives the impression that insufficient stuffing has been used, whereas a clean diamond looks full and well padded. In practice this cleaning presents difficulties, as the material itself, especially leather, will not always respond readily to the regulator, however skilfully manipulated. The skin may be papery or too thick, or the upholsterer may have been at fault in miscalculating the amount of fulness to be given. Insufficient stuffing also causes difficulty when endeavouring to clean or work the diamonds. On the other hand, some moroccos require but little working, the skin being of a nature which responds readily to the regulator. A clean effect in leather work should not be obtained by cramming or plugging the slack places in the leather with stuffing as this generally leads to faulty work, hard in some places, soft in others. Inexperienced

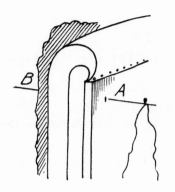

FIG. 350

FIG. 351

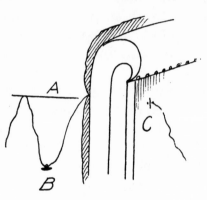

FIG. 352

FIG. 353

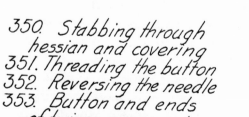

350. Stabbing through
    hessian and covering
351. Threading the button
352. Reversing the needle
353. Button and ends
    of twines prepared
    for drawing into
    position
354. The knot tied and
button in floating
position

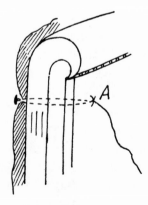

FIG. 354

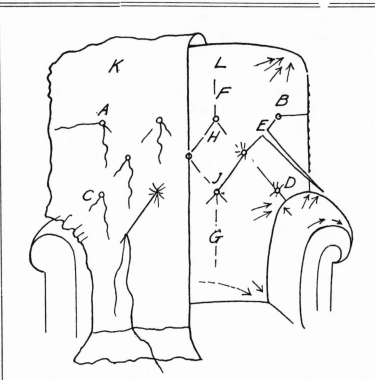

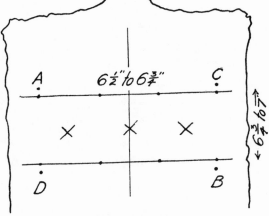

FIG. 356

E. Setting the
fulness into a fold
or pleat
A. left half shewing
the buttons floating
and tied for a
spring back
L. right half shews
buttons drawn down
and tied from the
outside back

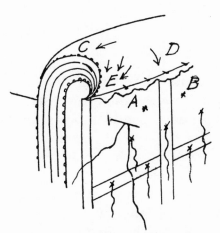

FIG. 355

To clean the top the
fulness is diverged
beneath the back D
The single arrows
indicate where least
strain is required

FIG. 357
Marking the back

To clean the fulness at top
and bottom of back, the
holes are pritchawled
outside the line A. D. C. B
about $\frac{1}{4}$"

A $6\frac{1}{2}$" to $6\frac{3}{4}$"   C

$6\frac{3}{4}$" to 6"

D   B

upholsterers need to be specially warned against this practice. When it is found that the fulness cannot be removed by legitimate means it is better to leave it alone than to risk faulty workmanship by the cramming in of additional material. It must not be inferred that the cleaning of the fulness in leather forms the essence of good upholstery, although incidentally the more skilful the workman the better is he able to manipulate the pleats, and the surer is his judgment as to the amount of fulness required in a covering.

The marking out of both the ground work and covering is most important. An irregular line of buttons at once offends the eye, and lines of pleats, such as those in the back of FIG. 358, if not carefully regulated and set at equal distances give the work an inferior appearance. The cleaning of leather work is frequently obtained at the expense of softness. When a heavy stuffing material is used in connection with buttoned work the clean effect is generally obtained without regard to any degree of softness. Such upholstery looks well but is often deceptive as regards comfort. Hair is the ideal stuffing material for buttoned leather work, but it requires considerably more working than flock. It is therefore clear that a clean piece of work is in itself no guarantee of excellence of workmanship. Rows of buttons set true and even, in conjunction with uniform proportion of the stuffing and a medium softness, together with pleats correctly set, are the chief characteristics to look for in high class work.

Buttons can be obtained in various sizes. Those most generally used for upholstery are known as " twenty-fours," but for small work " twelves " are employed. It is important to see that the shank of a button used for leather work is strong, as a considerable strain and pull is entailed. Exactly how a button is placed in position is shown at FIGS. 350 to 354. A needle 10in. or 12in. long and a length of (buttoning) twine are needed. Stout, thick twine is useless for this work, it must be pliable, free from kinks, so that in travelling through the stuffing material and fabrics in upholstered work it may be drawn from either end with ease. FIG. 350 shows the needle stabbed through about $\frac{1}{4}$in. one side of the mark A to the corresponding hole on the covering B. When the stuffing material is hair the covering of wadding must be broken with the finger sufficiently to allow free passage for the twines. The button A, FIG. 351, is then threaded on the needle. B indicates the end of the twine for tying the knot. The button is passed over the eye on to the single twine, B, FIG. 352, the needle A stabbed through the covering to C, leaving a space between the two twines of about $\frac{3}{4}$in., and drawn through as shown

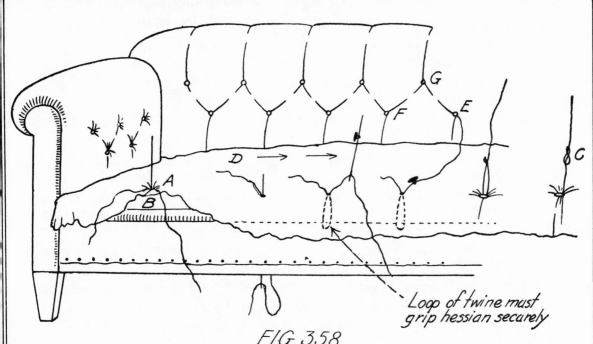

FIG. 358

Method of fixing buttons

The corner buttons and back row
D are placed first. Successive
stages in the placing of a button
are shewn

Loop of twine must
grip hessian securely

FIG. 359

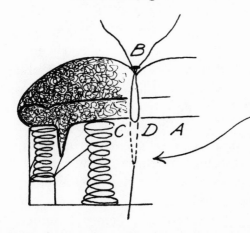

Section of seat shewing
the position of twine

A. The spring hessian
B. The button
The dotted line shews
the passage of the needle
When the point of the needle
is clear of C. a space of 1"
must be allowed before
stabbing through at D

at Fig. 353, A and B. The two ends may now be pulled taut, but before this is done they should be run backward and forward several times to make sure that the twine responds easily and freely before tying the knot, A, Fig. 354. Such a knot as was shown at Fig. 113 is made having a short and a long end of $1\frac{1}{2}$in. and 6in. or 7in. respectively. The long end is required for the gradual pulling of the button into its place from the floating position shown in the left half of the example at Fig. 356 to the final position. The appearance of a back with the ends "tied off" is shown at Fig. 355, A and B. When strained down to the desired position an ordinary slip knot is formed and the two ends cut off, Fig. 358, C. In such an example as is shown at Fig. 356 or backs of similar style, the corner buttons should be placed first, A, B, C, and D, because when this is done the stuffing is not so liable to become displaced. The buttons must not immediately be drawn down tightly, but left in a floating position as shown on the left-hand side of the sketch. The drawing down process should be commenced by pulling the twines gradually, the outside buttons A, C, and B and D, a little deeper than the centre ones. While this is being done the fulness of the leather will assert itself in the shape of wrinkles which must be gathered up into a fold or pleat by means of the flat end of the regulator E. Much depends on these pleats. When placed regularly and evenly they are pleasing in appearance; any displacement of the stuffing can be adjusted with advantage from the outside back with the pointed end of the regulator. The head F, and the bottom swell G, are cleaned, instead of forming pleats at top and bottom as previously described. This does away with the necessity of drawing the leather too taut. The single arrow in the sketch indicates where the minimum strain is required. In addition to creasing the leather, as already described, it is helpful to hammer out the pleats on the reverse side. This is best done on a flat stone slab or very smooth hardwood. The fold of the leather is beaten out on the line of crease, care being taken to ensure that the pleat is placed in the correct position (downwards) and downwards from the buttons H and J, and the leather is strained on either side. It will be obvious that the fulness caused by the increased size of the diamond on the covering requires careful manipulation. Fig. 355 shows where it may be tacked to the best advantage, and the arrows indicate where the greatest strain is required. To avoid making the head too firm a little fulness should be allowed at C and disposed equally when cutting before hammering. In cleaning the tops and bottoms of backs much also depends on the

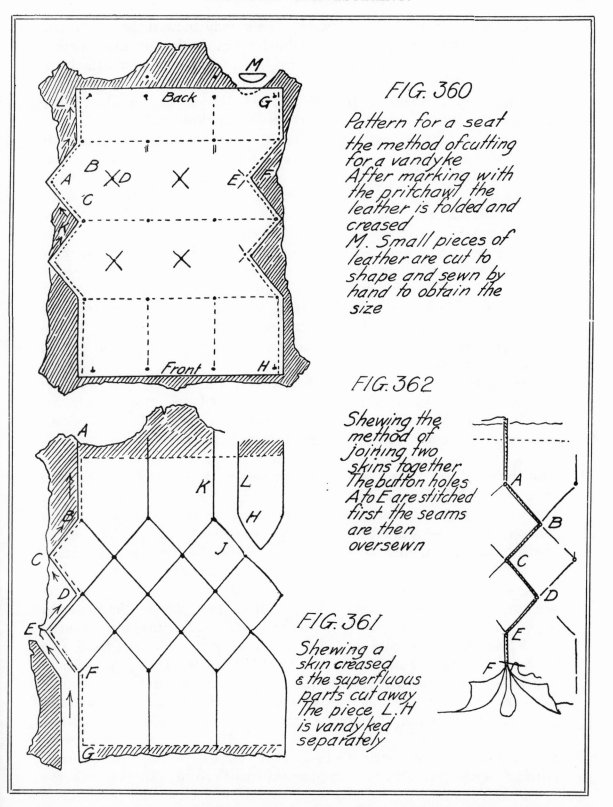

FIG. 360

Pattern for a seat the method of cutting for a vandyke
After marking with the pritchawl the leather is folded and creased
M. Small pieces of leather are cut to shape and sewn by hand to obtain the size

FIG. 362

Shewing the method of joining two skins together
The button holes A to E are stitched first the seams are then oversewn

FIG. 361

Shewing a skin creased & the superfluous parts cut away
The piece L.H is vandyked separately

marking out, but there are so many factors which must be taken into account that success cannot be attained without considerable practice. A back such as FIG. 356 upholstered in a pliable, medium-thickness skin if marked on the ground work 6in. by 6½in. would need a minimum of fulness up and down ¼in. to ½in. and ½in. or ¾in. in the width. The position for the buttonholes is shown at FIG. 357.

The buttoning of seats is similar to that of backs, differing only in the method of placing the needle, which is generally a long one, 14in. or 16in., according to the depth of the seat. The eye of the needle, FIG. 358, A, is stabbed through first. The position of the buttonhole is found by placing the hand beneath the stuffing B. When the point of the needle is clear of the hessian it must grip not less than ¾in., see section, FIG. 359, A. Considerable care must be exercised when buttoning seats to avoid the entanglement of the twines with the coils of the springs. After the buttons are drawn "home" a slip knot C is run down close to the button, the two ends cut off and tucked beneath the button with the flat end of the regulator. The back (half diamond) if sprung would be treated exactly as the seat.

Patterns are necessary for buttoned leather work, see Chapter 36, and where two or three skins are required for a seat they are vandyked, a term which is derived from the serrated edge of the pattern when cut. FIG. 360 shows a pattern cut for the seat of FIG. 358 and placed on a skin. Any marks or blemishes in the skin must be cut out if very pronounced or if of a minor character should be hidden in a line of a pleat. It will be seen that the button A cannot be obtained; a piece of leather the size of the diamond would be vandyked to the following button D. The position for the pattern having been found it should be temporarily tacked to the skin and the holes stabbed with a pritchawl. After removing the pattern and before creasing, the superfluous parts of the leather are cut way commencing at G to K and L, FIG. 361, in the direction of the arrow, tapering the cuts slightly when near the button hole, see F; about ⅜in. should be allowed for sewing. The left-hand side of FIG. 361 when vandyked to the right-hand side of FIG. 360, would appear as a continuous piece of leather when buttoned to a seat, the folds of the pleat covering the join so that if the skins are uniform in colour the vandyke cannot be detected without raising the pleats. The method of sewing the vandyke is similar to that of the welt, i.e., oversewn. The button holes, FIG. 362, A to E, are securely stitched with fine thread, leaving sufficient room for inserting the

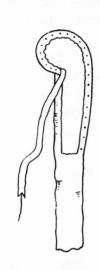

FIG. 363

Leather tacked
with ¼" tacks
on the reverse
side of a wood
facing

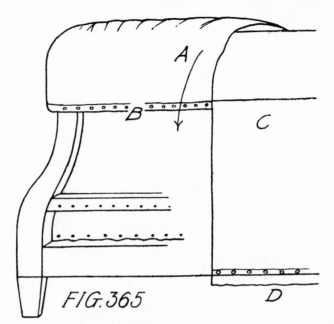

FIG. 365

METHOD OF BACK-TACKING
A. The reverse side of outside arm
B. A strip of buckram
C. The neat appearance. when
   pulled over, no tacks visible
D. This portion is tacked beneath
   the frame and covered with
   a bottom hessian

FIG. 366

Grooved semi-circular
piece of brass filled
with lead
Small panel pins
inserted at intervals
as required

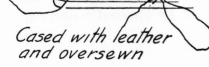

Cased with leather
and oversewn

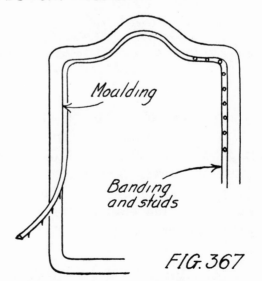

Moulding

Banding
and studs

FIG. 367

needle. Fig. 363 shows the reverse side of a wood facing prepared to fix in position at D, Fig. 364. The method of back tacking is shown at Fig. 365. The leather is tacked temporarily on the edge of the reverse side A. A strip of buckram or a double fold of a hessian lining is tacked so that the covering B when strained over presents a neat appearance. This form of tacking for outsides is also economical, trimming being unnecessary.

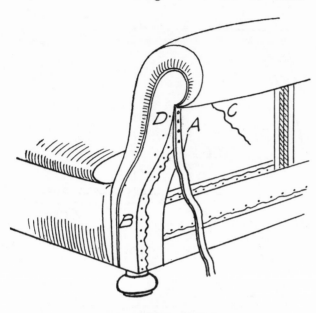

FIG. 364

A. Continuation of welt
B. This part of leather back-tacked
C. Cord to hold the wood facing in position
D. When the facing is fitted nails are placed on the outer edges

Although banding and studs is the finish generally used for leather work there is nothing to compare with a leather covered moulding, Fig. 366. Unfortunately the expense of this frequently militates against its use. The upholsterer does not as a rule attempt to fix this form of finish, the makers of the moulding usually doing it themselves. In comparison with a moulding the disadvantage of studs used in conjunction with banding is that owing to their projection they show signs of wear earlier than the rest of the work. There are several kinds of oxidised nails made of superior appearance which are more durable than leather studs when used with banding. At Fig. 367 is shown a chair back which indicates the difficulty of manipulating banding and studs to fit the various curves. A moulding covered as already described is a far neater and more suitable finish. In order to avoid breaking the face of the leather in driving leather covered studs the head of the hammer should be covered with a piece of stout leather.

CHAPTER 38.

CHARACTERISTICS OF STUFFING MATERIALS.

Materials of various kinds are used as stuffings for upholstery, either singly or in combination, and the upholsterer should make himself acquainted with their characteristics and uses in first and second stuffing. As has already been mentioned, hair is the ideal stuffing material from every point of view. Its value lies in its resiliency. It is unnecessary in the first stuffing to use hair of too good a quality (unless extra soft upholstery is specified) because owing to the various stitchings required to produce the edge, a short, loose hair is preferable and stitches better than long hair. The less expensive qualities are known in the trade as common hair, and these are generally used for the first stuffing of upholstery.

ALL HAIR.

Upholstery that is first and second stuffed complete with hair is known as "all hair." This term is used to distinguish such work from "part hair" and "hair stuffed" work. A chair first stuffed with fibre or wood-wool and second stuffed with hair is correctly described as "part hair" or "hair stuffed," but it is incorrect to state that it is "all hair." In the broad sense, materials other than hair are only substitutes for it. Upholstery of the highest class should be stuffed with hair throughout, and the work will then retain its shape and buoyancy for a longer period than if hair is used in combination with other materials.

PART HAIR.

This term implies that the first stuffing consists of any material but hair, which, in part hair work, is used for second stuffing only, or as a casing over some other stuffing. The term is of various application, and may stand for any of the following combinations :—

First stuffed, fibre ; second stuffed, hair.

First stuffed, fibre ; second stuffed, hair, seat only (arms and back of flock).

First stuffed, fibre ; second stuffed, flock and hair.

In some manufacturing houses the term implies that fibre is used for the first stuffing, and hair of no specified quality used entirely for the second stuffing. " Part hair" upholstery is an excellent combination, and the next best grade to all hair work.

Black Fibre and Hair.

Fibre dyed black resembles hair, but does not possess the same buoyancy. It is a very serviceable material for first stuffing but not for second stuffing. Upholstery first stuffed with fibre and second stuffed with hair should be described as " part hair," it is not correct to describe such a combination of materials as " all hair."

Green Fibre and Hair.

Green fibre varies somewhat in texture. When fine it is an excellent substitute for hair, but the coarser varieties are not so satisfactory from the upholsterer's point of view. A first stuffing of fine green fibre produces firm edges. The upholsterer who wishes to produce good work must exercise care in the selection of the green fibre he uses as uneven edges are frequent when a fibre which is too coarse is employed. Upholstery with a second stuffing of hair on a first stuffing of the best grade of green fibre is almost equal to " all hair" work.

Fibre and Cased Hair.

This term indicates a first stuffing of fibre throughout, and a second stuffing consisting of (1) flock and hair or (2) fine quality Algerian fibre in combination with hair, a layer of which is spread over the fibre. If a good, white flock is used, upholstery finished in this way is very durable; but inferior flocks that are seedy or lumpy are not satisfactory, as however carefully the upholsterer may finish the work it soon develops faults, because when the material becomes dead and lifeless the outer covering sags, and consequently the stuffing material becomes displaced. The term " cased hair" occasionally gives rise to misunderstandings, for it will be obvious that when a maker desires to produce an inexpensive article there is a tendency to use the maximum amount of flock or fibre and the minimum of hair.

From a practical point of view, a layer of hair spread on the flock produces a more even surface in the finished work because of the tendency of flock to become seedy or lumpy; unless cased with

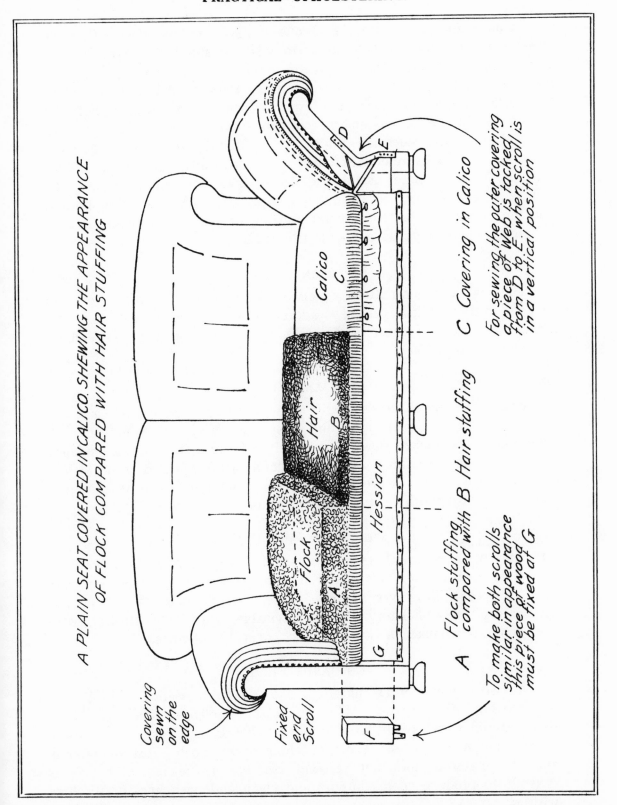

A PLAIN SEAT COVERED IN CALICO, SHEWING THE APPEARANCE OF FLOCK COMPARED WITH HAIR STUFFING

A Flock stuffing, compared with B Hair stuffing   C Covering in Calico

Covering Sewn on the edge

Fixed end Scroll

For sewing the outer covering a piece of Web is tacked from D to E, when scroll is in a vertical position

To make both scrolls similar in appearance this piece of wood must be fixed at G

hair, this defect is noticeable through the outer covering. On the other hand, the customer is liable to misunderstand the term "cased hair," and to imagine that a greater quantity of hair is used in the composition of upholstery described thus than is actually the case. The term frequently leads to disputes when renovating upholstery stuffed in this way; customers complain that the hair has not been replaced, and the salesman finds some difficulty in convincing them that only a small amount of hair was originally used. In second stuffing, fibre is more useful for backs than for seats because the tacks are not subject to so much compression. It does not possess sufficient resiliency for the second stuffing of seats, and tends in time to lose its buoyancy; as a result, the covering may sag.

FIBRE AND FLOCK.

This is a combination which is largely used; and, provided that a fairly thick layer of wadding is placed over the flock, it makes one of the most serviceable forms of stuffing for medium class or cheap work.

ALVA AND FLOCK.

From the upholsterer's point of view, alva produces a smoother edge than hair. It is light and easy to work. Alva for stitched edges should be tacked down very firmly; if too soft, it has a tendency to sag. It is sometimes used for second stuffing cased over with a thick layer of flock. A great merit of this material lies in its immunity from attack by moth. It should never be used damp.

WOOD-WOOL AND FLOCK.

Wood-wool is now extensively used for some classes of upholstery. The finer qualities of this material produce excellent edges, but like alva it needs filling very firmly. The coarser qualities are not so satisfactory for upholstery. It is advisable when first stuffing with this material to place a layer of flock over the springs.

COCOANUT FIBRE.

As with many other materials used for upholstering the quality of cocoanut fibre varies. The practical upholsterer does not view this material with favour, as it is hard to work, and takes considerable time to loosen and open. When stitching edges much effort is required, and the material does not respond readily to the regulator. It is difficult to produce good contours and clean and even lines of stitching with it.

Down and Feathers.

Down and feathers are employed for filling the loose cushions and pillows used in some classes of upholstery in combination with a hair-stuffed foundation. Waste is likely to occur if these fillings are used indiscriminately in the workshop, and this is best avoided by setting apart a special room for down and feather work. If the feathers are too coarse the stalks will soon work through the outer coverings unless the cushion case is made of a stout fabric such as a swansdown or other specially prepared material. The practice of rubbing a layer of soap on an unsuitable fabric is useless. The ideal cover for an inside case (but a very expensive one) is kid. The skins are, as a rule, small, and many of them are needed to cover a cushion of moderate size; the charge for labour is, therefore, a heavy one. In a previous chapter on " Cutting," the method of case-making for cushions has been described. The most general fault with down and feather cushions for upholstery is that they are made too firm. The inside case is bound closely in addition to the outer cover, and this renders the cushion to some degree airtight. This must be taken into consideration when filling. A cushion moderately filled responding freely to the touch before sewing will produce suitable firmness when enclosed in the outer covering. An upholstered seat that is to be fitted with loose cushions should be stuffed proportionately and its surface must be flat, rising slightly at the front edge in order that the cushion will set snugly and not become displaced.

Kapoc.

This vegetable down is used extensively for upholstery. In comparison with hair it has a tendency to lose its buoyancy under compression, but a good quality kapoc soon recovers its natural resiliency when beaten or well shaken. Complaints made by customers with regard to kapoc filled cushions are very often due to their own neglect, as a cushion filled with this material should be frequently shaken up in exactly the same way as are the pillows when beds are made. A kapoc seat or back cushion will respond to such treatment and keep its shape well. Kapoc is used in a variety of ways in upholstering. It serves as an excellent substitute for wadding as a covering for either hair or flock. In combination with fibre it may be used freely in backs and arms. The filling of cushions with kapoc is economical compared with down or feathers. A kapoc filled cushion should be firm to the touch; if filled too lightly it has a tendency, especially in the cheaper qualities, to become lumpy. It is not advisable to second stuff entirely with kapoc, but it may be used with advantage in connection with a more. heavy stuffing.

Wadding.

Wadding is used in upholstery as a covering for flock and hair. If the flock is of good quality and not seedy or lumpy the wadding may be dispensed with ; but in connection with hair a covering of wadding is essential in order to obtain a clean, even surface for the outer covering, and to prevent the hair working through the fabric. Wadding is also useful for covering edges, especially if they are filled with coarse fibres. Upholstery that is second stuffed with an under-lining of calico has a layer of wadding placed between it and the final outer covering

SLIP COVERS (LOOSE COVERS).

HOW TO CUT AND MAKE THEM.

CHAPTER 1.

It is estimated that the cutting of loose covers is understood by only about 10 per cent. of upholsterers. Nine out of every ten workmen, if requested to cut a cover for any particular piece of work they were finishing, would probably decline on account of lack of knowledge of the subject. It is the cutting of the various stiles or blocks in such work which the beginner fears to undertake, though why this should be so is not quite clear, for the competent upholsterer should fully understand it. There was a time when loose cover cutting was paid for at a lower rate than stuffing, but as far as remuneration is concerned there is now no disadvantage, as case cutting and the stuffing is paid for at a uniform rate. If the upholsterer is content to limit himself to the stuffing he thereby restricts himself to working inside a factory, for loose case cutting is essentially outdoor work. The cutter has first to take his material to the customer's house, plan and cut out the necessary covers, and then hand over the work to a machinist to be made up in accordance with his particulars and measurements. The man, therefore, who is capable of cutting covers has more variety in his work, and is also able to fill up the slack time which, as far as the upholstery trade is concerned, occurs regularly at certain seasons of the year. It is possible that one of the reasons why upholsterers do not readily take up loose case cutting is because they have to shoulder the responsibility for the satisfactory fit of the covers after they leave the hands of the machinist. A good machinist is invaluable to a cutter, as she soon gets to understand his particular style of cutting and other technical details, thus saving unnecessary explanations. Another reason why upholsterers do not enter this branch of the trade is that loose case cutting is generally associated with the more complicated art of drapery cutting. Loose covers are becoming increasingly popular, and the fine fabrics now used for upholstery make protective covers of some kind imperative.

It is hoped that these detailed instructions and explanatory diagrams will give every upholsterer the necessary knowledge and confidence to enable him to undertake this interesting and remunerative branch of the trade.

There are two kinds of covers used for upholstery: (1) the loose cover, (2) the dust cover. The difference between these is that

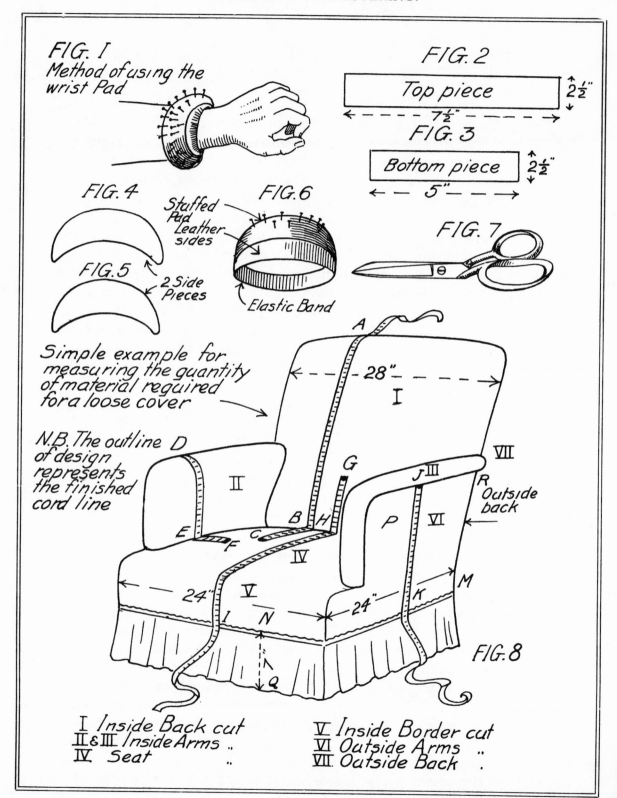

FIG. 1
Method of using the wrist Pad

FIG. 2
Top piece   2½"
7½"

FIG. 3
Bottom piece   2½"
5"

FIG. 4

FIG. 5   2 Side Pieces

FIG. 6
Stuffed Pad
Leather sides
Elastic Band

FIG. 7

Simple example for measuring the quantity of material required for a loose cover

N.B. The outline D of design represents the finished cord line

28"
I
VII
G
J III
R
Outside back
II
P
VI
B H
E
F C
IV
24"
V
24"
M
K
I
N
Q

FIG. 8

I   Inside Back cut   V   Inside Border cut
II & III Inside Arms   VI   Outside Arms   "
IV   Seat   "   VII   Outside Back   "

the loose cover requires careful fitting, while the dust cover is cut roughly to the shape of the work, and could not be used for the same purpose as a loose cover. Dust covers are usually made up of plain fabrics, such as hollands or linings, and cut to the floor so that the piece of furniture is entirely hidden. Dust covers are essential in connection with upholstery work that is used only at certain seasons and for use during the period of annual cleaning. Tapestries, silks, and other coverings soon become shabby if constantly exposed and not used. Loose case making is essentially women's work, consisting as it does of the using of pins, the cutting of darts, the manipulation of pleats, folds, and fulness. In connection with loose covers, terms associated with dressmaking, such as collars, gussets, frills and flounces are frequently used.

Before actually cutting loose covers, the upholsterer must ascertain by correct measurements the number of yards of material required for any particular piece of work. Measurements are taken with a tape measure, which is indispensable to the loose case cutter. As far as tools are concerned they are few in comparison with those required by the upholsterer. They are enumerated below :—

A sharp pair of scissors is indispensable. Those of French pattern, FIG. 7, are to be preferred because the blades are light, and the shape of the hand holes fits the thumb and fingers so that no inconvenience is felt even after hours of cutting. A pair of scissors of the ordinary type is useful for intermittent cutting.

A wrist pad for pins, shown at FIGS. 1, 2, 3, 4, 5 and 6 is an easily-made article.

A tape measure with brass ends should be used. It should be of good width, with bold and distinct numbers.

Pins for the temporary joining of the material should not be too large or clumsy, as a great variety of shapes, corners and out-of-the-way cuts will have to be pinned. The pins should be stout rather than fine, and about 1⅛in. in length.

A yard stick completes the list of tools which the loose case cutter requires.

FIG. 1 is a diagram of the pad so placed on the wrist that the pins in it are within easy access whatever portion of the work is being manipulated. Such a pad saves much time, and is indispensable for a cutter. FIG. 2 is a strip of any strong soft material. FIGS. 4 and 5 are the side pieces cut crescent shape, and FIG. 3 the bottom piece; 3, 4 and 5 are preferably of leather. The fitting of these together, as shown at FIG. 6, need not be described in detail, but it should be mentioned that hair makes the best filling for the wrist pad. Fabrics used for the making of loose covers are usually soft and pliable, such as cretonnes, linings, hollands, chintzes, printed linens, etc., and as these vary in width particulars must be ascertained in order to obtain correct calculations.

A beginner should first attempt the simplest style of chair, such as is shown at Fig. 8. This is devoid of borders, facings, and scrolls, and consists of straight cuts without any additional pieces being required other than those cut off the length of material. Assuming the material to be a cretonne, a single width measures about 32in.

The names by which the different cuts are distinguished are numbered I.-VII. at Fig. 8. In this particular design No. V. cut is omitted because the seat and borders are in one continuous piece forming what is known as a pull-over seat. The tuck-away of a loose cover is very important. When a cover is fitted the part known as the tuck-away is invisible, being tucked in between the seat and arms and between the seat and inside back. This serves a double purpose: (1) it keeps the cover taut; (2) the material range of the arms and back being joined to the seat the pattern may be set in correct position. The size of tuck-aways is important. If too small, the compression when the chair is used will cause the cover to become displaced and unsightly. If too large the material cannot be dispensed with without much juggling with the cover.

Before commencing to take measurements, a survey of the style of the chair is made, and the width of the material must be compared with the widest parts to be covered to ascertain if extensions are necessary. Extensions are the pieces added to the material by seaming in order to increase its width, and at certain parts the pattern requires matching, otherwise the appearance will be patchy and unsightly. Such extensions to be seamed must be noted. This is important when taking measurements, and guess work will not do. A number of pieces of material of the necessary size for making extensions may be available but be useless for the purpose on account of difficulties in matching the pattern. For example, a cretonne 32in. wide placed on a piece of work measuring 40in. requires extensions on both sides to be matched and so form the full width. In work of large dimensions extensions are numerous, especially if the material is a narrow one. At this juncture it should be pointed out that seams in materials are a bugbear to the cutter and also to a critical customer, who may have approved of the material in its uncut state, but regards it as unsatisfactory because of the seams when it is made

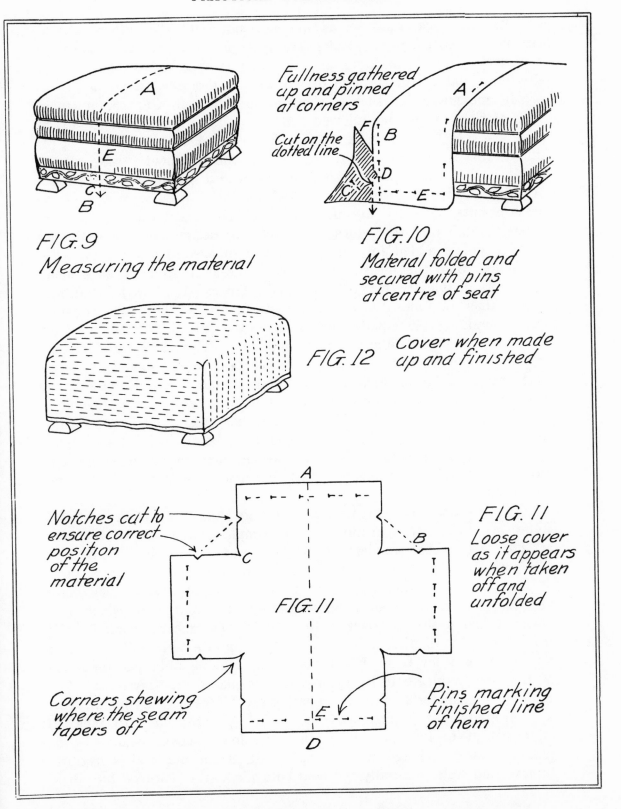

FIG. 9
Measuring the material

Fullness gathered
up and pinned
at corners

Cut on the
dotted line

FIG. 10
Material folded and
secured with pins
at centre of seat

FIG. 12   Cover when made
up and finished

Notches cut to
ensure correct
position
of the
material

FIG. 11

FIG. 11
Loose cover
as it appears
when taken
off and
unfolded

Corners shewing
where the seam
tapers off

Pins marking
finished line
of hem

up. In some materials seams are not noticeable, in others almost invisible. Unsatisfactory results are generally due to a combination of a narrow width material and a design which seams badly. The selection of fabrics of suitable design will be described later.

In measuring for such a chair as is shown in FIG. 8, a tuck-away of 6in. should be allowed, as shown at inside arm E to F, inside back B to C, seat H to G. From D, A and J to the top of frill K 1in. should be added to the net measurement. Care should be taken that the tape is placed at the widest portion of the surface for insides. It must be remembered in this first example that no measurements of width are necessary, it being assumed that a 32in. material will çover the widest parts of the design. For the flounce N to Q 3in. is added for turnings to the finished depth of 7in. For the fulness take the measurement round the base from M back again to M and double it; in no case should the extra allowed for fulness be less than $1\frac{1}{2}$ times the length round the base. The base measures 96in. round, which equals three times the width of the material. To get the requisite fulness this should be doubled, and we, therefore, arrive at six widths of 10in. deep. Unavoidable waste sometimes occurs when using a fabric with a large design, but the odd pieces can generally be used by a skilful cutter. It must also be remembered in taking measurements that additional material must be allowed for the welting; on some occasions odd pieces may be used for this purpose, but where from the nature of the various cuts to be made no such pieces are available provision must be made for the welting when measuring.

The methods of cutting loose covers vary with the different styles of work. An example of a simple slip-on cover is shown at FIG. 12. The simplest form is here shown, as the beginner will gain experience and confidence by first attempting small pieces of work, making covers for them in the different styles. The sketch at FIG. 9 is a footstool measuring 14in. by 10in., for which it is assumed that a slip-on cover is to be cut. The measurement is taken from the base of the frame C to the opposite side, allowing $1\frac{1}{2}$in. for hemming from C to B on all sides. Having obtained the centre of the stool, indicate it by means of pins placed lengthwise at A and E. Cut the material, fold it in half, place the fold exactly in the centre as indicated by the pins, and secure in this position with pins. It is important to fix securely so that the folded cover cannot be displaced. After making sure that each side of the material is free from fulness and sets naturally without dragging, the corners are drawn

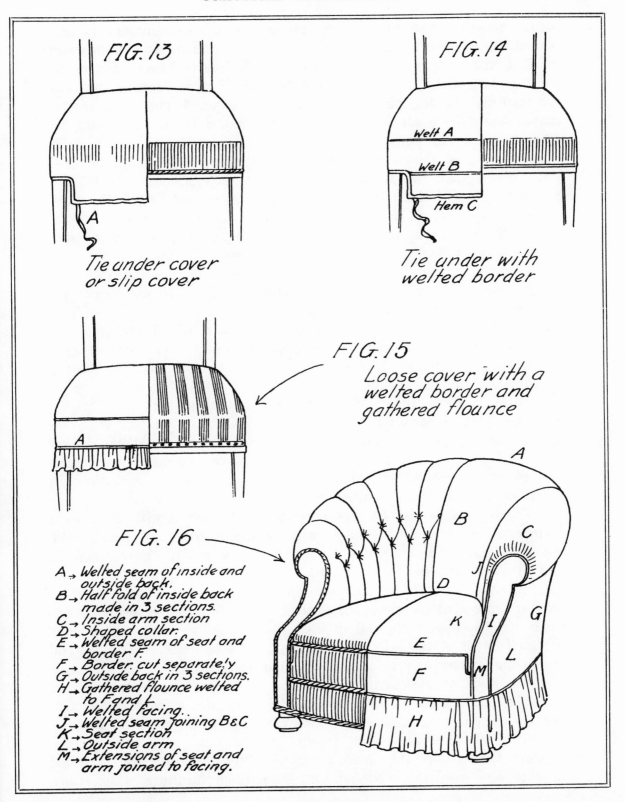

FIG. 13

A

Tie under cover
or slip cover

FIG. 14

Welt A

Welt B

Hem C

Tie under with
welted border

FIG. 15

A

Loose cover with a
welted border and
gathered flounce

FIG. 16

A → Welted seam of inside and
     outside back.
B → Half fold of inside back
     made in 3 sections.
C → Inside arm section
D → Shaped collar.
E → Welted seam of seat and
     border F.
F → Border. cut separately
G → Outside back in 3 sections.
H → Gathered flounce welted
     to F and L
I → Welted facing.
J → Welted seam joining B & C
K → Seat section
L → Outside arm
M → Extensions of seat and
     arm joined to facing.

lightly together and temporarily pinned at C. The corner is then pinned closely, working from the centre D upwards and downwards. At E a row of pins will denote the finished line of hem. To cut the corners start with the scissors from the top F, first making sure that the material is not pinned too tightly. A small notch of triangle shape should be made at D to guide the machinist when making up. The cover when unfolded will now appear as at FIG. 11. The triangle notches should not be cut too deeply, and should be of a lesser depth than the amount taken up in the seaming. A, D (FIG. 11) is the line of the fold, B the triangle-shaped notches, C the acute angle at the corners, E the line of hem. When made up the cover should fit as shown at FIG. 12. Before attempting any description of the more complicated designs, the beginner is advised to study the examples of different styles shown at FIGS. 13, 14, and 15. FIG. 13 is called a tie-on or slip cover. The material is in one piece, and cut to allow a margin of 2in. or 3in. underneath the seat. Two tapes are attached at each corner, and these are tied round the legs and hold the cover in position. Covers such as these are not very elegant, and even if cut by an experienced man have a somewhat amateurish appearance.

At FIG. 14 a tie-on cover is shown with a border, which at once gives it a superior finish. The reason for this is that the fulness can be cleaned, and if this does not serve to remove it that which remains can be equalised by means of the separate border. The top A is welted. The border can be made in one piece from A to C, or divided by a further welt at B.

The style shown at FIG. 15 is welted and finished with a gathered flounce. Covers such as these, when correctly cut and well fitted, are very dainty and neat. Tapes are necessary at the corners A, and are tied underneath, as noted when describing FIGS. 13 and 14. At FIG. 16 this style is shown adapted for an easy chair. Various cuts are indicated by means of letters. In a loose cover such as this tapes are dispensed with, and in their place hooks and eyes, or buttons, are used either at the sides G or centre of outside back. The method of cutting a loose cover for such a chair is described later.

The style of loose cover illustrated at FIG. 17 is known as the box pleated flounce. To be effective it requires a careful selection of the material of which the loose cover is to be made. It is a favourite in connection with chintz, as the nature of the material displays the folds of the pleats advantageously. Loose covers finished in this way are more suitable for dining-room furniture, while frilled

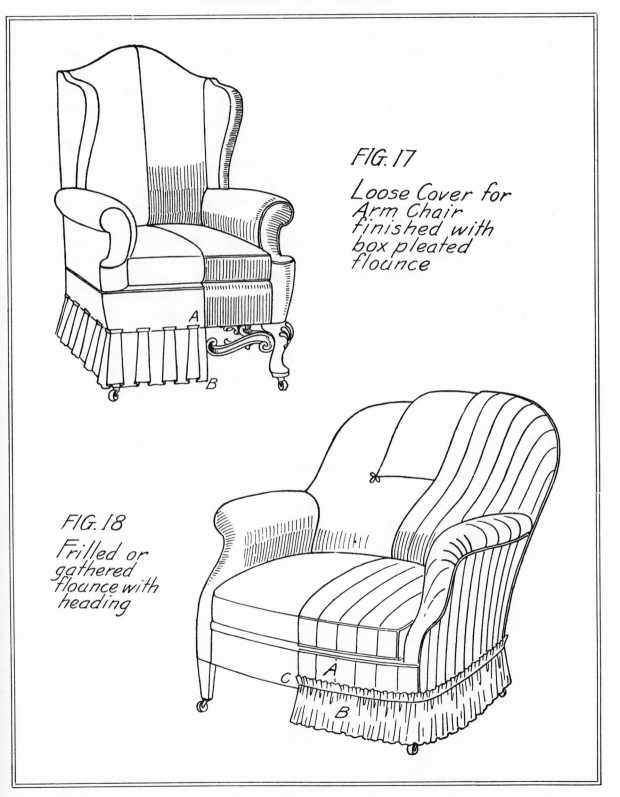

FIG. 17

Loose Cover for
Arm Chair
finished with
box pleated
flounce

FIG. 18

Frilled or
gathered
flounce with
heading

borders are more general for use in drawing rooms. The depth
of such borders is governed by the design and the height of the edge,
but in this particular finish a deep flounce looks better than a narrow
one, and for medium size easy-chairs it should not be less than $7\frac{1}{2}$in.
from the heading A to the hem B. Flimsy material is unsuitable
for box pleating, as the folds, even if carefully ironed, soon become
displaced. Where the upholsterer is called upon to advise he should
consider the interior of the room as a whole in connection with the
number of covers to be cut in the same pattern. The effect of box-
pleated flounces is too square and heavy if a great number of pieces
of upholstery in one room is treated in this way. Further, the
box pleat finish is not so satisfactory in appearance on concave or
convex shapes, showing to much better advantage on large, straight
work such as the fronts of settees, box ottomans and lounges. The
measurements of FIG. 17 will be referred to in a subsequent chapter.
The illustration at FIG. 18 shows a loose cover finished with a frilled
or gathered flounce with a heading, the border A and the flounce
B being welted together. The flounce is gathered at C about 1in.
or $1\frac{1}{2}$in. from the top in order to form an independent heading of the
material. This style is neat and satisfactory in appearance. If it
has a disadvantage it is that unless the material used is a stout one
the heading tends to become displaced. There are further variations
of the above styles which are cut in a similar way but differ in
making up. These will be described subsequently.

CHAPTER 2.

THE MAKING OF DARTS.

In order to follow intelligently the instructions given in subsequent chapters the reader should acquaint himself with the various technical terms used in describing the different cuts and parts of a loose cover. The similarity of many of the terms with those used in dressmaking has already been noted—fulness, gusset, and dart being instances of this.

Fulness in the making of a loose cover is more difficult to deal with than in upholstery. The upholsterer may strain his material taut to equalise or clean the surplus material, and then tack it to keep it in position, but with a loose cover this is not possible; it must be so cut and manipulated that it will lie correctly. Fulness occurs on the most simple style of loose cover, and the skill of a cutter is apparent not so much in measuring and planning as in the methods by which he disposes of the slackness or fulness which forms on various parts of a loose cover. There are several ways in which fulness in loose covers may be disposed of: the upholsterer should study them carefully, as they differ radically from those to which he is accustomed when treating fulness in fixed coverings.

In loose covers fulness must be either (1) gathered in the form of frills; (2) folded into pleats; (3) cut out; (4) equalised.

Before coming to a decision as to the best method to employ for any particular part of the work, the following points must be considered :—(1) the nature of the material; (2) the amount of fulness to be regulated. Some materials cause the cutter more difficulty than others. Chintz in particular may be mentioned. Fulness in a material such as this is far more difficult to deal with than in a soft cretonne. Material of a texture that folds easily and naturally into pleats, or that can be gathered up into a series of frills, is best left uncut; on the other hand, when dealing with a stiff fabric the fulness may be best disposed of by cutting away and forming what are known as darts, which derive their name from the appearance of the cuts when sewn and pressed. When there is a large amount of fulness to be disposed of the formation of darts is advisable, but as the operation requires considerable skill in order to ensure that the darts set naturally the beginner is advised to make his first attempts by pleating or equalising the fulness.

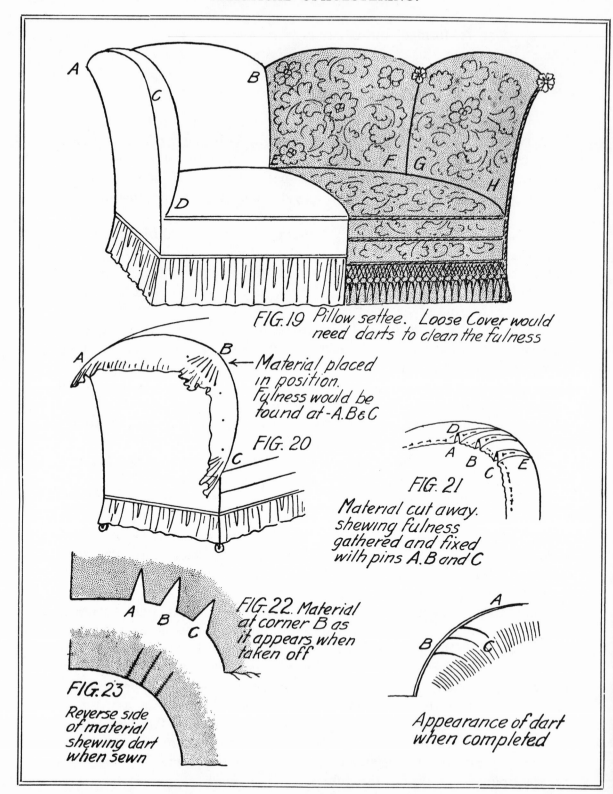

FIG. 19 Pillow settee. Loose Cover would need darts to clean the fulness

B ← Material placed in position. Fulness would be found at - A.B & C

FIG. 20

FIG. 21

Material cut away. shewing fulness gathered and fixed with pins A. B and C

FIG. 22. Material at corner B as it appears when taken off

FIG. 23

Reverse side of material shewing dart when sewn

Appearance of dart when completed

A dart is formed by cutting away the fulness of parts of the material, and sewing the edges to a fine tapered point. It is chiefly on semi-circular or crescent-shaped work that fulness occurs to such an extent as to ruin the appearance of the work unless it is carefully cleaned. The crescent-shaped settee, Fig. 19, is a piece of upholstery in connection with which, when making up a loose cover, the formation of a series of darts would be advantageous. At all the parts A/H fulness would be encountered, and it would be more pronounced at A, B, C, and D than at the lower part E/H. As already mentioned, the nature of the material is an important consideration before deciding which method to employ to clean the fulness. Its tractability or otherwise may be tested by slightly straining the cover at one of the corners. If it responds, and the slackness disperses or cleans itself, equalisation of the fulness will be the best method to follow. If, on the other hand, the fulness is pronounced, and when cleaned in one part merely makes itself apparent in another, better results are obtained by cutting a series of darts. Fig. 20 is a diagram showing the material laid loosely over the work, and it will be found that fulness will gather at the points A, B, and C. At Fig. 21 the darts have been formed and pinned together preparatory to cutting off, and D and E on either side of the darts have been cleaned by the treatment. Fig. 22 is an enlarged view of the appearance of the material taken off and spread out. The edges at A, B, and C are sewn together, and the reverse side, after the sewing has been done, is shown at Fig. 23. At Fig. 24 the completed cover is placed in position, and the darts tapering to a fine point are indicated. Some expert machinists are very skilful in the making of such darts, and the sewing can be so beautifully done that the vanishing point is scarcely discernible. This gradual dying away is what should be aimed at in this method of cleaning fulness.

CHAPTER 3.

HOW TO FORM GUSSETS.

Fulness can be disposed of with advantage by the cutting of darts at the parts indicated on FIGS. 24 to 26. Show-wood furniture lends itself particularly to this method, because of the many projections of the wood not met with in stuffovers. Although this way of cleaning the fulness by cutting out has many advantages, it is not wise to form too many darts, because the joins in the material cannot be treated in the same way as welts, that is, by oversewing to prevent the material fraying at the edges. It is very necessary for all the seams of loose covers to be strongly sewn, because they are cleaned at frequent intervals and the material thereby subjected to much strain; as a result seams loosely or carelessly sewn soon become faulty.

The gussets of a loose cover are triangular pieces of material inserted in cuts made to take them. They are used for two reasons: (1) To increase the angle; (2) for additional strength. A gusset is sometimes called a gore, but the former is the more usual term among upholsterers. Gussets are very helpful at those parts of a loose cover where the material falls short in but a slight degree, and also in cases where a number of pieces meet at one point and extra strength is required.

The dart and the gusset fulfil opposite functions: the dart cleans the fulness while the gusset creates fulness by the insertion of more material.

FIGS. 25 and 26 are chairs with backs which are semi-circular in shape, and the material must be cut as between A and B, FIG. 25, in order to spread it; V pieces or gussets are inserted in the cuts to create fulness, and thus a tuck-away is formed.

FIG. 27 represents the material for an inside back as it would appear after cutting at D, E, F. The dotted line at A is the sight line of seat, and the depth between A and B indicates the tuck-away.

It is important to avoid cutting too deeply at the point C, as allowance must be made for the sewing of the gusset piece.

Three cuts are shewn. It is inadvisable to have too many, but the upholsterer must be guided by the nature of the material; a harsh fabric requires more cuts than one which is soft and pliable.

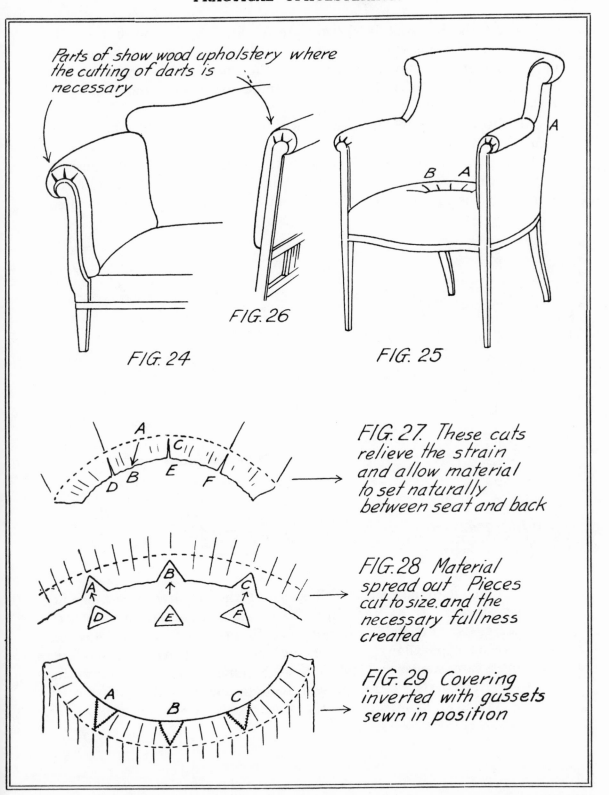

Parts of show wood upholstery where the cutting of darts is necessary

FIG. 26

FIG. 24

FIG. 25

FIG. 27. These cuts relieve the strain and allow material to set naturally between seat and back

FIG. 28 Material spread out Pieces cut to size. and the necessary fullness created

FIG. 29 Covering inverted with gussets sewn in position

At FIG. 28 the material is shewn spread out. D, E and F are the gusset pieces for insertion at cuts A, B and C. These pieces are cut ½in. larger all round: the depth of the gusset is governed by the cut, and the width according to the number of gussets and the shape of the curve.

At FIG. 29 the material is shewn inverted, with the gussets A, B and C sewn in position.

FIGS. 30 and 31 indicate those parts of a chair at which gussets or V pieces are frequently used, either to give added strength or to increase the width when the material falls short by two or three inches.

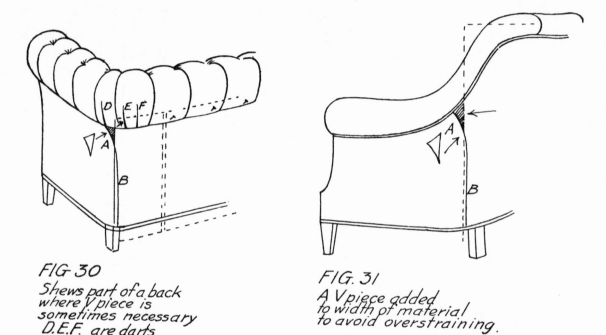

FIG 30
Shews part of a back
where V piece is
sometimes necessary
D.E.F. are darts

FIG. 31
A V piece added
to width of material
to avoid overstraining.

In joining materials which fall short of the required measurement by a few inches, as at the top of the seam B, FIG. 30 and 31, a gusset serves a twofold purpose: (1) It prevents the dragging of the material; (2) allows of economy in the cutting. Gussets in loose covers are similar to and serve the same purpose as collars in upholstery, though the latter present more difficulty unless the cutter possesses practical knowledge of the work.

CHAPTER 4.
POSITION OF SEAMS.

The number of seams in the material in making loose covers should be reduced to the minimum. Unnecessary seams are sometimes caused by starting to cut before adequate planning. Presuming the covering to be of a conventional pattern and that a length has been cut for either a seat or back without planning for the subsequent cuts, seams will be found necessary at unexpected places. Planning should not be discarded even when there is plenty of material available. The only safe rule is first to set out the various cuts and mark them with pins or chalk. In this way the position and number of the seams become apparent and the various cuts may be utilised to the best advantage. Although seams are of necessity governed to a great extent by the width of the material, customers are often fastidious about them, and some of them apparently expect a cutter to be something of a conjurer as well.

It often happens that the matching of the material encroaches 2in. or 3in. on either side of the selvedge, thus reducing the made-up width by several inches. In the showroom materials are shown gracefully draped ; a customer likes the pattern, and seams do not enter into the question at all, but the salesman who possesses some knowledge of the theory of loose cover work would be able to advise as to the suitability of one width or another as applied to particular styles of work. The expert loose-case-cutter is frequently called upon to hide as far as may be the faults which should never have occurred had the salesman been able to point out that the material chosen by the customer was quite unsuited for the purpose. Unfortunately, it is only when the work is made up that the faults become apparent.

Economy as regards material should not be practiced at the expense of seams which are necessary and when placed correctly not displeasing to the eye, especially if the material has been skilfully matched. Such an example as FIG. 17 lends itself to a single or double width material. In the single width (30in.) no seam would be necessary. In FIG. 18 the use of a double width material would obviate the use of seams on the shoulders in front of the inside back which would be required if a 30in. material was employed. A single width material could be used with advantage in such a pillow settee

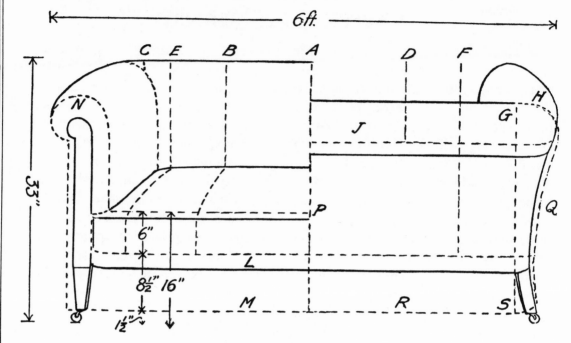

FIG. 32

A. A 30" material placed for seaming at the centre A. to C

B to D. Front & back view of seam, each side of the centre

E to F. Position of seams for a double width material

G. Back view of seam for 30" material

H. Mitre seam of back and arm

J. Line of welted seam of inside & outside back

L. Cutting line of border

M. Hemmed line of flounce

N. Welted line for facing

P.Q. Two positions for openings of a settee cover at back

R. Continuation line of flounce

S. A finishing point for flounce not required all round

as is shown in FIG. 19, as in this case the necessary seam in centre of seat would correspond with that of the inside back. A double width material if used from the half width would require seams at the corners A and D. If the design does not permit of cutting from the half width a single width would be more economical than a double width. In large pieces of work, such as chesterfield settees, either single or double widths are suitable. The former is, generally speaking, more economical, allowing the seams to be placed with greater advantage, see FIG. 32. The making of seams may frequently be avoided if a margin over and above the net quantity of material is allowed. The cutter is often compelled to form a seam at a conspicuous part of the work because (1) he has bare net quantity of material or (2) a difficult pattern to match.

The proportions and shape of the work govern the position of the various seams, and it is only by practice and experience that a beginner in loose cover cutting can judge correctly and gain confidence in knowing how and where to cut to the best advantage.

The best advice that can be given to any man who aspires to become a good cutter is that he should plan the material before cutting and visualise the position of the seams. If he follows these rules he will gain confidence, being assured that he has a sufficiency of material at hand, and be able to gauge the number as well as the size of the various pieces while proceeding with the work. The method of case-cutting for such a piece of upholstery as is shown in FIG. 32 will be described in a subsequent chapter.

CHAPTER 5.

TIE-UNDER COVERS. HOOKS AND BUTTONS.

To commence cutting a simple style of tie-under cover for a small chair such as FIG. 13, the measurement would be obtained from the bottom edge of the moulding at the back to the front, and from side to side, with an additional allowance of 3in. to 4in. all round. FIG. 33 shows the covering folded in half and pinned to the seat. A diagonal is cut at A finishing about $\frac{3}{4}$in. from the wood; the material is gathered up at the corner C and pinned close to the under covering, then cut away as B to the top E. A slanting cut D is made about $\frac{1}{2}$in. from the moulding for the flap pieces to be hemmed, taped, and tied beneath the seat separately, or at the back legs only. A half-plan of the covering is shown at FIG. 34.

FIG. 14 shows a small chair covering (tied under) but made up of two pieces, a seat and welted border. For the size of the seat the measurements are obtained from the top of edge, back to front and side to side at the widest part, with an allowance of 1in. all round. The covering is folded in half, pinned in the centre of the seat, also temporarily pinned on the edge as A, B, C, FIG. 35. The pieces of material for the front, sides and back are termed borders; for these measure from E to F, allowing 3in. or 4in. (to G) for tying beneath as in the previous example. The borders are first set, then pinned to the loose seat cover, about $1\frac{1}{2}$in. apart. It is important that the border should set naturally and easily; if any drags appear the pins must be released and the material slackened or gathered up as required. This is of frequent occurrence in large pieces of work, but in straight cuts of small chairs if the threads are kept straight the need for re-pinning may generally be avoided. A half plan of the seat and border is shown at FIG. 37. When a cover is to be finished, bordered and flounced, as FIG. 15, the depth of the borders is governed by the proportions of the chair. In loose covers (especially for small work) borders and flounces, if cut too narrow or too deep, are apt to appear clumsy. The frill or flounce should be slightly deeper than the border; for the example shown the top border is cut $3\frac{1}{2}$in. to finish $2\frac{1}{2}$in., the flounce cut $4\frac{1}{2}$in. to finish $3\frac{1}{4}$in. In cutting

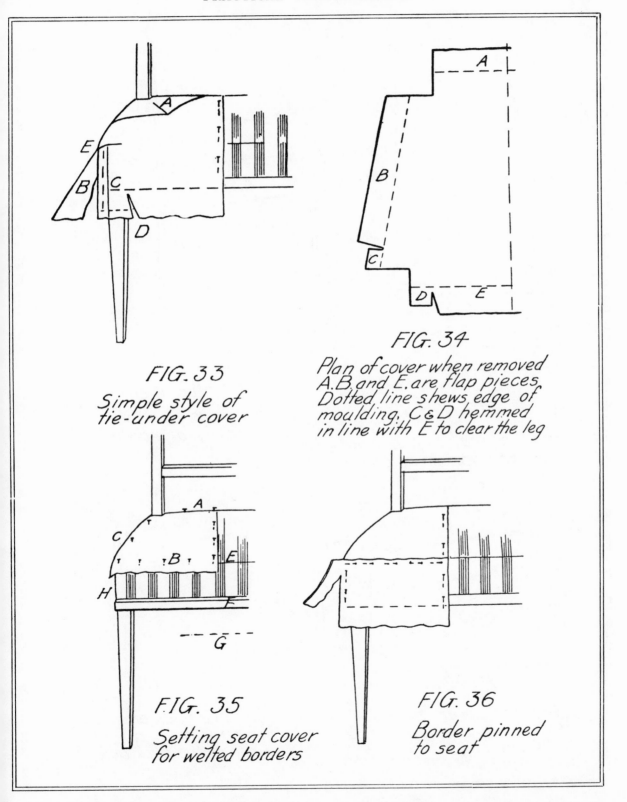

FIG. 33

Simple style of
tie-under cover

FIG. 34

Plan of cover when removed
A. B. and E. are flap pieces.
Dotted line shews edge of
moulding, C & D hemmed
in line with E to clear the leg

FIG. 35

Setting seat cover
for welted borders

FIG. 36

Border pinned
to seat

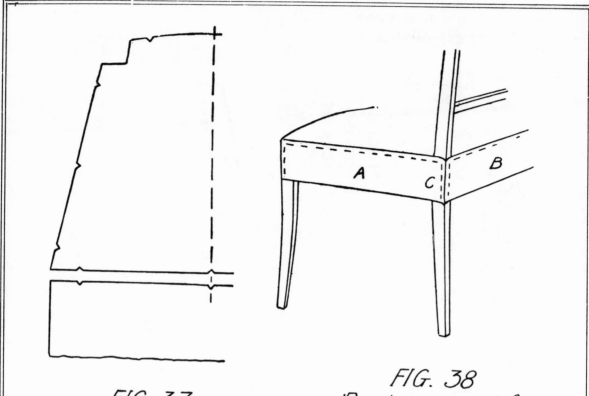

FIG. 37
Plan of seat and border
and position of notches

FIG. 38
Borders pinned for
buttons or hooks

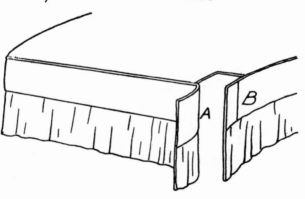

FIG. 39
Shewing cover made up
Separate pieces are basted
at A and B

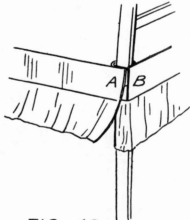

FIG. 40
The cover fastened to
the continuation
piece of the back border

these simple styles of covers, two points previously mentioned may be reiterated : (1) Allow a sufficient margin of material from the pins for seaming ; (2) notches are important, they form the only guide for placing the various pieces together, after being taken apart and reversed for sewing.

Small chair covers that are fixed to seats by means of tapes do not, as a rule, set gracefully unless placed by an experienced hand, the tapes are invariably drawn too tight, causing ugly drags of the covering ; this fault is minimised when the cover is finished with hooks and eyes or buttons fastened at the back of the chair, see FIGS. 38, 39, 40. The borders A, B, FIG. 38, are continued, pinned together and cut in the same manner as shown at front corners, FIG. 33.

The flaps, A and B, FIG. 39, are additional pieces basted on by the machinist, buttoned-holed or fitted with hooks and eyes. FIG. 40 shows a cover in position. Covers such as this, correctly cut and machined, present a neat and superior finish. In addition to the line of pins at C, FIG. 38, a pencil mark should be added on both borders, to indicate the outline of the wood frame. This is very helpful to the machinist when making up, as it is important that a fastening should be neither too slack nor too tight.

CHAPTER 6.

CUTTING ON THE DOUBLE.

In cutting loose covers for chairs which are symmetrical in shape the experienced man usually follows the method of cutting on the double, as shown in previous examples, but the beginner is advised to make a start by cutting on the single—*e.g.*, covering the whole of the work with the material and cutting on either side. By following this plan he will be able to judge of the appearance of the work as he proceeds and to trace the position of the various cuts. Work that is not equally balanced, such as couches and various kinds of show wood furniture, must be cut singly for the simple reason that a duplicate of one side cannot be obtained from the other when cutting on the double.

When working on the double, first plan the material, making sure that the central parts of the patterns, if any, are placed in a suitable position on the work. Also visualise the number and size of the pieces that may be required for seams. When each length has been marked, either by pinning or with the pencil, proceed to cut, but not before. The importance of careful planning cannot be over-stated. To cut the example shown at FIG. 17—an easy chair with a loose cushion—the cushion would be cut independently and an allowance made for the tuck-away, just as in the case of an ordinary seat. There is no fixed rule as to where to commence. Some cutters place the seat first, others the inside back or inside arms. The shape of the work forms the best guide, and in this connection it should be remembered that each piece should be so placed that it can be manipulated without too much displacement of the others. After removing the cushion the measurements of the various cuts are obtained as described in Chapter 1, FIG. 8. The seat and back pieces are folded in half and pinned to the marked centres of the work. The cuts of the tuck-away in a loose cover are generally made the reverse way to those of upholstery cuts, see A and B, FIG. 41, as it is necessary that the material should lie flat without any fulness. A plan of the inside pieces is shown at FIG. 42, the notches forming a guide for making up. Those at the top of the inside back would correspond with those of the outside back; also the inside arm and the outside

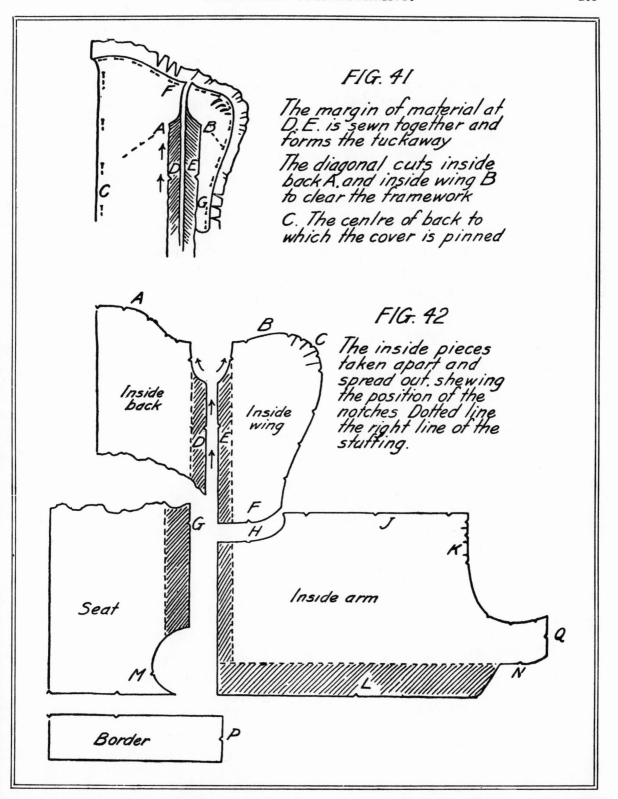

FIG. 41

The margin of material at D.E. is sewn together and forms the tuckaway

The diagonal cuts inside back A. and inside wing B to clear the framework

C. The centre of back to which the cover is pinned

FIG. 42

The inside pieces taken apart and spread out. shewing the position of the notches. Dotted line the right line of the stuffing.

Inside back

Inside wing

Seat

Inside arm

Border

arm. Extra notches are necessary at C for the equalisation of the fulness. The shaded parts at D and E represent the tuck-away, F and H are joined, one notch only being required. The notch G would correspond with L on the inside arm and M would correspond with N. Too many notches tend to confuse the machinist. Extra notches are more necessary where fulness is pronounced, as at the wing C rather than in the straight part of the inside arm, J. The notches P and Q would meet those of the outside arm. The cutter must remember that before making the cover the machinist must reverse the work, and that badly shaped cuts, notches which are too deep, or incorrectly placed, parts of the work uncut or unevenly trimmed, will occasion considerable trouble in joining the various pieces together. For the example in question twelve pieces are necessary, independent of those required for the flounce or frill. The method of cutting the cover for the cushion is described in the following chapter.

CHAPTER 7.

THE CUTTING OF COVERS FOR LOOSE CUSHIONS.

There are two methods of obtaining the measurements for a loose cushion—(1) by means of a paper template; (2) the use of a tape measure (see Fig. 8). When the cushion is a shaped one the former method is to be preferred. A badly fitting loose cover for a cushion spoils the appearance of the work, however well the other parts of it have been done. To cut by means of a template lay the pattern over the cushion, temporarily fixing at the four corners with pins, and mark the outline with pencil or chalk. Before cutting away the superfluous parts, remove and spread out on the board. If the pattern does not appear evenly balanced reduce or enlarge to rectify this and then trim off. To true the template obtain the centres of back and front, then fold it in half. It is advisable to test it further by placing it again on the cushion, at the same time noting if the net size of the pattern will allow sufficient for sewing, then make a note on the pattern and cut accordingly. When the corners of a cushion are square if they are cut too sharp they will appear clumsy when made up. A better effect is obtained by slightly rounding the corners of the covering at top and bottom (see Fig. 44). This may be done after cutting from the pattern. When the sizes are obtained by means of the tape, a measurement is taken from back to front B and side to side, at A and C, allowing $\frac{1}{2}$in. all round for sewing: also the depth of the border D. When a cushion placed in a chair shows only the front border the joins for the seams are best placed one or two inches from the front corner E and the back corners at F. To insert the cushion in the cover it is necessary to have an opening, Fig. 45. This is best made at the back when the shape permits. When made up a clean surface is then obtained on one side and the opening is out of sight. A welted or plain seamed cushion should be finished an inch from each corner before leaving the opening D, E, Fig. 45. Additional pieces are basted and sewn to the seat and border to carry hooks or buttons used for fastening.

Whatever the style of cover to be cut there is little difference of principle, if any, in working; the various pieces for the insides and outsides must be cut, placed temporarily on the work, fulness manipulated, equalised, pleated, and cleaned by converting into darts

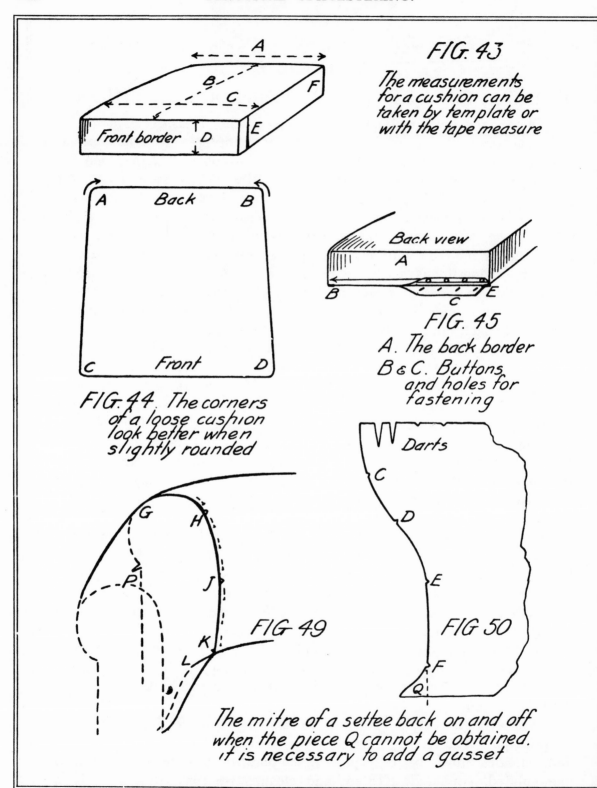

FIG. 43

The measurements for a cushion can be taken by template or with the tape measure

A. The back border

A. Front border

Back view

FIG. 44. The corners of a loose cushion look better when slightly rounded

FIG. 45

A. The back border

B & C. Buttons and holes for fastening

Darts

FIG. 49

FIG. 50

The mitre of a settee back on and off when the piece Q cannot be obtained. it is necessary to add a gusset

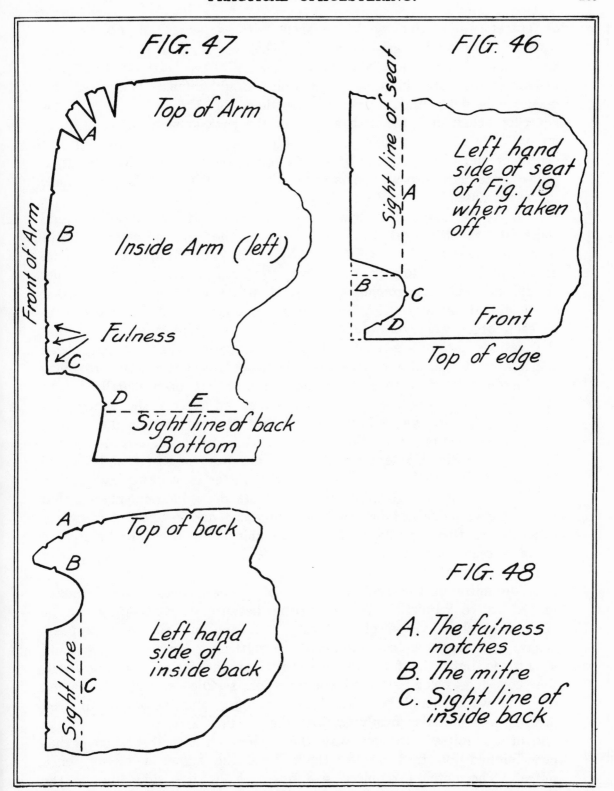

FIG. 47

Top of Arm

Front of Arm

A

B Inside Arm (left)

Fulness

C

D E

Sight line of back

Bottom

FIG. 46

Sight line of seat

Left hand side of seat of Fig. 19 when taken off

A

B

C

D Front

Top of edge

A Top of back

B

Left hand side of inside back

Sight line

C

FIG. 48

A. The fulness notches

B. The mitre

C. Sight line of inside back

or gussets, and the whole finished with a series of notches for reassembling after being taken apart. Wherever possible openings should be avoided because a cover is more easily fitted without them and fastenings of any kind are generally troublesome. The need for openings is determined by the proportions of the work. A loose cover for a chair or settee with a rake in the back must have an opening: on one side of the outside back in the case of a chair, and at the centre or end of the outside back for a settee, see FIG. 32. At FIG. 19 a pillow settee is shown without any facings. Fulness would be pronounced in this because of the contour of the back, arms and sides, see FIG. 20. A plan of the seat after being cut with the position of notches and sight line is shown at FIG. 46. Few notches are necessary at the front because the border is straight. The most important notches are C and D. FIG. 47 represents the arm piece. At the corner A fulness will be pronounced, and it will be necessary to equalise it or cut it away by forming darts; notches should be made close to each other wherever much fulness is to be treated to ensure that the various pieces are placed together properly. FIG. 48 represents the left hand side of the back after being cut, and the close proximity of the notches at A indicates where fulness has been equalised. In large pieces of work such as chesterfields and settees the same rules must be followed—*i.e.*, folding the pieces, and cutting on the double, assuming, of course, that the work is evenly balanced. In seats and backs of considerable length the pieces are best matched and seamed together before cutting, though when the cutter is working away from the shop this is not always convenient. It must be remembered that a cover after being cut has to be taken apart and reversed for sewing. Notches are therefore liable to become misplaced when the matching up of a seam gathers up too much material, or an insufficient quantity has been allowed.

The mitre of the back and arm of a chesterfield or any similar shaped settee requires care in cutting because no tuck-away can be allowed at the division of the mitre. If too full the work appears baggy and suggests bad judgment in cutting. On the other hand if cut too tight the fold will be visible at the facings on the front, the covering being strained instead of setting easily. To avoid this the work should be tested after pinning and before cutting by pressing the material firmly against the stuffing with the hand on the line of the mitre. In this way the cutter can test if the cover has been pinned too taut or too slack. FIG. 49 shows a section of a mitre. The notches required are few. K is the side line of the back, L the end of the seat tuck-away, P the join of the inside and outside back. FIG. 50 indicates the shape of the mitre after being removed. The notches C, D, E and F are those shown in the section of mitre G, H, J, and K, at FIG. 49.

If has been mentioned that the notches which form the guide for the correct reassembling of the various pieces are best cut small (not more than $\frac{1}{4}$in. deep) rather than large. This must not be taken as a hard and fast rule, because the threads of some fabrics when cut fray at the edges, and in consequence the notch which is too small cannot be traced owing to the ragged ends of the unravelled threads. Coverings of this nature require larger notches and also an increased margin of material left for the purpose of sewing. On the other hand, in materials which cut cleanly and evenly only small notches are necessary. Notches are best cut after the whole of the work is pinned and the superfluous pieces removed. It sometimes happens that a notch has not been duplicated on one or other of the pieces. In order to avoid this the two pieces should be levelled together with the thumb and forefinger of the left hand close to the position where the notch is to be made, and the notch made in both pieces at the same time. When a cover is complete and ready to place on the work any alterations necessary owing to the misplacing of notches are very difficult to rectify. Those parts where fulness occurs, especially if not made exactly to the cutting position, when on the work cause the material to drag and appear faulty, however carefully they may have been cut in the first instance.

INDEX